Economic Liberalization and Stabilization Policies in Argentina, Chile, and Uruguay

A World Bank Symposium

Economic Liberalization and Stabilization Policies in Argentina, Chile, and Uruguay

Applications of the Monetary Approach to the Balance of Payments

Edited by

Nicolás Ardito Barletta
Mario I. Blejer
Luis Landau

THE WORLD BANK
Washington, D.C., U.S.A.

Editor   James E. McEuen
Book design   Brian J. Svikhart
Cover design   George P. Parakamannil

Library of Congress Cataloging in Publication Data
Main entry under title:
Economic liberalization and stabilization policies in
   Argentina, Chile, and Uruguay.
   (A World Bank symposium)
   Includes bibliographical references.
   1. Monetary policy—Southern Cone of South America—
Addresses, essays, lectures. 2. Balance of payments—
Southern Cone of South America—Addresses, essays, lec-
tures. 3. Southern Cone of South America—Economic
policy—Addresses, essays, lectures. 4. Economic
stabilization—Southern Cone of South America—Addresses,
essays, lectures. I. Ardito Barletta, Nicolás.
II. Bléjer, Mario I. III. Landau, Luis, 1936-   .
IV. World Bank. V. Series.
HG810.S68E36 1984   339.5'098   83-25958
ISBN 0-8213-0305-8

Contributors

The affiliations shown are those at the time of the symposium, May 21-22, 1982.

Nicolás Ardito Barletta
Vice President
Latin America and the Caribbean
    Regional Office
The World Bank

Leonardo Auernheimer
Associate Professor of Economics
Department of Economics
Texas A&M University

Mario I. Blejer
Economist
Research Department
International Monetary Fund

Guillermo A. Calvo
Professor of Economics
Department of Economics
Columbia University

Krishna Challa
Senior Operations Officer
Projects Department
Latin America and the Caribbean
    Regional Office
The World Bank

Vittorio Corbo
Professor
Instituto de Economía
Pontifical Catholic University of Chile

José María Dagnino Pastore
Economic Consultant
(Buenos Aires, Argentina)
    and
Professor
Argentine Catholic University

Jaime DeMelo
Economist
Development Research Department
The World Bank

Rudiger Dornbusch
Professor of Economics
Department of Economics
Massachusetts Institute
    of Technology

Sebastian Edwards
Assistant Professor of Economics
Department of Economics
University of California, Los Angeles

Carlos Elbirt
Country Economist
Country Programs Department II
Latin America and the Caribbean
    Regional Office
The World Bank

Jacob A. Frenkel
David Rockefeller Professor
    of International Economics
Department of Economics
University of Chicago
    and
Research Associate
National Bureau of Economic Research

Joseph Grunwald
Senior Associate
Foreign Policy Studies Program
The Brookings Institution

James A. Hanson
Professor of Economics
Department of Economics
Brown University

Arnold C. Harberger
Professor of Economics
Department of Economics
University of Chicago

Linda M. Koenig
Assistant Director
Western Hemisphere Department
International Monetary Fund

Luis Landau
Senior Economist
Office of the Regional Vice President
Latin America and the Caribbean
    Regional Office
The World Bank

Enrique Lerdau
Director
Country Programs Department II
Latin America and Caribbean
    Regional Office
The World Bank

Rolf Lüders
Managing Director
Empresas BHC
(Santiago, Chile)

Arturo Meyer
Senior Economist
Country Programs Department II
Latin America and the Caribbean
    Regional Office
The World Bank

Guy Pierre Pfeffermann
Chief Economist
Office of the Regional Vice President
Latin America and the Caribbean
    Regional Office
The World Bank

Larry A. Sjaastad
Professor of Economics
Department of Economics
University of Chicago
    and
Professor
Graduate Institute
    of International Studies
    (Geneva, Switzerland)

José B. Sokol
Country Economist
Country Programs Department II
Latin America and the Caribbean
    Regional Office
The World Bank

Pablo T. Spiller
Assistant Professor of Economics
Department of Economics
University of Pennsylvania

Vito Tanzi
Director
Fiscal Affairs Department
International Monetary Fund

Simón Teitel
Economic Advisor
Economic and Social Development
    Department
Inter-American Development Bank

John Williamson
Senior Fellow
Institute for International Economics

Roberto Zahler
Economic Affairs Officer
Economic Commission for Latin America/
    Latin American Institute
    for Economic and Social Planning
United Nations

Contents

Part III. Evaluation and Lessons from Experience

Definitions

"atraso cambiario"	Exchange rate lag
billion	Thousand million
CPI	Consumer price index
"financiera"	In this book, refers to a variety of nonbank financial institutions whose liabilities are predominantly time deposits, some of which can be very short term
GDP	Gross domestic product
GNP	Gross national product
LIBOR	London interbank offered rate
"tablita"	Preannounced schedule of exchange rate devaluation
WPI	Wholesale price index

Preface

Following the oil shock of the early 1970s, most Latin American countries began a search for alternative economic strategies to cope with the long-standing problems of acute external payments contraints, wildly fluctuating inflation rates, and difficulties in sustaining a rapid pace of economic growth. This search included a reassessment of the interventionist and protectionist policies that many countries had followed until then. Thus, several countries introduced a gradual liberalization of foreign trade and financial markets.

The "Southern Cone" countries (Argentina, Chile, and Uruguay) in particular launched bold economic programs by the middle of the decade to open up their economies to foreign trade and international capital flows; in other words, programs intended to integrate their respective economies with the world economy. The theoretical framework that served as a basis for these new economic programs is known as the "monetary approach to the balance of payments."

By the early 1980s, the application of these programs was well under way in the three countries. However, there were important differences among them in the sequence and speed with which different aspects of the programs were carried out. The underlying economic conditions were also quite different, as evidenced by the rates of inflation, the role of the public sector in the economy, the size and complexity of the industrial exports that had grown under high protection, and so forth. Also, the results obtained in bringing down inflation and accelerating economic growth were mixed. Respected professional economists who had spent time analyzing these experiments disagreed sharply in their assessments of economic performance in the three countries. Doubts were raised about the validity of the theoretical framework and about the internal consistency of the policies that had been applied in each country.

In view of the great importance that these experiments have as lessons for policymakers elsewhere, the Latin America and Caribbean Regional Office of the World Bank decided, in the spring of 1982, to organize a symposium to analyze and discuss these questions. Some of the most distinguished economists, representing different points of views, were invited to participate. To ensure a frank and uninhibited discussion, it was decided not to include in the symposium government officials who could be personally identified with the execution of the policies to be analyzed. (Two of the participants, however, later became the heads of the economic teams in their respective countries.) The meetings were held at the World Bank, in Washington, D.C., on May 21 and 22, 1982.

The lessons obtained from the experiences of these three countries should provide useful guidance for policymakers in Latin America and in other regions as well, including the industrialized countries. For this reason we have decided to make the proceedings available to a wider public.

Nicolás Ardito Barletta
Vice President
Latin America and the Caribbean
Regional Office
The World Bank

An Overview

Mario I. Blejer and Luis Landau

The Latin America and Caribbean Regional Office of the World Bank organized a symposium, "Liberalization and Stabilization—Recent Experience in the Southern Cone," held at headquarters on May 21 and 22, 1982. The purpose of the symposium was to review the recent economic experiences of Argentina, Chile, and Uruguay. In very general terms, the three countries based their economic policies on the theoretical framework known as the "monetary approach to the balance of payments." There were, however, considerable variations in the policies actually carried out, and the results have been mixed.

SCOPE OF THE SYMPOSIUM

The symposium was expected to draw practical lessons for policymakers from what actually happened in these countries. In particular, it was asked to address the following types of issues:

- Empirical evidence regarding the major assumptions and implications of the monetary approach to the balance of payments. For example, the "law of one price" in goods and capital markets; the effects of devaluation on real economic variables; and the determinants of the supply of money—foreign capital availability and the role of monetary policy.
- Dynamic aspects and costs, including topics such as gradualism versus shock in the adoption of stabilization and liberalization measures; the speed of adjustment of relative prices between traded and nontraded goods; the advantages of alternative foreign exchange rate regimes (fixed, crawling, floating, preannounced); the sequencing of liberalization measures in the commercial and financial markets; and financial market integration and the problem of interest rate convergence.

The emphasis was on comparative empirical evidence. Although there were few formal papers, all participants had carefully prepared their presentations in advance of the symposium. An intense discussion followed each presentation and continued in a wrap-up session. For publication, the papers and proceedings of the symposium have been substantially rearranged, and cross-references added, to facilitate the review.

ORGANIZATION OF THE VOLUME

The eight chapters of the volume are divided into three parts that have substantially different structures. In the first part, the salient characteristics of the theoretical framework underlying the Southern Cone experience are analyzed in the papers by Mario I. Blejer and Jacob A. Frenkel. The second part concentrates on the analysis of country experiences. A detailed paper by José María Dagnino Pastore considers the developments in Argentina, and the common and different elements in the implementation of the stabilization programs in Argentina, Chile, and Uruguay are addressed from different angles by twelve participants whose remarks are included in chapter 4. The third part is devoted to the evaluation of the elements of success and failure that have arisen from the implementation of the programs, and the discussion is centered on the practical lessons to be learned. This section includes papers by Larry A. Sjaastad, Simón Teitel, and James A. Hanson. In the last chapter, seventeen of the participants discuss and evaluate the implications of the experience, drawing general conclusions about the applicability of the monetary approach as a policy framework.

SUMMARY OF THE ISSUES ADDRESSED

The question of how to characterize the nature of the policies followed in the Southern Cone within the context of broad analytical models is addressed by Mario Blejer in the first chapter. After outlining the main tenets of the monetary approach, he claims that the two central ideas that emerge from this approach, ideas that have concrete policy implications, are that the overall balance of payments largely reflects monetary forces in the economy and that, under fixed exchange rates, the aggregate money supply is an endogenous variable. Following a review of some of the salient features of the strategies adopted, in connection with the framework presumptively being applied, Blejer concludes that the experience of the three countries is not fully relevant to evaluating the performance of the monetary approach as an operational instrument. That is so because a variety of policies—such as the use of the exchange rate for stabilization purposes and of liberalization policies for structural purposes—were being implemented in conjunction with the stabilization plans. In his comments to Blejer's paper, included here as part of chapter 8, Rudiger Dornbusch sharply disagrees with this conclusion, claiming that the Southern Cone served as a most appropriate testing ground for the monetary propositions, including the macroeconomic framework that is implied in the monetary approach to the balance of payments. This basic disagreement, between those criticizing the theoretical framework and those who have raised doubts about the consistency in the implementation of the policies, is a central issue in most of the papers as well as a focal point in the discussions summarized in chapters 4 and 8.

Two conceptual matters related to the framework within which policies were applied are considered by Jacob Frenkel in chapter 2. He concentrates first on the proper sequencing of liberalization measures, claiming that, because of different speeds of adjustment in goods and capital markets, liberalization measures should not be adopted simultaneously in both. Frenkel's view is that the trade account should be opened up first and that the liberalization of capital flows should be slowed down until domestic goods markets are better integrated with the world markets. The second issue discussed by Frenkel is the optimal design of stabilization programs, in which the choice between the gradual and the drastic application of stabilization measures is central. He makes a case for drastic treatment, based on the arguments that a major policy shock will minimize the total output costs of seriously reducing the inflation rate and that budget cuts, crucial to reducing the rate of inflation, are very difficult to implement gradually.

Chapter 3, opening part II of the volume, is a complete and careful analysis by José María Dagnino Pastore of the Argentine experience in implementing stabilization and liberalization programs. After a detailed examination of the evidence, he concludes that the partial and temporary benefits attained by the anti-inflationary experiment in Argentina were offset by large and lasting costs. Dagnino Pastore attributes the blame for the difficulties in Argentina partially to implementation errors but mainly to the model itself, since in his view the crucial assumptions underlying the model are not empirically valid in that country.

The fourth chapter of the book is based on the discussions, by twelve participants, of the individual experience of the three countries. Most of the discussion on the Argentine case is based on comments to Dagnino Pastore's paper. Although some of the participants agree with his basic conclusions, others describe in some detail the problems and implications arising from inconsistent policies having been applied together, and point out that most of the complications have come from deficient and incomplete implementation of the programs.

With respect to the Chilean experience, there was much broader agreement between the participants. The problems faced by that country in 1982 were mainly attributed not to the trade liberalization policies but rather to inadequate macroeconomic management, especially the fixing of the exchange rate at an unsustainable level given external developments affecting the Chilean economy. The other two aspects of the Chilean reforms that were the subject of lengthy discussions were the effects of liberalization of trade and capital flows on the level of employment and on the level of real interest rates. With respect to the lack of convergence of interest rates to the world levels (adjusted for exchange rate expectations), it was generally agreed that market imperfections may have played a central role. This issue is the focal point of the presentation by Pablo Spiller in chapter 4. He analyzes the lack of competitiveness in the Uruguayan capital market, reaching the conclusion, based on econometric evidence, that the banking system in that country has been characterized by the presence of noncompetitive practices. This fact helps to explain why interest rate parity did not emerge in Uruguay, and probably in the other Southern Cone countries, despite the external opening of the capital market. Part II of the volume concludes with the paper by Roberto Zahler, which provides a detailed regional view of recent experience. He compares the incidence of similar policies among the three countries and stresses the need for flexibility as well as consistency in the various policies included in an economic program.

The third part, dealing with the evaluation of the experience and with the lessons that can be learned from it, opens with a comprehensive study by Larry Sjaastad, in chapter 5, that elaborates on the common aspects and the various differences between the Argentine and the Chilean developments. He draws a number of conclusions and poses various policy implications, which are summarized in the last part of his paper. Among the lessons indicated, Sjaastad stresses that the discipline of the fixed exchange rate system can and did reduce the rate of inflation, but that it is not sufficient, even if combined with free capital mobility, to guarantee low real interest rates. Fixed exchange rates are inconsistent with large and persistent fiscal deficits and with additional numeraires, such as the wage indexation policy followed in Chile. Sjaastad also stresses that, as the economy becomes more open, external developments such as changes in the terms of trade and exchange rate fluctuations among major currencies should be considered with more attention in the design of stabilization programs.

In chapter 6, Simón Teitel analyzes the adjustment and liberalization programs of the Southern Cone from a different perspective, considering first the background and the regional context within which the programs were adopted, and then providing an evaluation of the costs and benefits of the programs implemented. Teitel sees the policy reforms of the late 1970s as a reaction to events in the economies of the Southern Cone countries during the 1950s and 1960s, when these countries were engaged in policies intended to improve income distribution. These policies lacked adequate budgetary provisions and led to monetary expansion, inflation, and sociopolitical tension. The reaction to this state of affairs was the attempt to liberalize the economy drastically, both internally and externally, and to reduce as much as possible the magnitude of government deficits and government interventions. In his evaluation of the costs and benefits of the policies adopted, Teitel is skeptical about the achievements, pointing out that many of the distortions caused by the programs, particularly the large-scale unemployment of human and physical resources, have been too persistent to be considered simply costs of adjustment.

Various aspects of the policy implications the monetary approach to the balance of payments has had in the Latin American context are analyzed by James Hanson in chapter 7. He describes the monetary approach as a general analytical framework that is not dependent on many of the assumptions criticized by other participants and that is useful in setting the limitations of monetary policy in an open economy operating under fixed exchange rates. In his analysis of the countries' experiences, Hanson stresses the importance of consistency between the different instruments applied and the need to be realistic in the design of reform packages. He elaborates in detail on the implications of the policies adopted for the behavior of interest rates and on the consequences of using alternative strategies of exchange rate management. Hanson also discusses the problems of the proper sequence of liberalization and the velocity at which the programs should be applied. He agrees with the points made by Frenkel in chapter 2 and with the need for rapid action, but he does not consider crucial the sequence at which the reforms are introduced, particularly given his preference for fast application of all the measures included in the package.

The last chapter of the volume contains the observations of seventeen participants. Some of the remarks take the form of comments on previous chapters, while others reflect the general views of the participants about the experience of the countries as well as their opinions on some of the issues that emerged during the symposium. Although there was clearly no consensus, the lively debate reflects the fact that the experiences of the Southern Cone countries have raised a diversity of new and renewed interest in topics of applied economic theory and policy. At the same time, the discussion presented here indicates that the process is currently in a stage where it is too early to attempt a final and definite evaluation. This openness of debate is reflected in the extensive list of further reading that has been compiled for the interested reader.

ACKNOWLEDGMENT

James E. McEuen, of the World Bank's Publications Department, played a major role in the production of the volume. He initiated and carried out, in consultation with the other editors, an extensive restructuring of the symposium records, edited the formal papers and the transcribed proceedings, and corresponded with all the contributors to ensure that their views were correctly summarized in the manuscript that emerged. In short, his resourceful participation was critical for this project.

PART I
The Conceptual Framework

1

Recent Economic Policies
of the Southern Cone Countries
and the Monetary Approach to the Balance of Payments

Mario I. Blejer

In making these remarks I do not intend to discuss in detail the analytical characteristics of the policies adopted in the Southern Cone countries of Latin America, or to evaluate the results obtained in each specific case. My objective here is simply to elaborate on some of the broad elements that constitute the framework within which policy was conducted and to make some observations on the nature of the strategies adopted.

The first part of this discussion concerns what I think is a problem of semantics but one that, nevertheless, has practical implications. The kinds of policy packages that have been implemented in the countries of the Southern Cone have been labeled with different generic names such as "monetary approach to the balance of payments," "monetarist," "free market," and the like. I think that it is important to clarify to what extent the policies that were adopted and the manner in which they were carried out are indeed consistent with the theoretical frameworks that presumably were being applied. Clarification is important to avoid judging and valuing the applicability of general analytical frameworks on the basis of the results obtained in specific historical experiences that may not have been relevant for the intended purpose. More specifically, if we conclude that the experience of the Southern Cone countries has not been successful, we may also conclude that liberalization is an inapplicable strategy or that the policy recommendations arising from the monetary approach to the balance of payments are intrinsically harmful. Whether or not this is true, generalization from a specific country's experience may be largely misleading without the appropriate qualifications.

THE FRAMEWORK OF THE MONETARY APPROACH

An adequate starting point for considering the connection between the theoretical formulations and the policies implemented is to elaborate briefly on some of the well-agreed central tenets of the monetary view of the balance of payments and to evaluate the extent to which actual policies have conformed to those central ideas. From the extensive writings on this topic, two basic ideas emerge that, although not particularly original, are largely stressed by the monetary approach and have concrete policy implications.

First, the overall balance of payments largely reflects monetary forces in the economy. Ex ante disequilibrium in the money market (that is, mismatch between the demand for real balances and the real value of the outstanding money stock) will be resolved by a combination of changes in the price level, the nominal rate of interest, the level of economic activity, and the "money account" of the balance of payments. Although it does not disregard other equilibrating channels, the monetary approach concentrates on the evolution of the money account in response to monetary disequilibrium. The money account simply represents the changes in a country's gross international reserves, and therefore the monetary approach is largely eclectic about which of the specific accounts that record transactions of diverse goods, services, and capital items would be most affected.

With respect to the specific distribution of monetary imbalance between prices, output, and the balance of payments, the distribution clearly depends on a large number of variables such as the exchange rate regime, the degree of openness of the economy in both the goods and the capital markets, the proportion of traded and nontraded goods, the level of resource utilization, and so forth. Many of those elements have been specifically modeled within the framework of the monetary approach, and the effects of considering different sets of alternative assumptions have been carefully analyzed. The monetary approach to the balance of payments, however, does not need to make intrinsic assumptions about the nature of those variables and does not require an economy with specific characteristics. The monetary approach neither assumes that all goods are traded nor that the "law of one price" holds; it does not require perfect capital mobility and interest parity; it does not assume full employment and perfect competition in all markets. It is a macroeconomic general equilibrium framework, centered on the money market and designed to analyze the interrelationship between the monetary and the external sectors of an economy in the context of the specific characteristics of that economy. It will yield different predictions and will generate different dynamic paths when alternative assumptions about the characteristics of the economy are made, but in no way is it restricted to a specific set of assumptions.

It is true that, in a very stylized characterization of the monetary approach, changes in international reserves have been directly linked to the money market by the condition that, under fixed exchange rates, the change in external reserves must equal the difference between the change in the real demand for money and the change in the domestic component of the money supply. But this is a characterization based on very restrictive assumptions, such as the full integration of domestic and foreign goods and capital markets (with perfect arbitrage predetermining the prices of domestic commodities and of financial assets and the independence of real economic activity from monetary shocks. It is also a characterization of the long-run equilibrium conditions, and it is consistent with many possible short-run paths of adjustment. As mentioned above, most of the restrictive assumptions on which this outcome is based have been relaxed, and alternative—in general, more realistic—results have emerged. Overall, the more general framework preserves the relationships between the monetary and the external sectors postulated by the monetary approach (that is, the spillover of monetary disequilibrium into the balance of payments), and these relationships are robust enough to emerge under many different assumptions. Therefore, the discussion of the monetary approach exclusively in terms of its long-run formulation based on ideal assumptions is a distorted and narrow characterization.

Second, the money supply is endogenous under fixed exchange rates. In any economy, the real demand for money is determined by the public. Equilibrium in the money market is attained by changes in the nominal money supply or the price level, or by a combination of both. When the exchange rate is controlled by the monetary authority, the balance of payments becomes one of the channels through which the nominal money supply is adjusted. Therefore, the nominal supply of money is no longer within the direct control of the monetary authorities and becomes an endogenous variable of the system. The monetary authority, however, does retain control over the volume of domestic credit, which is one of the sources of money creation. The distinction between money and domestic credit becomes crucial: the central bank controls the latter but not the former. Given a rate of growth in the demand for money, an equivalent growth in the supply can be derived by an appropriate increase in domestic credit. However, if the rate of domestic credit expansion falls short or exceeds the growth in demand, net foreign assets, and hence the money supply, will change to ensure monetary balance.

This simple analysis has a very concrete policy implication. Because by fixing the exchange rate the monetary authority can affect the composition but not the overall level of the money supply, domestic credit policy becomes the central instrument for monetary and balance of payments control. Given a balance of payments target, the design of credit policy should therefore be consistent with the monetary preferences of the public.

THE MONETARY APPROACH IN THE SHORT RUN

In addition to the two general characteristics discussed above, and to place the type of liberalization and stabilization policies adopted in the Southern Cone within the context of the monetary approach to the balance of payments, it is convenient to describe some of the short-run operational features arising from this analytical framework. Because in the three countries there was no intention to allow exchange rates to be freely determined by market forces— rather, exchange rates were set and periodically (sometimes daily) altered in discrete amounts by government fiat—the nominal supply of money remained beyond the control of the authorities, particularly after the elimination of exchange controls. The principal instrument of monetary policy was, in these circumstances, the volume of domestic credit creation, which is largely determined by the fiscal and the financial considerations of the government. When the rate of monetary expansion from domestic sources is inconsistent with the expansion in the demand for real monetary assets, the monetary disequilibrium so created spills over to the commodity and financial markets. The exact nature of the adjustment depends, of course, on the conditions in each country. In addition to income effects, which in the short run depend on the degree of resource utilization and on how much the public has anticipated the monetary expansion, the excess demand in the commodity market, caused by excess supply in the money market, will lead to a combination of price increases (which reduce the real value of the outstanding stock of money) and balance of payments deficits (which, by depleting the level of reserves, reduce the level of the nominal money stock). The effects of monetary disequilibrium will fall more heavily on the domestic price level (and on the domestic interest rate) and less on the balance of payments the lower is the degree of commodity and capital mobility. Therefore, (1) the larger is the proportion of nontraded goods, (2) the heavier are the restrictions to international transactions in goods and securities, and (3) the more prohibitive are the tariffs, quantitative restrictions, and exchange controls, the higher will be the effect of monetary imbalance on the domestic rate of inflation. Domestic inflation will, in addition, be affected by the behavior of the traded goods prices. This in turn is a function of world inflation and of the exchange rate policy followed.

In general, therefore, the domestic rate of inflation can be expected to depart from the world rate both when the exchange rate is altered and when domestic credit policy is not in line with the evolution of the demand for real monetary assets. The departures will be larger and more persistent the larger are the structural and policy limitations to the free movement of goods and services. A similar picture emerges in the capital market. In the absence of capital and exchange controls, interest rate differentials between the domestic and the "world" rate should be explained by expected changes in the exchange rate. In addition to such factors as transaction costs and differential taxation, departures from this condition are the result of imperfect substitution between domestic and foreign assets arising from factors such as political, exchange, and default risk—which, in other words, imply that some domestic assets may be nontradable despite the absence of capital controls. Furthermore, departures from interest parity can also be caused by less than competitive practices in the domestic banking industry that prevent its integration with the world market. Again, domestic policies will have greater effect, and for longer periods, on the domestic interest rate and will have less effect on the international movement of capital the more restricted and the more controlled is the domestic capital market.

The long-run versions of the monetary approach, however, have assumed that capital and commodities arbitrage will eventually prevail because of the substitutions in consumption and the linkage at the factor level between the production of traded and nontraded goods. Although this is a desirable property of this class of models, it is not a necessary assumption and not a conclusion of the analysis. It is quite evident that this long-run view was not the one considered as the operative policy framework for the short-run stabilization programs in the Southern Cone—although, at least in some cases, it was viewed as a desirable long-run goal. An assumption widely made was that arbitrage does take place relatively rapidly in the traded goods sector.

ECONOMIC POLICY IN THE SOUTHERN CONE

Let us now consider, in very broad terms, the economic policies followed by the Southern Cone countries and the connection of these policies with the ideas of the monetary approach. The specifics of the strategies implemented cannot be easily generalized; their characteristics can be described in many different ways, according to the basic beliefs of those describing them. The descriptions range from "an attempt to transform a bourgeois democracy with strong welfare state and socializing tendencies into a reactionary dictatorship," as described by Lawrence Whitehead (Thorp and Whitehead 1979), to what Roque Fernandez (1982) in his review of Thorp and Whitehead's book has called the transformation, in the case of Chile, of a centrally planned economy into a market-oriented economy. In general terms, it can be said that a central feature of the policies adopted is the concentrated effort to introduce far-reaching trade and financial reforms based on deregulation, on the opening up of the economy to external forces, and on the adoption of an outward-looking development strategy.

These reforms, however, were introduced during a period of extreme external and internal disequilibrium that was characterized by high—even uncontrolled—rates of inflation, balance of payments pressures, and, at least in the case of Chile, a serious problem of unemployment. The process of liberalization was therefore adopted in conjunction with the implementation of comprehensive stabilization plans. Clearly, both sets of policies—stabilization and liberalization—interact, but they are not necessarily part of a single package, and analytically they could be treated independently. They are designed to attain quite different objectives, and their results should be considered within the context of these objectives. Whereas the goal of stabilization policies was the relatively rapid reduction of inflation while labor market equilibrium was attained or preserved, the objective of the liberalization policies was to eliminate distortions in the allocation of resources and to change the basic economic structure of the countries. The targets of both sets of policies were to be reached within the general constraints imposed by the external sector, but continuous balance of payments equilibrium was not a central objective. For the real sector, it was clear from the start that stopping the acute inflationary pressures and attaining the desired structural change could not be achieved without real costs during the transition, but it was expected that the resulting outcome would be a more efficient economic performance that would lead to more rapid and sustained future income growth.

Even though there is obvious feedback between both types of policies, and disentangling their results is not always possible, it is important to consider the results within the proper framework. Thus, the lack of success of the Argentine program in bringing about a substantial fall in the rate of inflation should not be an indication of the unfeasibility or lack of merit of opening up the economy. And the large spreads between domestic and foreign interest rates in all three Southern Cone countries should not be seen as an intrinsic failure of the stabilization strategy.

An additional issue to consider is the time dimension. Although the stabilization efforts were designed to drive the economy toward equilibrium within a relatively short period of time, the liberalization policies were designed to change the structure of the economy and the patterns of development in the long run. Therefore, although results of the adjustment policies became evident in the short run, it still may be too early to attempt a full evaluation of how the relaxation or elimination of exchange and trade restrictions have worked.

It is indeed difficult to fit the design, and particularly the implementation, of the specific liberalization and stabilization programs followed by the three countries within the framework of the monetary approach. Some of the main elements of the programs—especially the fiscal, commercial, and exchange rate components, and some of the credit market policies as well— can generally be associated with the monetary approach, but still there are many additional policies (such as some incomes policies) that do not seem to be related to the model.

Fiscal and Commercial Policies

Fiscal policy had the effect of reducing the rate of growth of the domestic component of the money supply through a drastic cut in the rate of expansion of credit to the public sector. This was designed to slow down inflationary and balance of payments pressures and to attain a reduction in the level of government intervention in the economy.

Commercial policy was designed to open the economy to foreign competition. The process of tariff reduction was part of a broader liberalization of restrictions on foreign trade that included the gradual elimination of nontariff barriers and the relaxation of limitations to foreign investment and foreign credit. The main objective of the liberalization policy was to reverse the import-substitution strategy, thus to eliminate distortions, to improve the allocation of resources, and to induce more rapid economic growth. This policy, however, was also expected to fulfill a role within the stabilization effort. With trade barriers eliminated and the flow of commodities facilitated, it was expected that the proportion of traded goods would rise, the linkage of goods markets would increase, and monetary pressures would have less effect on internal inflation. In addition to this flow effect of increasing the extent of arbitrage, the reduction of tariffs was expected to have a direct anti-inflationary effect by reducing the price of traded goods.

The set of reforms adopted in the capital market had similar objectives. The reforms entailed the full liberalization of interest rates and the elimination of the highly centralized banking arrangements that were preventing the growth of domestic financial intermediation. Exchange controls were eliminated, and barriers to free capital movements were largely reduced. The main objective of the reforms was to improve resource allocation and to reduce the role of government in directing financial flows. Again, some benefits were also expected from the stabilization program because the free flow of funds would induce interest arbitrage and reduce the impact of money disequilibrium on the cost of credit to the private sector.

Exchange Rate Policy: The "Tablita"

One of the most important policy instruments used was the exchange rate, which was directed to attain both policy objectives. Although during the first phase of the programs a policy of managed crawl was followed, after 1978 the plans of the three countries were characterized by the preannouncement of the path to be followed by the exchange rate over a specified horizon (the "tablita"). This is a variation of a fixed exchange rate system (and indeed shifted to a fixed rate in Chile by mid-1979), but it had some special characteristics associated with its being part of a comprehensive plan and with its being adopted during periods of substantial inflation. The monetary authorities did not allow for any feedback between domestic and foreign variables during the announcement period, but some adjustments were made in the exchange rate movements that occurred beyond the period of overlap between old and new schedules. If the rates of devaluation implied by the announced schedules are lower than those of the recent past, there is also a direct effect on inflation arising from the lower rate of price change in the traded goods sector. This was not, however, the main objective of the policy. The anti-inflationary role of the preannouncement was to be played mainly through the effects of lowering overall inflationary expectations. In the context of the monetary approach, a reduction in expected inflation tends to induce an increase in the real demand for money, and, for given rates of monetary expansion and income growth, the increase in the money demand will have stabilizing effects on the price level. To have this stabilizing effect, however, the signal coming from the exchange rate policy should be credible and noticeable. The preannouncement of a gradual reduction in the rate of depreciation of the exchange rate may meet these conditions if it is regarded as indicating a commitment on the part of the monetary and fiscal authorities to take the necessary steps to reduce inflation to rates consistent with the announced policy.

The policy of preannouncing the exchange rate was also designed to help the process of opening the economy. The objective was not to induce real appreciation of the domestic currency and thus swamp the domestic economy with imports, as it has been described many times, but to foster the establishment and growth of trade in the wake of the tariff reductions. When the exchange rate is unstable and unpredictable, exchange rate fluctuations increase the risk that the profit opportunities arising from the trade reforms will not be maintained, and this reduces the incentive to incur the initial cost entailed in exploiting any opportunity for arbitrage. The preannouncement of the exchange rate increases the likelihood that international competition will actually emerge. Similar effects were expected to take place in the capital markets because the reduction in exchange risk would induce a larger response to the elimination of exchange controls.

Obviously, all these are once-and-for-all effects of the preannouncement, and they will tend to be reversed if confidence in the policy starts to erode and the announced exchange rate is widely perceived as unsustainable given the prevailing inflation differentials, the balance of payments position, and the effects of the policies on domestic production and employment.

The announced exchange rate policy may indeed become unsustainable if the system is called upon to absorb unexpected external or internal shocks that are too large or too many in too short a time, or if the other elements of the economic program, such as domestic credit policy and the assumed speed of market integration, are inconsistent with the rate of devaluation implied by the exchange rate schedules. This will happen, for example, if the trade reforms have not been extensively implemented, or if they fail to produce rapid results in commodity arbitrage, and, at the same time, the government's financing requirements and credit policies imply a rate of expansion of domestic credit inconsistent with the evolution of the demand for monetary assets. In this case the rate of domestic inflation may exceed the world rate by more than the announced rate of devaluation. The consequent deterioration in the balance of payments, the contraction in domestic activity, and the distortion in the ratio of traded to nontraded goods prices will erode confidence in the announcement, producing capital outflows and forcing the eventual abandonment of the program.

IMPLEMENTATION OF ECONOMIC POLICY

What actually happened as the policies were implemented? Without describing the specific experiences of the three countries, a number of general features related to the framework discussed above can be mentioned. A significant amount of success was attained in the fiscal area (especially until 1980). The size of the state, including public enterprises, began to shrink, and the magnitude of fiscal imbalance was largely reduced. In Chile and Uruguay the fiscal deficit was actually eliminated, while in Argentina the deficit remained relatively significant but, in 1978 and 1979, was not financed by central bank credit but through the domestic and foreign markets.

In the liberalization area the developments were much more ambiguous. Argentina largely opened the capital market, but trade reforms were more selective and much less far reaching. Uruguay followed a similar pattern but with a lower degree of opening of the goods market, and Chile went far in the liberalization of the goods market but retained some controls in the capital market. The adjustment to the liberalization measures was, however, neither as fast nor as large as expected. Imports did increase sharply, but price arbitrage was not widespread. In the capital markets, interest rates failed or took a long time to converge with the world rate adjusted for the announced rate of devaluation. The slow pace of arbitrage can be related to nonuniform rules followed in different markets, to the persistence of implicit bureaucratic and institutional restrictions, and to the various initial costs associated with organization, marketing, and learning, which tend to be high when the economy has been restricted for a long period.

In addition, the concept of trade and financial liberalization should be distinguished from the idea of perfect competition. Many domestic markets, given their size and organization, reacted in an oligopolistic manner to the opening of the economy. Producers became importers and were able to maintain control over their market. In the financial market this situation is quite notorious. The domestic market is largely segmented because not all financial agents have the same degree of direct access to international borrowing, especially when new financial institutions specializing in international intermediation are not yet developed. Given the fixed set-up costs and the structure of the domestic banking system, the development of new institutions requires a substantial period of time. In the meantime, borrowers without direct access to international markets must obtain credit from domestic financial intermediaries that can borrow abroad and lend to domestic agents. In such a situation, the domestic interest rate is not determined solely by the foreign interest rate, the expected rate of change in the exchange rate, and the existing risk premium; it is also strongly influenced by domestic market conditions, including the domestic demand for and supply of credit, the structure of the domestic financial system, and the state of inflationary expectations. A situation like this was more evident in the case of Chile, where the process of opening was conducted together with the process of privatization, and a limited number of economic groups were able to control a large fraction of real and financial activity.

Under these circumstances sustained capital inflows, attracted by the opportunity of achieving fast financial profits, can take place and may result in an excess supply of money, with consequent excess demand for commodities. If the proportion of traded goods remains limited, this excess money supply cannot be eliminated solely through the balance of payments; rather, it creates inflationary pressures and, given the fixed path of the exchange rate, also results in an overvalued currency. It is possible, however, that the observed capital inflows responded to a rise in the real demand for money brought about by the reduction in the average rate of interest in the economy following the liberalization. In that case, no pressure in the goods market should be felt, since the capital inflow does not lead to excess supply of money.

A process such as this affected all three countries to some extent, but it was particularly evident in the Argentine economy through the first quarter of 1980. In Chile and Uruguay the absence of fiscal pressure, with the consequent drastic drop in the rate of inflation, made this factor less important.

The subsequent evolution of events in Argentina can also be framed within the same general structure. Although the rate of inflation was halved by 1980, it still remained very high in relation to the announced rate of devaluation. The schedule was not adapted to unexpected or uncontrolled developments and remained largely inconsistent with the monetary evolution in the country. The large volume of capital inflows that took place and the rising price of beef (with its disproportionate incidence in the consumer price index) were factors that prevented, until 1980, the reduction in the rate of inflation. During and after 1980, several developments took place that led to the virtual collapse of the Argentine stabilization efforts. In the fifteen months from the announcement of the program (in December 1978) to March 1980, most of the monetary growth was from the external sector, and the monetary base from internal origin grew by only 35 percent. Two months later it was doubled, and by the end of March 1981 it grew to about twelve times its original value. Such a spectacular increase was caused by a rise of more than 1,100 percent in the credit to financial institutions and of 760 percent in the financing of the central government. These two changes, moreover, were substantially independent, both in cause and in timing. The increase in credit to the financial system was caused by the domestic financial crisis, which started in March 1980 as the central bank announced the liquidation of the largest private investment company and of the nation's second largest private bank. These events triggered a major transfer of deposits from private to official banks. To restore confidence, the central bank introduced a special discount facility that disbursed, in two months, more than US$2.7 billion. This scheme—and the eventual liquidation of four large banks, with the consequent need to repay guaranteed deposits—induced an expansion in the credit to the banking system of an equivalent of about 40 percent of Argentina's international reserves (which were still high at that time).

Although the financial crisis was the central cause for expansion of the base in the second quarter of 1980, the period July 1980 through March 1981 was characterized by the rapid growth of central bank credit to the central government, which increased fourfold in the second half of 1980, mainly to finance the growing fiscal deficit.

Faced with this extreme change in the rates of credit expansion, the central bank did not adapt the exchange rate schedules despite the growing overvaluation of the Argentine peso. The uncertainty about the sustainability of the program led to a substantial transfer of funds abroad that put increasing pressure on the balance of payments. After the change of government in February 1981, two large devaluations marked the end of the Argentine stabilization program.

At the core of the monetary problems created by the Argentine financial crisis is the distinction between the liberalization and opening of the financial market on the one hand and the role of the public sector in that market on the other. Although in the three countries the state reduced its role as regulator of financial activity, only in Chile was there a significant drop in the role of public institutions in financial intermediation. In Argentina, about 50 percent of deposits were held by public institutions, and, following the opening up, the share of foreign banks increased substantially. The reinforcement of the deposit guarantees, which were instrumental in the failure of the stabilization effort, was indeed necessary to prevent the disintegration of private commercial banking. Clearly, the consequences of deregulation and opening financial markets in the presence of a predominant public sector activity in those markets is a topic that demands further analysis. [See Pablo Spiller's comments in chapters 4 and 8.]

The performance of the stabilization plans in Uruguay and Chile was quite different from that in Argentina and will not be discussed here. The crucial difference was the drastic reduction in the fiscal deficit that was central to the ability to control inflation, which has been drastically reduced in both countries, but some balance of payments and fiscal problems have recently arisen (Foxley 1982).

CONCLUDING REMARKS

To summarize, I do not believe that the experience in the Southern Cone is very relevant to evaluate the performance of the monetary approach to the balance of payments as an operational framework for stabilization policies. Those experiences were characterized by the attempt to use exchange rate policy as a central instrument in the stabilization program, and this attempt has little to do with the monetary approach. Liberalization policies were followed for structural and long-run purposes and were not intended to force upon the economy the assumptions of the monetary approach—in fact, as I have mentioned above, the law of one price is not an integral part of this approach. It is clear, however, that the expansion of the array of goods and assets directly exposed to foreign competition was expected to complement the stabilization effort by reducing monetary pressures on domestic prices and by directing these pressures toward the balance of payments.

In the critical area of domestic credit management, the basic principles of the monetary approach were not actually followed. Although the nominal quantity of money becomes an endogenous variable, the authorities intended several times to control it so as to neutralize the influence on domestic interest rates stemming from foreign sector conditions. If anything, the Argentine experience illustrates that the monetary approach does have some predictive power. Domestic credit expansion at the rates observed after 1980, under a practically fixed exchange rate and with an only partially open economy, was bound to produce the inflationary and balance of payments effects actually realized. Moreover, the relatively high dispersion of the rates of domestic credit expansion can easily be related to the observed dispersion of interest rates and price changes, especially in the nontradable goods sector.

I have not touched here on other crucial aspects of the policies, such as the effects on real wages, on the distribution of income and wealth, on employment, and on the accumulation of foreign debt. I would like to mention, however, that the recessions that followed the policies in all cases are definitively undesirable outcomes from the narrow viewpoint of the monetary approach. Recession is clearly not a policy recommendation of that approach because a reduction in the level of economic activity is bound to increase monetary pressures on prices and on the balance of payments by contracting the demand for monetary assets. The causes of the recessions could be attributed to the very high real interest rates arising from market segmentation and from the bad financial position of many enterprises and to the apparent overvaluation of the domestic currency. The recessions also reflect the process of adjusting the structure of production to changing incentives following liberalization. The loss of real income is indeed a real cost associated with the change in development strategy. What requires elucidation is the degree to which this cost has been increased by the specific application of the instruments and the framework of the monetary approach.

REFERENCES

Fernandez, Roque B. 1982. "Review" of Thorp and Whitehead 1979. Journal of Political Economy, vol. 90, no. 2 (April), pp. 441-42

Foxley, Alejandro. 1982. "Towards a Free Market Economy: Chile 1974-79." Journal of Development Economics, vol. 10, no. 1 (February), pp. 3-29.

Thorp, Rosemary, and Lawrence Whitehead, eds. 1979. Inflation and Stabilization in Latin America, p. 65. New York: Holmes & Meier.

2

Economic Liberalization and Stabilization Programs

Jacob A. Frenkel

My remarks concentrate on two major issues. The first concerns the optimal design of economic liberalization programs, in which the proper sequencing of liberalization measures—specifically, the order of economic liberalization of international transactions in goods and financial markets—is crucial. The second concerns the optimal design of stabilization programs, in which the choice between the gradual application and drastic application of stabilization measures is central. I will close my remarks with a few notes on the pegging of a currency to a basket of foreign exchange.

THE SEQUENCING OF ECONOMIC LIBERALIZATION

The question of the optimal process of economic liberalization involves one of the most difficult aspects of the theory of economic policy, namely the transition toward equilibrium. The prescription of economic theory is very clear when applied to first-best situations. Economic theory is much more reserved when it comes to evaluating and comparing distorted situations. Evaluating alternative strategies for economic liberalization involves comparisons among various distorted situations that characterize different paths an economy may take in its approach toward the undistorted, first-best equilibrium. Consequently, views about the "proper" sequencing of liberalization measures should be put forward with great care and modesty; economic theory does not provide unambiguous instructions. With these reservations in mind, I will propose what might be a proper order for economic liberalization.

Consider an economy that suffers from numerous distortions in goods and capital markets, and suppose that it has many barriers to international trade in goods and capital. Suppose that the economy wishes to remove the distortions and to liberalize trade in goods and capital. Under these circumstances the general rule is that the first step in the liberalization process should be the removal of domestic distortions in goods and capital markets and the attainment of fiscal order so as to reduce the need for a heavy reliance on inflationary finance. In the second step, the economy can turn its attention to the liberalization of its links with the rest of the world. This external liberalization should also proceed in two phases. The first should reduce distortions to the free flow of goods by liberalizing the balance of trade. The capital account of the balance of payments should be opened up and liberalized only in the second and final phase of the liberalization program. In what follows, I offer some arguments in support of the proposed order of liberalization of the trade and the capital accounts of the balance of payments. This order is advocated by McKinnon (1982), and the subsequent arguments here are adapted from Frenkel (1982).

The key distinction between the effects of opening up the trade and the capital accounts of the balance of payments stems from the fundamental difference between goods and asset markets. As is known, the speed of adjustment in asset markets is much faster than the speed of adjustment in the market for goods. Asset markets are more sensitive to expectations about the distant future, and new information that alters expectations is reflected in asset prices much faster than in the prices of goods and services. This intrinsic difference in the basic characteristics of goods and assets has several implications.

First, since the economy under consideration has been distorted for a significant period of time, nobody (including the economist) can be certain about the precise paths that the various sectors in the economy will follow after the liberalization. Under such uncertainty prudence is called for. The order of liberalization that first opens up the trade account has the virtue of providing the policymaker with the opportunity to examine the market's reaction and to correct an error if an error is being found. The inverse order of liberalization is not likely to provide such an opportunity, since once the capital account is opened up the initial reaction is likely to be very fast, and the resulting capital flows are likely to be huge. Thus, while eventually it will be desirable to have an open capital account, prudence calls for a gradual transition so as to facilitate the required change in institutions and economic structure.

An analog to the economy that is recovering from a long history of distortions can be seen in the individual who recovers from a heart condition and coronary bypass surgery. Although it is envisaged that the patient will fully recover, nobody would recommend that the patient start a rehabilitation program by signing up to run a marathon race. The implications of the different speeds at which the trade and capital accounts adjust can be visually illustrated by imagining a carriage that is being pulled by two horses, one of which is a fast runner and the other slow. Surely if the two horses were to run at different speeds the carriage would overturn. To avoid a disaster, the speed of the two must be coordinated and brought into line. This could be achieved by speeding up the slow horse or by slowing down the fast one. It stands to reason that the first solution would not be sustainable, whereas slowing the fast horse could be achieved with little effort. Analogously, the overall balance of payments constraint requires that the trade and the capital accounts be brought into line with each other; thus, even though the two accounts tend to respond at different speeds, the overall constraint implies that the two must be harmonized. It seems that such consistency could be achieved with less effort by slowing down the volume of capital flows than by speeding up the rate of trade flows.

Second, it is easier (and is likely to be cheaper from the social viewpoint) to reverse wrong portfolio decisions than to reverse wrong real investment decisions. This potential difference in social costs also supports the proposed sequence of liberalization measures. When the authorities remove distortions in the commodity markets and open up the trade account, real investment in the economy will be based on a less distorted environment—a situation that is more consistent with the long run. Portfolio investments will continue to be based on the distorted capital market as long as the capital account is not opened up. Once the capital account is liberalized, some of these portfolio decisions will have to be reversed. If the capital account is opened up first, portfolio decisions are likely to be in closer correspondence with the long-run undistorted conditions, but real investment will still be carried out in a distorted environment as long as the trade account is not opened up. Because of the distortions, the social cost of the investment is likely to exceed the private cost. These real investments will have to be reversed once the trade account is liberalized, and because of the difference in private and social costs it is likely that the first order should be preferred. Noted, however, that the distortions to the flow of goods affect both the trade account <u>and</u> the capital account; by the same token, the distortions to the flow of capital also affect both the trade account and the capital account. It is likely, however, that the <u>relative</u> effect of each distortion on the two accounts differs. The effect of the distortion to the flow of goods on the trade account relative to its effect on the capital account is likely to be larger than the corresponding effect of the distortion to the flow of capital. This difference in the relative sensitivities of the two balance of payments accounts to the two distortions underlies the recommended order of liberalization.

Third, the cost of a distortion depends on the distortion itself and on the volume of transactions that take place in the presence of the distortion. Thus, when the trade account is opened up first, the cost of the remaining distortion—that is, of the closed capital account—is proportional to the volume of trade, which, because of the slow adjustment of the market for goods, is likely to be relatively small. But when the capital account is opened up first, the cost of the remaining distortion—that is, of the closed trade account—is proportional to the volume of capital flows, which, because of the high speed of adjustment in asset markets, is likely to be very large. Thus, a comparison of the cost of distortions also supports the proposition that the trade account should be opened up first.

The various arguments that were outlined above rationalized the different treatment of the trade account and the capital account by reference to the different speeds of adjustment in goods and asset markets. In view of these different speeds of adjustment, the synchronization of the two balance of payments accounts was brought about through dis-synchronization of the liberalization measures. An alternative strategy for accommodating the different characteristics of the two balance of payments accounts could be an adoption of a dual exchange rate regime. Such an exchange rate system allows for a separate exchange rate for commercial transactions in goods and services and for a different (typically floating) exchange rate for capital account transactions. By this system, the different speeds of adjustment in goods and asset markets are reconciled through an adjustment of the relation between the two exchange rates. It is important to emphasize, however, that, although a dual exchange rate system may solve the synchronization problem, it does introduce the economy to the potentially dangerous path of multiple exchange rate regimes. The danger of such multiple rate regimes is that they are typically characterized by a complex set of distortions, by a complicated bureaucratic system, by an involved structure of rent-seeking activities, and by a costly allocation of rents. And, as is typically the case, it is much easier to introduce and to create the distortions and the distribution of rents than to remove them. Furthermore, experience suggests that the dual exchange rate regime cannot be sustained if the difference between the exchange rates for commercial transactions and for capital transactions becomes too large. In other words, it seems that the dual exchange rate system might be capable of introducing an additional viable and effective instrument as long as the need for a reliance on that instrument is not too great. But because the synchronization problem might be severe during a liberalization program, it is likely that during such a period the sustainability, and therefore the usefulness, of the dual exchange rate system might be limited. Under these circumstances, the proposed sequencing of liberalization measures might be the more viable.

The removal of various distortions in the market for goods—including various taxes, subsidies, and tariffs—will yield a new equilibrium price level, a nominal exchange rate, as well as a new real exchange rate. Before embarking on such a path, however, the initial conditions have to be set correctly so as to reflect the new equilibrium exchange rate and prices that will follow the removal of the distortions. Several attempted liberalizations have resulted in accelerated, uncontrolled inflation. These outcomes can be explained, in part, by the nature of indexation clauses. To avoid such failures, it is critical that the initial (once-and-for-all) changes in prices that result from the removal of subsidies and other distortions be excluded from the indexes that are used for wage indexation.

As was emphasized earlier, it is essential that the liberalization program is preceded by a restoration of a fiscal order that reduces the government's dependence on inflationary finance. It is especially important that this fiscal order be restored before opening up the capital account of the balance of payments, because liberalization of the capital account is likely to encourage the process of "currency substitution." This phenomenon causes an effective reduction of the "tax base" for inflationary finance. Unless the need for inflationary finance is reduced, the opening up of the capital account, and the resultant shrinkage of the inflationary tax base, might give rise to an accelerated rate of inflation as the government attempts to collect the needed sum of inflationary tax from a smaller tax base.

Because some sectors in the economy are being harmed more than others during a liberalization program, this differential incidence of hardship is likely to induce strong pressures for accommodative monetary and exchange rate policies. It is important, therefore, to emphasize that the course of monetary and exchange rate policies should not be designed to alleviate such sectoral difficulties. Monetary and exchange rate policies are aggregate policies that should not be guided by intersectoral considerations. These intersectoral considerations are extremely important, and some of them should be dealt with, but the proper instruments to be used are fiscal policies rather than monetary or exchange rate policies.

Finally, since the success of the liberalization program depends crucially on expectations concerning the feasibility and credibility of the program, it is essential that the various measures undertaken interact in a consistent way. Trust and confidence, which can be built only with great difficulty, can be destroyed very easily. Therefore, it is important not to start with the program until all loose ends are tied up. The economic system—through the mechanism of memory, which builds itself into expectations—shows little tolerance of errors. Thus, while slight delay in the introduction of the program will not be fatal, the premature introduction of an inconsistent plan might be.

STABILIZATION PROGRAMS: GRADUAL VERSUS DRASTIC MEASURES

In many cases the decision to embark upon a liberalization program coincides with the decision to embark upon a stabilization program. The reason for this coincidence can be easily understood. Both liberalization and stabilization programs are associated with short-run costs, and both require political courage as well as broad political support to implement. The circumstances that are likely to generate these requisites are typically those of deep economic difficulties, widespread distortions, and galloping inflation. Although liberalization and stabilization programs have tended to be introduced together, the two are distinct programs, and they need not necessarily accompany each other.

One of the central questions concerning the initiation of a stabilization program is the choice between a gradual and a drastic application of the stabilization measures. The case for gradualism is well known; it rests on prudence and on the possibility for fine tuning and midcourse corrections. In what follows I will outline some arguments in favor of a drastic treatment. Some of the subsequent arguments in this section draw on Fischer and Frenkel (1981). As for the question of liberalization, however, economic theory does not provide an unambiguous answer for the choice between gradual and drastic treatments. It is especially inappropriate, therefore, to approach this issue dogmatically.

The first argument for drastic treatment is that, since there are numerous problems of nonsynchronized changes of money and wages in the economy, a major policy shock will minimize the total output costs of seriously reducing the inflation rate. A sharp reversal of policy is likely to ensure that many preexisting contracts are reopened and that economic agents adapt their behavior to the likely course of policy. If the policy is well planned, the initial conditions that it will produce should be close to the new steady-state equilibrium of the economy.

The second argument for drastic treatment is that gradualism may not in practice reduce the inflation rate. Underlying the gradual approach is the fear that attempts at restrictive policy will produce unemployment. It is precisely these fears that make it likely that any future inflationary shock will not be resisted but accommodated. Under such circumstances, slower implementation of stabilization measures may well end up gradually increasing the inflation rate, rather than reducing it, as inflationary shocks are accommodated and deflationary shocks are allowed to feed into higher output at the same inflation rate.

The third argument for drastic treatment rests on the recognition that there is a vital importance in reducing the budget deficit as part of any program to reduce inflation. There is little doubt that the single most important factor in reducing a galloping rate of inflation is a significant cut in the budget deficit. Such cuts are by their nature very difficult to implement. They are likely to be even more difficult to implement gradually. The short-run pressures are usually to expand the budget deficit, for one worthy cause or another; unless the problem is addressed directly and as a whole, the budget deficit is not likely to be cut. But once the problem is confronted, the opportunity is at hand for making a concentrated attack on the inflation rate.

One of the major arguments against drastic measures is that there are uncertainties about the effects of the anti-inflationary package that is put in place. But any policies that are followed in an economy that is in need of a stabilization program have a highly uncertain outcome. Nor are the consequences of pursuing a gradualist policy by any means certain. It is, as argued above, quite possible that gradualism will increase the inflation rate and thus merely postpone the application of drastic treatment.

The central factor determining the success of the stabilization program is its impact on the public's expectations. It is crucial that the introduction of a new policy should be consistent, credible, and broadly based. The main components of any stabilization plan are the fiscal and monetary policy measures that are adopted. It is essential that these measures be viewed and perceived as viable, consistent, and sustainable.

One of the difficulties in implementing a drastic remedy is that the distorted economic system has grown over many years and has become deeply embedded, and any drastic change would be disruptive by rendering many existing investment projects uneconomical. It seems, therefore, that the desirable solution to the question of the choice between gradual and drastic stabilization measures should be a plan that incorporates the best elements of each. An example of such a solution could be preannouncement of a feasible path for the policy instruments. Thus, if the stabilization involves a cut in government spending, a reduction in the rate of monetary growth, and the like, gradual reduction coupled with the preannouncement of the entire path would avoid the undesirable consequences of immediate drastic cuts. At the same time, the feasibility and the consistency of the plan would testify to the government's long-term commitment and would enhance credibility and promote a stabilizing of expectations.

Finally, any stabilization program must have two primary objectives and areas of operation. First, the program must adopt policy measures that rapidly reduce the high rate of inflation. Second, the program must begin the process of institutional reform that will reduce the susceptibility of the economy to future inflationary shocks and will make it possible to keep future inflation under better control. A key factor in controlling future inflation is the presence of a nominal anchor guiding the course of monetary policy. Such an anchor could be the money supply, the nominal exchange rate, or another nominal quantity.

BASKET PEGGING

The large variability of bilateral nominal and real exchange rates has led to proposals that some of the Southern Cone countries peg their currencies to a basket of foreign currencies rather than to a specific leading currency such as the U.S. dollar. [See, for example, Larry Sjaastad's recommendation in chapter 5.] These proposals have many positive features, but they also raise some important practical and conceptual issues that I do not believe have been fully addressed.

First, as should be obvious, all weighted averages (with positive weights that sum up to unity) vary to a lesser degree than some of their individual components. Therefore, it is clear that pegging the currency to a basket of foreign currencies will yield a smaller variance of the exchange rate expressed in terms of the basket. But, as is also clear, averages tend to mask great diversity. The relevant question, then, is whether introducing stability into the weighted average should be the desirable route independent of the degree of instability in the components that constitute the average. Specifically, shifting from bilateral pegging to basket pegging will stabilize the value of the currency in terms of the basket, but it will destabilize the value of the currency in terms of the individual currency to which it was previously pegged.

Is it obvious that the stability of a weighted exchange rate is to be preferred to the stability of a bilateral exchange rate vis-a-vis a major currency? In analyzing this question it is worth remembering that the discussion of the welfare cost of inflation also deals with related matters. There, the distinction is drawn between the cost associated with the variability of the price level and the cost associated with the variability of relative prices. Drawing on this analogy, one wonders whether those who emphasize the need for stability of the weighted exchange rate instead of the stability of bilateral rates would also place less emphasis on the cost of fluctuations of individual relative prices compared with fluctuations of the aggregate price level. Prior to adoption of a new pegging strategy, there is the need to specify the nature of the costs of benefits from the relevant alternatives.

Second, pegging to a basket in itself will not eliminate many of the difficulties with and objections to flexible exchange rates unless there is an actual asset that represents the basket and unless that asset can be traded freely in futures markets.

Third, there is the practical question of choosing the weights for the composition of the currency basket. The typical procedure has been the adoption of a trade-weighted basket. The choice of the proper weights, however, is not just a technical question, since it begs the conceptual problem of the role of the capital account. Specifically, because a large fraction of international transactions involves international capital markets, what role should these transactions play in determining the proper weights that should be assigned to the currencies that make up the basket?

The success of a new exchange rate regime, like the success of liberalization and stabilization programs, depends on the adoption of a consistent set of policy tools and on a reasonable understanding of the implications of each course of action. It will be irresponsible to experiment with new systems just to learn how they work out. As with liberalization and stabilization programs, the cost of delaying the adoption of new pegging arrangements until their full implications are understood is likely to be small relative to the cost of a premature start.

REFERENCES

Brunner, Karl, and Allan H. Meltzer, eds. 1982. Economic Policy in a Changing World. Carnegie-Rochester Conference Series on Public Policy, vol. 17. Amsterdam: North-Holland; New York: Elsevier.

Fischer, Stanley, and Jacob A. Frenkel. 1981. "Stabilization Policy in Israel." Report prepared for the Bank of Israel. Jerusalem, July. Processed.

Frenkel, Jacob A. 1982. "The Order of Economic Liberalization: Lessons from Chile and Argentina: A Comment." In Brunner and Meltzer 1982.

McKinnon, Ronald I. 1982. "The Order of Economic Liberalization: Lessons from Chile and Argentina." In Brunner and Meltzer 1982.

PART II

Recent Experience
in the Southern Cone

3

Assessment of an Anti-inflationary Experiment: Argentina in 1979-81

José María Dagnino Pastore

This paper is a policy assessment and has no pretense to be an analytical contribution. It does purport to draw some lessons from the first of the anti-inflationary experiments in the Southern Cone to reach completion.

To this effect, a description of the Argentine context and an outline of the program are presented, followed by a somewhat detailed description of the process and by an evaluation of the results.

Subsequent sections explore the causes of the failure of the experiment. The deviations in the implementation of the global monetarist model, and the model itself, are described. The inadequacies, limitations, and shortcomings of the model are analyzed, and questions about the resistance of reality to policy-induced reforms are briefly posed. Finally, the observations in these sections are collected and summarized in a list of conclusions.

THE CONTEXT

The Videla-Martínez de Hoz team took power in Argentina in March 1976, with a time horizon of three years for their administration. At the start, the government faced serious problems of security and order. The economic situation was critical on at least three counts:

- The foreign sector (no disposable reserves; sizable deficit in the current account)
- The public sector (deficit of 14 percent of GNP; revenues 25 percent of expenditures)
- The inflationary process (10 percent in December 1975, 20 percent in January 1976, 30 percent in February 1976, 50 percent in March 1976).

The goal of the government was to cure these economic pathologies by the end of its mandate, without creating open unemployment until it could reestablish security and order.

Toward the end of 1978, the term of the Videla-Martínez de Hoz government had been extended for two years (to March 1981), and the initially critical issues had evolved as follows:

- International reserves were equivalent to eighteen months of imports, and the current account showed a surplus.
- The fiscal deficit was 4 percent of GNP, and revenues were 70 percent of expenditures.
- The inflation rate could not bore through a floor of 150 percent per year.

Inflation had resisted successive attempts to bring it down: a price truce in early 1977, a credit squeeze in late 1977, and a "dirty float" since mid-1978. Output was recovering strongly from a sharp but short recession, and the unemployment rate was at an historic low.

Having thus far succeeded in achieving its other goals, the government chose as its paramount policy objective for the rest of its period the reduction of the inflation rate to at least the post-World War II average (30 percent annually), in order to leave the country economically healthy according to conventional Western criteria. It was decided to experiment with a novel approach to fight inflation. Thus, the Argentine experiment must not be confused with programs to stabilize variables, to achieve a structural opening of the economy (see the discussion of import tariff reductions in the next section of this paper), or to adjust the foreign sector.

THE EXPERIMENT

The anti-inflationary program of December 1978 was designed to weaken inflationary feed-back—expectations, informal and formal indexation—by preannouncing the growth rates of a few key variables controlled by the government:

- Public prices and wages at 4 percent monthly for eight months (for compliance, see table 3-1)
- Domestic credit at 4 percent monthly for eight months (for compliance, see table 3-2)
- The exchange rate at 5.4 percent in January 1979 and at 0.2 percent less in each succeeding month, successively extended until August 1981, but abandoned in March 1981 (see table 3-3); the initial devaluation schedule (or "tablita") was:

$$\tilde{E}_t = E_o \pi_{t=o}^8 (1.054 - 0.02t), \text{ where}$$

$\tilde{E}_t$ = preannounced exchange rate (pesos per U.S. dollar) at the end of month t
E_o = exchange rate (pesos per U.S. dollar) at the end of December 1978.

Table 3-1. Argentine Production Costs and Prices and Indebtedness, 1977-81

| Year and quarter | Quarterly percent change | | | | Private sector real indebtedness (thousand millions of Dec. 1978 U.S. dollars) |
	Real wage rate	Real public prices	Real private services prices	Real borrowing interest rate	
1977	10.1	12.1	n.a.	—	—
1978	5.9	−2.1	n.a.	13.4	12,394
I	−24.3	12.9	n.a.	89.0	11,161
II	0.0	−9.5	n.a.	4.3	11,534
III	5.9	−1.7	n.a.	24.8	12,455
IV	8.6	−2.5	n.a.	−8.5	14,426
1979	16.9	−17.7	n.a.	0.6	16,202
I	−0.1	−6.2	n.a.	−20.9	14,084
II	−0.5	−8.7	2.7	−18.1	14,963
III	3.3	−8.3	2.1	−3.2	15,981
IV	18.3	4.9	6.1	52.3	19,773
1980	24.0	26.6	23.4	18.9	23,536
I	2.1	4.0	7.6	18.7	21,593
II	1.5	3.5	4.3	10.8	22,680
III	6.8	6.6	7.9	34.2	24,686
IV	6.8	10.3	2.4	13.4	25,186
1981	−13.6	3.5	−6.6	10.6	21,357
I	−1.4	4.6	5.1	51.3	23,577
II	−15.2	−12.2	−8.9	−24.5	22,052
III	−13.8	8.9	−12.2	29.7	20,060
IV	5.6	3.5	−5.3	0.8	19,737

n.a. Not available; — not applicable.
Note: All figures have been deflated by the nonfarm WPI (wholesale price index).
Source: Econométrica SA data bank.

Table 3-2. Monetary Variables in Argentina, 1977-80
(quarterly percent change)

Year and quarter	Foreign assets (net)	Domestic credit	Money	Quasi-money
1977	—	262.0	148.9	451.3
1978	897.5	159.4	133.7	195.3
I	65.3	28.6	19.5	39.2
II	59.6	25.8	35.2	32.9
III	38.6	24.7	6.7	39.8
IV	8.8	28.6	35.3	14.2
1979	132.0	205.6	135.8	229.5
I	22.2	29.0	15.0	35.7
II	31.8	30.1	25.6	37.4
III	30.3	28.8	15.0	38.3
IV	10.5	37.3	41.9	29.5
1980	−51.7	−110.0	95.0	104.4
I	4.0	21.3	11.7	22.1
II	−20.7	21.6	24.1	11.0
III	−5.9	19.7	9.9	24.9
IV	−37.7	18.9	28.0	20.7
1981	−44.7	119.0	68.5	99.4
I	−39.1	13.2	−20.8	1.7
II	4.4	14.4	21.2	18.2
III	−0.1	28.2	12.0	30.0
IV	−13.0	32.0	56.7	27.6

— Not applicable.

Sources: Through 1980, IMF, International Financial Statistics, several issues; for 1981, Central Bank of Argentina, Statistical Bulletin, several issues.

-

All these rates were clearly inferior to the prevailing inflation rate (consumer price index, CPI, 30.2 percent and wholesale price index, WPI, 26.9 percent in the last quarter of 1978).

Simultaneously, a schedule for import tariff reduction was announced. Import tariffs were to fall, in equal quarterly steps, from their current levels to a uniform 30 percent at the end of the fifth year. This partial trade liberalization fell short of a structural opening of the economy because it neglected imports. The initial tariff reduction schedule was:

$$A_{jt} = A_{jo} - (A_{jo} - A_{jT})\frac{t}{T} = A_{jo} - A_{jo}\frac{t}{T} + A_{jT}\frac{t}{T}$$

$$= A_{jo}(1 - \frac{t}{T}) + A_{jT}(\frac{t}{T}); \ (T=20); \ (t=1,\ldots 20); \ \text{where}$$

A_{jt} = import tariff on product j (ad valorem) in quarter t

A_{jo} = import tariff on product j (ad valorem) at the end of December 1978

A_{jT} = import tariff (percent value added) at the end of reduction schedule.

For all j, $A_{jo} \geq$ 30 percent = $>A_{jT}$ = 30 percent, and

$A_{jo} <$ 30 percent = $>A_{jT} = A_{jo}$.

Later, there were anticipated reductions for producers goods and for some products that experienced unjustified price increases.

Table 3-3. Argentine Inflation, International Inflation, and Devaluation of the Peso, 1978-81
(quarterly percent change)

Year and quarter	Preannounced devaluation (1)	Observed (2)	International prices of tradables (3)	WPI (4)	CPI (5)	Simple inflation[a] (6)	Cumulative gap (7)
1978	—	13.9	1.3	24.9	28.2	11.1	—
I	—	20.7	1.3	26.6	31.8	7.8	—
II	—	9.5	1.3	24.5	28.6	16.0	—
III	—	9.9	1.3	21.6	22.3	9.9	—
IV	—	15.8	1.3	26.9	30.2	11.0	—
1979	13.6	12.6	3.5	23.0	24.5	6.8	—
I	15.3	15.3	−1.9	28.4	30.6	15.5	15.5
II	13.9	13.9	4.3	28.2	25.5	5.6	22.0
III	11.8	11.8	9.7	29.8	27.6	4.0	26.9
IV	9.9	9.9	2.2	7.2	14.7	2.1	29.5
1980	5.3	5.3	2.2	17.1	17.1	8.8	—
I	8.0	8.0	5.3	12.8	19.5	5.1	36.1
II	6.1	6.1	−1.0	17.5	18.8	13.1	53.9
III	4.3	4.3	4.5	9.0	13.1	3.8	59.8
IV	3.0	3.0	0.1	9.1	16.9	13.5	81.4
1981	—	55.1	−0.5	29.4	23.3	−17.1	—
I	3.0	18.9	5.8	12.9	15.8	−7.9	67.1
II	—	90.7	−4.9	44.1	26.9	−30.0	47.0
III	—	28.3	−2.3	32.1	27.5	1.7	49.2
IV	—	82.5	−0.4	30.3	23.4	−32.1	33.4

— Not applicable.

Sources: Column (1) Ministerio de Economía, Boletín Semanal de Economía, several issues.
         Columns (2)-(7) Econométrica SA data bank.

a. Computed as: $\left[\dfrac{1 + \text{col. (5)}/100}{[1 + \text{col. (1)}/100] \cdot [1 + \text{col. (3)}/100]} \right] \times 100.$

The government expected that the reductions to be effected in the growth rates of the variables under control—and their anticipated disclosure—would provoke a fast decline of inflation toward those rates.

In particular, there was confidence that the growth rate of import and of export prices—which was smaller than the initial inflation rate and was decreasing given the government's control over the behavior of the exchange rate, tariffs, and rebates—would place a "ceiling" on the growth rate of domestic prices: on the import side, given by

$$\frac{dMP}{MP} \leq (1 + \frac{dMP^*}{MP})(1 + \frac{d\tilde{E}}{E})(1 + \frac{d\tilde{A}}{A}), \text{ where}$$

MP = import price (pesos)

MP^* = import price (U.S. dollars)

$\tilde{E}$ = preannounced exchange rate (pesos per U.S. dollar)

E = initial exchange rate (pesos per U.S. dollar)

$\tilde{A}$ = preannounced import tariff (ad valorem)

A = initial import tariff (ad valorem);

Table 3-4. Argentine Domestic Interest Rates, International Interest Rates, and Preannounced Devaluation, 1978-81
(quarterly rates)

Year and quarter	International interest rates (1)	International financial costs (2)	Domestic borrowing interest rate (3)	Domestic lending interest rate (4)	Financial cost gap[a] (5)
1978	2.47	15.8	28.4	23.5	7.7
I	2.17	20.8	38.1	29.5	8.7
II	2.30	11.7	26.5	21.8	10.1
III	2.57	12.1	24.9	21.8	9.7
IV	2.83	18.6	24.2	20.8	2.2
1979	3.14	17.5	23.9	21.3	3.8
I	3.02	23.5	23.2	20.8	−2.7
II	2.87	17.1	23.2	20.8	3.7
III	3.12	15.3	25.7	23.2	7.9
IV	3.79	14.1	23.5	20.5	6.4
1980	3.6	9.1	18.4	15.7	6.6
I	4.1	12.4	19.4	16.4	4.0
II	3.3	9.6	18.1	15.1	5.5
III	3.0	7.4	18.2	16.1	8.7
IV	4.0	7.1	17.8	15.1	8.0
1981	4.2	61.6	31.6	26.2	−35.4
I	4.2	23.9	26.9	21.6	−2.3
II	4.3	98.9	32.7	27.8	−71.1
III	4.67	34.3	39.2	32.4	− 1.9
IV	3.8	89.4	28.1	22.9	−66.5

Sources: Column (1) LIBOR (London interbank offered rate) plus a 1.2 percent yearly spread.
Column (2) Preannounced devaluation and international interest rates (observed devaluation until last quarter of 1978 and since first quarter of 1981; commercial exchange rate since third quarter of 1981).
Column (3) FIEL, Informe de Coyuntura, several issues.
Column (4) Central Bank of Argentina.
a. Column (4) − column (2).

on the export side, given by

$$\frac{dXP}{XP} \leqslant (1 + \frac{dXP^*}{XP^*})(1 + \frac{d\tilde{E}}{E})(1 + \frac{dS}{d}), \text{ where}$$

XP = export price (pesos)
XP* = export price (U.S. dollars)
S   = export rebate (ad valorem).

These prices were going to "converge" rapidly toward the ceiling at the mere threat of imports or of loss of foreign markets and the resulting product and factor substitutions.

It was also expected that the domestic interest rate was going to approach the international interest rate adjusted for the preannounced rate of devaluation, with account taken of some costs and a negligible exchange risk premium (see table 3-4). On the active operations side, a floor was set by:

$$PI \geqslant (1 + PI^*)(1 + \frac{d\tilde{E} + d\tilde{U}}{E})(1 - PG) - 1, \text{ where}$$

PI = passive domestic interest rate
PI* = passive interest rate (U.S. dollars)

$d\tilde{U}$ = expected additional devaluation

PG = additional (percent) expenses in U.S. dollar placements.

On the passive operations side, a floor was set by:

$$AI^* \geq (1+AI^*)(1+ \frac{d\tilde{E}+d\tilde{U}}{E})(1-AG), \text{ where}$$

AI = active domestic interest rate (AI = PI + peso spread)

AI^* = active interest rate in dollars ($AI^* = PI^* + $ U.S. dollar spread)

AG = additional (percent) expenses in dollar borrowings.

This premium was due not only to some, although at the beginning small, uncertainty as to the compliance of the devaluation schedule, but also to the fact that until July 1980 the minimum term for borrowing abroad was twelve months and the preannounced devaluation schedule initially lasted eight months (later it was less), as mentioned by Rodríguez (1979).

The rate of domestic credit creation was to accompany the process, regulating the level of international reserves.

THE PROCESS

But the reality was different. The WPI, which weights tradables more heavily, grew faster than the ceiling during the first nine months of 1979: by 12.3 percent in the first quarter, by 7.9 percent in the second, and by 5.8 percent in the third, accumulating a gap of 28.2 percent before roughly converging during the next twelve months and picking up again later on. The CPI, which includes services and ponders foodstuffs (exportables) less, rose even faster, accumulating a gap of 26.9 percent during the first nine months, of 53.9 percent during the first eighteen months, and of 116.5 percent during the whole twenty-seven-month period until the change in government—diverging rather than converging. (These figures do not take into account the reduction in the average tariff levels which declined at about 6 percent annually; thus, they overestimate the ceiling and underestimate the gap. See table 3-3.)

The delay in convergence had different causes:

- The initial presence of redundant ("water in the") tariffs, although there are reasons to doubt the importance of this cause, as shown by the FIEL study conducted by Manuelli, Nielsen, and Sturzenegger (1980) and by Wogart and Marques (1979)
- Lags in imports, accounted for mostly by the time required to establish new international trade relations and marketing channels
- Delays until import penetration in domestic markets affected prices, recalling limited product substitutability, imperfect regional competition, oligopolistic market structures, and other elements affecting transparency
- The existence of natural protection, vastly more widespread than expected (including the nontraded value-added share of tradables), as stressed by Schydlowsky (1981)
- Disbelief in the sustainability of the experiment, which turned out to be a self-fulfilling prophecy.

Real Exchange Rate Appreciation and Balance of Payments Deterioration

Of course, the most important effect was the cumulative loss of competitiveness of local producers both in foreign markets (exporters) and in domestic markets (import substituters). The real exchange rate (1970 = 100) was given by

$$RE = NE \frac{(0.5XPI + 0.5MPI)}{NPI}, \text{ where}$$

RE = real exchange rate (pesos per U.S. dollar)

NE = nominal exchange rate

XPI = export price index
MPI = import price index
NPI = nonagricultural, nonfood WPI (proxy for nontradables).

It was 96.1 at the end of 1978 and declined to 74.5 one year later, to 61.8 two years later, and to 57.8 at the end of the Videla-Martínez de Hoz administration.

The real appreciation of the peso would not have hurt the competitive position of local producers so much had the peso been undervalued at the start. But this was not the case, as shown by Rodríguez and Sjaastad (1980).

At the end of 1979 it was fairly clear that the achievement of convergence was no longer sufficient for the success of the experiment. It was already too late. By then nothing less than an "overconvergence," which would have placed local producers in competition again, was required. But it did not happen.

The surplus of the current account of the balance of payments dwindled in the final quarter of 1978: a dirty float led to a real appreciation of the peso from May of that year. The balance became negative in the first quarter of 1979 and increasingly so afterwards (with the exception of a seasonal peak in the next quarter), reaching unprecedented levels in the economic history of Argentina—US$750 million per quarter—since the final quarter of 1979. (See table 3-5.)

Table 3-5. The Real Exchange Rate and the Argentine Current Account, 1977-81
(millions of U.S. dollars)

Year and quarter	Current account	Merchandise	Services	Real exchange rate (1970 = 100)[a]
1977	1,289.9	1,490.3	−200.4	107.8[b]
1978	1,833.6	8,565.8	−732.2	101.7
I	278.0	472.5	−194.5	110.5
II	755.0	937.1	−182.1	104.5
III	754.1	920.7	−166.6	95.1
IV	46.5	235.5	−189.0	96.1
1979	−550.1	1,098.4	−1,648.5	79.4
I	−64.2	350.7	−414.9	81.9
II	466.2	1,002.7	−536.5	80.8
III	−66.6	247.7	−314.3	80.2
IV	−885.5	−502.7	−382.8	74.5
1980	−4,767.8	−2,519.2	−2,248.6	69.8
I	−767.3	−223.2	−544.1	75.9
II	−988.7	−361.3	−627.4	71.2
III	−1,145.0	−746.6	−398.4	70.4
IV	−1,866.8	−1,188.1	−678.7	61.8
1981	−4,055.8	−134.0	−3,921.8	69.4
I	−2,068.5	−624.1	−1,424.4	57.8
II	−698.6	246.2	−944.8	70.4
III	−117.2	607.2	−724.4	75.2
IV	−1,191.5	−363.3	−828.2	74.4

Source: Econométrica SA data bank.

a. $RE = NE \frac{(0.5\ XPI + 0.5\ MPI)}{NPI}$, where

RE = Real exchange rate (pesos per U.S. dollar)
NE = Nominal exchange rate, daily average
XPI = Export price index
MPI = Export unit prices of industrial exporters.
NPI = Nonagricultural, nonfood WPI (proxy for nontradables).
b. Fourth quarter.

Table 3-6. Disaggregation of the Argentine Current Account, 1977-81
(millions of U.S. dollars)

| Year and quarter | Merchandise | | Services | |
	Exports	Imports	Real	Financial[a]
1977	5,651.7	4,161.5	346.8	−547.2
1978	6,399.5	3,833.7	−99.8	−632.4
I	1,330.4	857.9	−75.7	−118.8
II	1,808.4	871.3	46.2	−228.3
III	1,966.4	1,045.7	−45.8	−120.8
IV	1,294.3	1,058.8	24.5	−164.5
1979	7,809.9	6,711.5	−763.5	−88.5
I	1,549.3	1,198.6	−285.4	−129.5
II	2,383.0	1,380.3	−153.6	−382.9
III	2,160.7	1,913.0	−158.6	−155.7
IV	1,716.9	2,219.6	−165.9	−216.9
1980	8,021.4	10,540.6	−740.1	−1,508.5
I	2,059.2	2,282.4	−419.4	−124.7
II	1,924.4	2,285.7	−150.2	−477.2
III	2,035.5	2,782.1	−11.0	−387.4
IV	2,002.3	3,190.4	−159.5	−519.2
1981	9,146.0	9,280.0	−616.0	−3,305.8
I	1,989.9	2,614.0	−681.7	−742.7
II	2,848.2	2,602.0	−32.8	−912.0
III	2,719.2	2,112.0	71.3	−795.7
IV	1,588.7	1,952.0	27.2	−855.4

a. Includes unilateral transfers.
Source: Econométrica SA data bank.

The deterioration of the current account was led by sharp increases in the real services deficit (US$663.7 million) and in merchandise imports (US$2,877.8 million) from 1978 to 1979; these deficits reflected outbound tourism and nontraditional imports, as well as more traditional ones, following the 10 percent reactivation of global demand during the year. This deterioration occurred despite a recovery in the terms of trade (1970 = 100) from 66 in the final quarter of 1976, a trough, to 84 toward mid-1980. (See table 3-6.)

The capital account experienced record inflows—over US$1,000 million per quarter—that funded the jump in reserves to US$10,480 million by the end of 1979. Foreign debt grew ever more, to US$19,035 million, due to some gross outflows. The inflow of funds was a result of the reduction of minimum borrowing terms to one year and of the financial cost gap (the differential between borrowing at home and abroad), which averaged 6.4 percent per quarter with an increasing trend. (See table 3-7.)

Although domestic credit expanded by 207.2 percent in 1979 (faster than before), the smaller and declining increase in foreign assets (132 percent) and the higher rate of growth of quasi-money (222 percent) explain the lower monetary expansion of 135.8 percent (about the same as 1978). This figure compares with a declining CPI rate of growth of 139.7 percent and a WPI rate of growth of 128.9 percent. The government deficit growth rate declined during 1979 to 108.5 percent, slower than the expansion of monetary variables. (See table 3-8.)

The Financial Crisis and the Measures of July 1980

In the second quarter of 1980, following the detonation of a financial crisis in March—four gigantic defaults, three of them banks—the capital account became negative while the current account continued deteriorating (current reserves declined from the March peak). The crash

Table 3-7. The Interest Differential and the Argentine Capital Account, 1977-81

Year and quarter	Interest differential (quarterly percent change)	Capital account (millions of U.S. dollars)
1977	—	1,189.1
1978	7.7	1,366.2
I	8.7	1,097.1
II	10.1	489.6
III	9.7	30.0
IV	− 2.2	− 250.5
1979	3.8	4,927.8
I	− 2.7	1,055.8
II	3.7	1,032.8
III	7.9	1,239.2
IV	6.4	1,600.0
1980	6.6	2,253.3
I	4.0	1,204.4
II	5.5	− 758.7
III	8.7	1,543.7
IV	8.0	263.9
1981	− 35.5	622.7
I	− 2.3	− 761.7
II	− 71.1	897.9
III	− 1.9	93.0
IV	− 66.5	393.5

— Not applicable.
Source: Econométrica SA data bank.

Table 3-8. Fiscal Variables in Argentina, 1978-81
(quarterly percent change)

Year and quarter	Current revenues	Current expenditures	Financial requirements
1978	− 12.6	3.7	− 25.8
1979	145.7	162.9	138.6
I	n.a.	n.a.	n.a.
II	46.7	28.0	− 15.5
III	40.4	38.9	32.7
IV	21.9	21.0	16.9
1980	90.6	108.9	179.0
I	− 5.9	3.4	44.7
II	13.5	28.2	70.9
III	45.0	26.7	− 8.5
IV	15.4	18.7	28.5
1981	148.9	140.6	119.1
I	15.7	3.6	− 29.4
II	39.7	34.0	8.3
III	28.9	48.1	159.2
IV	24.0	36.4	71.9

n.a. Not available.
Source: Econométrica SA data bank.

was a result of the particular way in which the banking system had been liberalized in mid-1977, when several of the usual prudential rules were abolished. Because the central bank guaranteed bank deposits, the crash caused a sharp expansion of the money supply in the second quarter of 1980.

The government faced the decision whether to continue or to abandon the experiment, and it chose the first option. A package of measures, directed to bolster confidence in the peso and to improve the payments situation, was announced in July 1980, although it was partly applied later on. The main measures of the package were:

- Another extension of the preannounced exchange rate schedule
- Elimination of a minimum term for borrowing abroad
- Increased gross public borrowing abroad
- Extension and increased rates of the value-added tax and elimination of other taxes (mostly on labor), supposedly neutral in effect on revenue, which improved local competitiveness (applied in October 1980)
- Elimination of tourist import franchises
- Additional import tariff reductions and a schedule to reach a uniform level of 20 percent by 1984.

By then the cumulative gaps between the WPI and the CPI with respect to the ceiling, since the beginning of the experiment, were 36.0 percent and 58.9 percent, respectively.

The current account continued its steady deterioration—now because of the leveling of exports in nominal dollar terms, increased imports, and a doubling of the financial services deficit, all of which reflected the sharp decline in the net international position. The capital account reacted positively only in the third quarter of 1980, when it showed an inflow of short-term funds of US$1,543.7 million.

Although the growth rates of the WPI and the CPI fell markedly in the third quarter of 1980, they still did not converge. Monetary growth accompanied the CPI rise, but because of the change in expectations and the increased financial requirements of enterprises, as well as of the public sector, real interest rates jumped to yet higher levels.

At the beginning of the fourth quarter of 1980 the short-term impact of the July package of measures was exhausted, and the end of the Videla-Martínez de Hoz administration was only six months away. Realization that the experiment could not be extended beyond March 1981 became widespread. Consequently, both the WPI and the CPI undertook a path very divergent from the ceiling, to finish with cumulative gaps of 67.4 percent and 116.5 percent, respectively, in March 1981.

The current account gave a deficit of US$3,825.1 million in the last six months, with a marked increase in imports at the end of 1980 and a violent upsurge of the deficit in services, both real and financial, in the first quarter of 1981. This happened despite an improvement in the terms of trade from 84.1 at the end of 1979 to 96.5 at the beginning of 1981.

The interest differential between borrowing at home and abroad had exceeded 10 percent per quarter since mid-1980 and reached 19.6 percent in the first quarter of 1981. Despite this differential, the capital account was barely positive at the end of 1980 and showed a deficit of US$851.9 million in the first quarter of 1981.

The behavior of the capital and the current account, as well as large gross outflows, caused a drop in reserves to US$4,699 million by March 31, 1981 and a huge jump of foreign debt to about US$28,000 million at that date. (See table 3-9.) Overall, the deterioration of the net international position of Argentina over the twenty-seven months of the experiment added up to US$16,700 million.

Table 3-9. Argentine Net International Position, End 1977-81
(millions of U.S. dollars)

Year and quarter	Reserves	Debt	Net position
End of 1977	4,039	11,761	−7,722
1978	6,037	13,663	−7,626
I	5,224	n.a.	n.a.
II	5,770	n.a.	n.a.
III	6,251	n.a.	n.a.
IV	6,037	n.a.	n.a.
1979	10,480	19,035	−8,555
I	7,034	n.a.	n.a.
II	8,513	n.a.	n.a.
III	9,694	n.a.	n.a.
IV	10,480	n.a.	n.a.
1980	7,684	27,162	−19,478
I	10,667	n.a.	n.a.
II	9,190	n.a.	n.a.
III	9,492	n.a.	n.a.
IV	7,684	n.a.	n.a.
1981	3,877	32,000	−28,123
I	4,699	n.a.	n.a.
II	4,729	n.a.	n.a.
III	4,646	n.a.	n.a.
IV	3,877	n.a.	n.a.

n.a. Not available.
Source: Econométrica SA data bank.

During 1980 domestic credit grew 119.6 percent, but—because of the contraction of foreign assets (−52.7 percent), and despite the slower increase in quasi-money (86.6 percent)—the monetary expansion was 95 percent.

The government deficit contributed to raise interest rates and to expand domestic credit because it increased by 174.8 percent. In fact, the fiscal situation began its decline in the final quarter of 1980, when the tax package of July became effective and proved not to be neutral but to favor heavily deficit. Still, the rate of monetary creation did not substantially exceed the declining CPI growth rate of 87.6 percent, although it certainly did exceed the even slower WPI growth rate of 57.5 percent. Both the CPI and the WPI reached their trough in the third quarter of 1980.

These developments had a dampening and lagged impact on the level of output and employment. The former began to decline only in 1981, although manufacturing production declined throughout 1980.

High Real Interest Rates and the Business Sector

Real borrowing interest rates ("active" interest rates, or "activas"; those paid by first-rate enterprises to first-rate banks, deflated by the WPI) were negative—though declining in absolute values—during the first nine months of the experiment. They became strongly positive with the decline in the inflation rate in the fourth quarter of 1979 and remained so thereafter. Their fluctuations reflect more variations in the WPI than in nominal interest rates, with the exception of the first quarter of 1981—the last before the change of government—when nominal interest rates jumped. Thus, real borrowing interest rates declined from October 1979 to June 1980 (for an average annual rate of 31.2 percent) and increased from July 1980 to March 1981 (for an average annual rate of 44.2 percent). In the final quarter—especially in the final month—of the Videla-Martínez de Hoz administration, they exploded. (See table 3-4. If there is certainty of a devaluation at a given time, there is a floor to the domestic interest rate I given by

$$(1+I)^{T-t} = (1+I^*)^{T-t} (1 + \frac{d\bar{E}_T}{E_t}), \text{ where:}$$

$d\bar{E}_T$ = devaluation at time T

I^* = foreign interest rate

E_t = exchange rate (pesos per U.S. dollar) at time t.

As $t \to T$, $I \to \infty$.

By introducing uncertainty both in the timing and amount of the prospective devaluation, we might explain reality more closely.)

These extraordinarily high interest rates—substantially more so for other than first-rate firms—caught enterprises, especially in the industrial sector, in a generally weak position. Negative real interest rates for over thirty years made it rational for firms to operate with high debt-equity ratios, since high leverages paid off handsomely. The violent real appreciation of the peso made price increases difficult, whereas the main cost components of firms—interests, wages, public and private services—soared. (See table 3-1.) Although during 1979 the reactivation of global demand allowed for a return to the 1977 output levels, these declined steadily after the first quarter of 1980. Thus, the margins of contribution were sharply reduced, and results were often negative. Under those conditions, enterprises found it difficult to change their financial structure: low or negative rentability did not attract equity investment; high interest rates on riskless financial investment depressed the value of physical assets.

Consequently, enterprises kept paying the high interest rates and increasing their debts at a fast pace. In contrast, the financial system, faced with a general situation of uncollectability, chose not to make explicit the portfolio situation and renewed credits plus interests (Ribas 1981). Both the business and financial sectors hoped for a better future rather than force sudden defaults. Thus, the indebtedness of the private business sector to the financial system grew spectacularly—73.9 percent in real terms from the end of 1978 until the end of 1980.

The devastating effects that real interest rates of such magnitude (negative leverage) had on the net worth of enterprises, and the difficulty of the enterprises recovering, have been quantified in several studies. Carbajal (1980) determined the survival period of an enterprise as a function of the difference between the rate of return on assets and the interest rate for different initial debt-assets ratios. (For a difference of −30 percent between the annual rates and an initial debt-assets ratio of 0.67, a firm loses its net worth in 1.33 years.) Areosa (1981) estimated the period required for a firm to reach a 0.5 debt-assets ratio as a function of the same two variables. (For a difference of +10 percent between the annual rates and an initial debt-assets ratio of 0.75, it takes 4 years.)

But even this cover-up of the real situation could not avoid a marked increase in business failures—by 69 percent in 1979 and 62 percent in 1980—and the bankruptcy of over 10 percent of the financial system by March 1981.

THE RESULTS

The main objective of the Argentine experiment was to reduce the inflation rate. It succeeded partially and temporarily. The WPI growth rate dropped from 26.9 percent in the fourth quarter of 1978 to 9 percent in the third quarter of 1980, to finish at 12.9 percent, and increasing. The

CPI growth rate diminished from an initial 30.2 percent to 13.1 percent in the third quarter of 1980, to end at a stable 15.8 percent. But both indexes failed to converge to the ceiling, causing the real exchange rate to decline from 96.1 at the end of 1978 to 57.8 at the beginning of 1981. This led to an unsustainable foreign sector situation and, consequently, to an unavoidable rebound of the inflation rate.

Although it was not an explicit aim of the program, the terms of trade improved steadily, from an initial 66.1 to a final 96.5. But both the lack of an empirical explanation and the continued improvement after the March 1981 devaluation cast doubt on whether betterment of the terms of trade was due to the experiment.

From the point of view of output, real GNP grew 7.8 percent during the twenty-seven-month span; real GNP per capita grew 3.6 percent during the same period—not bad for stabilization times, but below the historical mean of 2.5-3.0 percent annually. Although total employment increased less than the total population, there was no open unemployment by March 1981. Real wages increased steadily: 16.9 percent in 1979 and 24.0 percent in 1980. Again, both output and employment had passed their peaks by the end of the period, and because of the foreign sector situation their levels were not sustainable.

As to the costs of the experiment, first there was the deterioration of US$16,700 million in the next international position—roughly 25 percent of the annual GNP. In a previous study (Dagnino Pastore and Durán 1981), we estimated that the main uses of the funds obtained by the increased foreign debt were, in decreasing order: outflows of funds, tourist expenditures and purchases, and nontraditional imports. (It has been argued that the main use was the import of military equipment. Our study does not show it; in any case, the main imports of military equipment date from 1978, before the experiment.)

Except for the eventual return of the capital outflows, which according to experience is at best very partial, and for some increase in capital goods imports, which in part replaced their domestic production, the asset counterparts of the increased liabilities have not added significantly to the capacity of the country to generate foreign exchange.

Meanwhile, the interest on the additional foreign debt posed an annual burden of roughly US$3,000 million on the balance of payments—more than 30 percent of total exports. Whereas years ago dollar interest rates were negative in real terms, this was no longer so. Thus, for some years there would be a jump in the exchange rate parity, since the other current items would have to generate an additional surplus of US$3,000 million annually. This can be interchangably called increase in competitiveness or decline in the standard of living.

Second, there was the fiscal deterioration. Although part of it was attributable to a lack of discipline on the expenditure side, the main cause was the already explained decline in revenues in real terms, which also reflected the incipient recession as well as the financial situation of enterprises. The government deficit was running at around 7 to 8 percent of GNP in the final quarters of the Videla-Martínez de Hoz administration.

A third significant cost of the experiment was its devastating impact on the profitability and financial structure of enterprises, specially those producing physical goods, and consequently on the solvency of the financial system. It was clear by March 1981 that, unless the government undertook general and exceptional measures of salvage, a large number of firms would default. This was even more apparent because the unavoidably huge devaluation was also going to hurt those companies that had not yet suffered because they had funded themselves abroad. Consequently, the need to solve this situation meant sizable additional government expenditures and future inflationary pressures.

These were the costs by the end of March 1981. After that time the experiment was abandoned, and not all later problems can be attributed to it. Yet some subsequent difficulties were unavoidable consequences.

In 1981 the devaluation was 263.8 percent; WPI grew 80.1 percent and CPI 131.3 percent. Thus, the real exchange rate recovered to 74.4 by the end of the year, but inflation was already at around the pre-experiment level. The balance of payments still showed a sizable deficit, and foreign debt had reached US$32,000 million. Despite some general relief measures by the government, business failures and bankruptcies continued at a high rate, and new official aid was likely. Real GDP declined by 6 percent, and unemployment jumped to its highest rate since the 1960s.

The crisis had not reached its trough yet but had instead already achieved—if not surpassed—the magnitude of the 1930-32 depression:

- The service of the foreign debt as a ratio of exports was higher than in 1932.
- The (forecasted) decline of industrial GDP for 1979-82 was −23.2 percent, compared with 17.7 percent in 1929-32.

One is thus tempted to share the concern of Rudiger Dornbusch (1981, p. 7) [see also his remarks in chapter 8 of this volume], that "the fact remains that in the last four years we have been accumulating substantial evidence that the new stabilization programs can turn out [to be] quite catastrophic."

THE IMPLEMENTATION

As Calvo (1981, p. 32) [see also his remarks in chapters 4 and 8 of this volume] wrote as an epilogue to his account of the experiment, "we economists must learn from the catastrophes of some...to try to improve the welfare of many others."

What were the causes of such lopsided results from the experiment? Were they errors in the implementation of the model? Or were they essential elements in the model? Or was it reality that did not conform to rational behavior as depicted by the model?

Let us first review the question of errors of implementation. At this point there is no quarrel about their existence in various aspects and stages of the experiment. The errors most usually mentioned are:

- The belief at the start—that various measures undertaken during 1976-78 had produced a substantial shift in the theoretical parity level of the peso—led to an appraisal that the currency was initially undervalued and that there was a buffer in case of delayed convergence; this did not prove to be true.
- In the same vein, the later failure to realize that the steady deterioration of the net international position, through its impact on the financial services deficit, was causing a gradual but continuous shift of the theoretical parity level of the peso in the opposite direction thus required an overconvergence to correct the situation.
- The increasingly unrealistic devaluation schedules preannounced, and the consequently increasing credibility gap, were an important cause of failure of this type of experiment, as analyzed by Blejer and Mathieson (1981).
- The failure to control domestic credit creation at rates compatible with a better performance of the net international position was attributable to the insufficient control of government expenditures.
- Along the same lines, the relatively faster opening of the country to financial as compared with commercial transactions caused an early and untimely inflow of funds, as explained by Frenkel [see chapter 2].

Such an extensive, although not exhaustive, list of deviations from the model in its application certainly creates a problem in identifying the cause of failure of the experiment.

An analysis of the figures involved, however, does not lend support to the hypothesis that the set of errors enumerated fully explains the results. Moreover, there are other aspects of the economy that did not behave according to the model and whose divergences are not easily explained by inaccurate application. Before exploring these, a summary of the model is in order.

The Model

The model behind the Argentine anti-inflationary experiment, explained in the second section above, can be summarized mathematically as follows:

(3.1) $P = EP^*$, where:

  P = domestic price level (pesos)
  E = exchange rate (pesos per U.S. dollar)
  P^* = foreign price level (U.S. dollars).

This is usually referred to as the "law of one price." In this case, since the foreign price level P^* is exogenous, the exchange rate E—a policy instrument—determines the domestic price level.

(3.2) $I = I^* + \dfrac{d\tilde{E}}{E} + \dfrac{d\tilde{U}}{E}$, where

  I = domestic interest rate
  I^* = foreign interest rate
  $d\tilde{E}/E$ = preannounced rate of devaluation of the peso
  $d\tilde{U}/E$ = expected additional rate of devaluation of the peso.

This is usually called the "law of one interest rate." In this case, since the foreign rate of interest I^* is exogenous, the rate of devaluation $d\tilde{E}/E$—a policy instrument—and the uncertainty about it, $d\tilde{U}/E$, determine the domestic rate of interest.

(3.3) $R = M^d - D$, where

  R = reserves
  M^d = money demand = M^s = money supply
  D = domestic credit.

This is the money market-clearing equation:

(3.3a) $R = P(aY - bI) - D$, where
  $M^d = P(aY - bI)$, the money demand equation
  Y = real income;

(3.3b) $R = EP^*(aY - bI) - D$, substituting equation (3.1)
    $= EP^*aY - EP^*bI) - D$;

(3.3c) $R = EP^*aY - EP^*bI^*E - P^*b\dfrac{d\tilde{E}}{E} - EP^*b\dfrac{d\tilde{U}}{E} - D$
    $= EP^*aY - EP^*bI^* - P^*bd\tilde{E} - P^*bd\tilde{U} - D.$

The level of reserves is a function of the (exogenous) foreign price P^* and interest I^* levels, of the (also exogenous, always full employment) real income level, of the (policy-determined) level and change in the exchange rate, and of the expectations about it, and of the (policy-determined) domestic credit level.

Under these conditions, the model can be summarized as follows.

• By the law of one price, the exchange rate level determines the domestic price level.

• By the law of one interest rate, the change in the exchange rate determines the domestic interest level—subject to changes in expectations.

• By the money market-clearing equation and the money demand equation, the domestic credit level determines the level of reserves—subject to changes in real income (always at full employment) or in the interest rate (under control). I cannot help noticing the inviting opportunities opened for two-tier market modeling by the fact that the international link between the goods markets is the level of the exchange rate, whereas the international link between the capital markets is the change in the exchange rate. [See discussions of this issue by Frenkel, chapter 2, and Dornbusch, chapter 8.]

This model qualifies as one of "global monetarism" in the sense that it assumes the law of one price and a full employment level of output, which is usual when the possibility of exchange rate changes (as the flexible exchange rate case) is allowed, as shown by Johnson (1976).

Limitations and Shortcomings of the Model

The observations collected about the experiment in Argentina, as well as reflections upon it, open two lines of criticism of the model: the validity of its empirical assumptions and the limitations of the model itself. Let us follow the first line.

The description of the process (see the third section above) shows that the law of one price did not hold for the Argentine case—Corbo (1981) [see also his remarks in chapters 4 and 8] provides different evidence for Chile. The findings for Argentina add to heavy econometric evidence in this regard, as reviewed by Kreinin and Officer (1978).

Observations of the process in Argentina showed that the widespread presence of non-tradable goods and services and significant nontradable value-added shares in tradable goods not only delay but may invalidate the law for the relevant time span. Consequently, the real effects of devaluation cannot be dispensed so easily.

The description of the process given earlier also casts doubt on the significance of the law of one interest rate. It seems necessary to go beyond the tautology of defining the risk premium as

$$(3.2a) \quad \frac{d\bar{U}}{E} = I - (I^* + \frac{d\bar{E}}{E}).$$

It is clear that there are operating costs, imperfect substitutability, and portfolio considerations involved.

But the lack of empirical validation of the behavioral assumptions of the model sheds light on other limitations: it does not adequately contemplate how deviations of observed from expected behavior feed back into the process.

If, as in the case of Argentina, those deviations occur in such a way that their effects on the level of reserves have opposite signs (they offset each other), the concentration of the model on the level of reserves leaves outside dynamic considerations that prove empirically important.

In fact, these limitations of the model are but a sample of more general shortcomings, its implicit assumptions about:

- The absence of "sterilization"
- The already mentioned presumption of full employment
- The independence, for periods relevant from a policy standpoint, of prices and income from domestic credit and interest rates
- The neglect of reverse causality—from reserves to expected devaluation and so on.

Frenkel and Johnson (1976, p. 25) dispose of criticism of the second assumption by claiming that the monetary approach should be viewed as a long-run proposition reflecting the assumption that full employment is "the historical norm rather than the historical rarity."

The economic literature flourishes with models that draw on the monetary approach and incorporate other elements to correct some of its limitations and shortcomings. In fact, the analysis conducted in the 1950s by the International Monetary Fund, a forerunner of the monetary approach, though less tightly knitted allowed for more flexibility and realism (see Robichek 1962). But it is also true that

- The experiment in the Southern Cone reflects a fairly crude version of global monetarism
- The incorporation of some of the sophistications would have provoked essential policy changes—making it difficult to keep the same name for the model before and after incorporating the changes.

So much for limitations and shortcomings. Let us now consider two necessary extensions of the monetary approach that seem to be useful.

• The indifference of some writers to whether changes in reserves are related to changes in the current or in the capital account is not justified. There is a substantial difference and widely diverging consequences between changes in assets based on a current surplus and those generated by increased liabilities—an elementary notion of business financial analysis.

• As Johnson (1977) has noted, "since the stock adjustment process enters into the determination of the international money flow in the money market, it must also enter into the determination of at least one of the flows in the other markets." By the same token, the arguments for the functions explaining the flows in the goods markets and in the securities markets must also enter into the determination of the flows in at least one of the other two markets. So, unless the goods and the securities markets are isolated from the money market, some of their arguments must enter into the determination of the money flows.

THE SOCIAL REFORM

All economic policies on the one hand operate within a context and on the other hand modify that context to a greater or lesser degree.

It has been shown that the anti-inflationary experiment in Argentina failed partly because of implementation errors, partly because of the inadequacy of the underlying model.

But one might ask whether the goal was to apply a model adequate to the context or whether it was more to modify reality so as to make it fit the model. If the objective was the latter, it was achieved to some extent during the process, but the final collapse of the experiment undid most of the achievement.

Additional elaboration of this point leads to questions not only of feasibility but also of desirability—and of comparison with alternative models to change the context. These questions lie well beyond the scope of this paper.

CONCLUSIONS

• The results of the anti-inflationary experiment in Argentina during 1979-81 are lopsided: partial and temporary benefits at huge and lasting costs.

• Multiple implementation errors pose a problem in identifying the cause of failure, but they do not explain the failure fully.

• The crude version of the model applied in Argentina has limitations in feeding deviations of observed from expected behavior back into the process.

• Thus, part of the failure must come from the model itself. Crucial assumptions of the underlying global monetarist model—notably the laws of one price and of one interest rate—cannot be validated empirically in Argentina.

• Some assumptions of independence between variables do not seem warranted, at least for periods relevant for a policy.

• Application of less simplistic models with monetary roots are likely to improve performance, but also to cause essential policy changes.

• A serious drawback of the monetary approach is its indifference to whether reserve changes correspond to the current or to the capital account. The difference is not at all immaterial for the dynamic behavior of the economic system.

• To join an already large chorus: the monetary approach will bear all its fruits when it is integrated with, rather than substituted for, the other balance of payments theories.

REFERENCES

Areosa, Mario N. 1981. "El sector productivo: Evolución de su estructura patrimonial." Buenos Aires (June 4). Processed.

Blejer, Mario I., and Donald J. Mathieson. 1981. "The Preannouncement of Exchange Rate Changes as a Stabilization Instrument." IMF Staff Papers, vol. 28, no. 4 (December).

Calvo, Guillermo A. 1981. Reflexiones teóricas sobre el problema de estabilización en Argentina. Documento de Trabajo no. 29. Buenos Aires: Centro de Estúdios Macroeconómicos de la Argentina (CEMA), October.

Carbajal, Celestino. 1980. "Rentabilidad, tasas de interés y supervivencia de la firma." Desarrollo Económico (Buenos Aires), vol. 20, no. 79 (October-December).

Corbo, Vittorio. 1981. "Inflation in an Open Economy: The Case of Chile." Paper presented at the Second Regional Meeting of the Econometric Society, Rio de Janeiro. Cuadernos de Economía (Santiago), vol. 19, no. 56 (April 1982).

Dagnino Pastore, José María, and Viviana Durán. 1981. "Deuda externa, 1972-80." Informe Interno (June). Buenos Aires: Econométrica SA. Processed.

Dornbusch, Rudiger. 1981. "Stabilization Policy in Developing Countries: What Have We Learned?" Paper presented at the Latin American Meeting of the Econometric Society, Buenos Aires, 1980. Revised December 1981. Final version in World Development, vol. 10 (September 1982), pp. 701-08.

Frenkel, Jacob A., and Harry G. Johnson, eds. 1976. The Monetary Approach to the Balance of Payments, and ch. 1 by them (same title). Toronto: University of Toronto Press; London: Allen and Unwin.

Guitián, Manuel. 1976. "The Balance of Payments as a Monetary Phenomenon: Empirical Evidence, Spain 1955-71." In Frenkel and Johnson 1976, ch. 15.

Johnson, Harry G. 1976. "The Monetary Approach to Balance of Payments Theory." In Frenkel and Johnson 1976, ch. 6.

_____. 1977. "The Monetary Approach to Balance of Payments Theory and Policy: Explanation and Policy Implications." Econometrica, no. 44, pp. 217-29.

Killick, Tony, ed. 1981. Adjustment and Financing in the Developing World. Washington, D.C.: International Monetary Fund.

Kreinen, Mordechai E., and Lawrence H. Officer. 1978. The Monetary Approach to the Balance of Payments: A Survey. Princeton Studies in International Finance no. 43. Princeton, N.J.: Princeton University, November.

Manuelli, R., G. E. Nielsen, and A. Sturzenegger. 1980. Apertura de la economía: El impacto de las modificaciones arancelarias, Argentina 1979-84. Buenos Aires: Fundación de Investigaciones Económicas Latinoamericanas (FIEL).

Ribas, Armando P. 1981. "Atila y el Banco Central." El Cronista Comercial, vol. 26, no. 2.

Robichek, E. Walter. 1962. "Monetary Analysis as a Tool for Credit Control." IMF Institute Training Program report no. TP-62-iv-2 (March 20). Washington, D.C. Processed.

Rodríguez, Carlos A. 1979. El plan argentino de estabilización del 20 de Diciembre. Documento de Trabajo no. 5. Buenos Aires: CEMA, July.

Rodríguez, Carlos A., and Larry A. Sjaastad. 1980. El atraso cambiario en la Argentina: ¿Mito o realidad? Ensayos Económicos no. 13. Buenos Aires: Banco Central de la República Argentina, March.

Schydlowsky, Daniel M. 1981. "Alternative Approaches to Short-Term Economic Management in Developing Countries." In Killick 1981.

Wogart, Jan Peter, and José S. Marques. 1979. "Price Stabilization through Trade Liberalization." Paper presented at the Second International Conference on Latin America and the World Economy. Buenos Aires: Instituto Torcuato di Tella. Processed.

4

Commentary on Recent Experience in the Southern Cone

The following is based on discussion of the monetary approach to the balance of payments as it was applied in Argentina, Chile, and Uruguay in recent years. Although some overlap with the commentary in part III is inevitable, part III is intended to be a broader and more widely ranging evaluation of the experience in the Southern Cone.

ARGENTINA

José María Dagnino Pastore

I have organized my comments in five parts, roughly in parallel with the structure of my paper [see preceding chapter].

Background. A few things must first be said about the Argentine context before the anti-inflationary experiment of 1979-81. The application to Argentina of the approach under analysis did not happen when the Videla-Martínez de Hoz government and economic team first came to power in 1976, but almost three years later. In March 1976 they faced, besides extra-economic problems, three critical areas in the economy: the foreign sector, the public sector, and inflation. In the foreign sector, liquid reserves were almost zero, and the current account deficit was US$1 billion. In the public sector, two indicators were: deficit, 14 percent of GNP, and the ratio of revenues to expenditures, 25 percent. That meant that only 1 out of 4 pesos of expenditures came through revenues. The rest was money or debt issue. And the monthly progression of inflation was: December 1975, 10 percent; January 1976, 20 percent; February 1976, 30 percent; and March 1976, 50 percent.

Inflation must be shown as a progression because everybody had a different theory of the course inflation would follow. This is the objective information. The peformance in the next three years until, say, December 1978 was very impressive, and this situation was completely reversed. The level of reserves came up to about US$6 billion, about a year and a half, of imports, which compares with OPEC (Organization of Petroleum-Exporting Countries) levels. The current account became positive—in the peak year it was positive, nearly US$2 billion. So the performance here was much better than expected. The public sector deficit came down to about 4 percent of GDP, and the ratio of revenues to expenditures was about 75 percent. Inflation showed some oscillation, but it could not go through a floor of 150 percent a year.

Initially, the government was supposed to complete its mandate by March 1979, but it was extended for two more years. Somewhere near the end of 1978 the priorities of economic policy were discussed, and the consensus was that two of the pathologies that had made Argentina a sick country among Western economies had been solved. Only one—inflation—remained, and this became the top priority of economic policy.

I cannot tell you the daily experiences, but any time there was an option between a decision that could hurt the fight against inflation (but help some other objective) and an alternative course of action, the decision was systematically taken to bring down inflation.

It is important to note that the policy being examined was not a policy of adjustment of the balance of payments. The balance of payments was favorable. And, although it incorporated some opening of the economy, which was a long-run objective, the policy had as its primary objective fighting inflation. In fact, questions will occur about the possibility of doing the two things simultaneously, as we shall see later on.

The program. This was the context. The measures to fight inflation were undertaken in December 1978. I do not want to make the story long. Before this period there were several attempts to bring down inflation that failed. One was a price truce; a second was monetary medicine, short-lived; and a third was to let the exchange rate float.

The package of measures in December 1978 came mainly from a diagnosis that expectations are important, that the mechanics of feedback are very important. I think it was an accurate diagnosis for a country such as Argentina, with its thirty-year history of inflation. The idea was to cut all these feedback links: expectations, informal indexation, and some forms of formal indexation. The instruments used were more or less the following.

The idea—to work through expectations—was to preannounce measures. So there was a preannouncement about the growth rate of public wages and prices; there was a preannouncement of the rate of domestic credit creation; there was a preannouncement of exchange rate devaluation (the "tablita"). And then there was a long-term measure—a gradual opening of the economy through reduction of tariffs over five years. The idea was more or less this: after five years there would be a uniform tariff of 30 percent; since there were different tariffs at the beginning, there would be a proportional convergence toward this 30 percent uniform tariff through quarterly decreases during the five-year period. This reduction of tariffs was the fourth element. It was reinforced through additional reductions from two sources. One was that, when some price increased beyond the level expected by the government, the firm making this price increase was punished by tariff reductions. The other was that there was a drop to zero level of some capital goods.

This was the group of measures undertaken, and the third measure (the preannounced rate of devaluation) was to be the driving force to make inflation decline. The theory was the following. There was relatively stable international inflation. If to this international inflation one added the rate of the devaluation of the peso, which was to decline over time, one obtained a ceiling for traded prices, both on the import and on the export side. The ceiling level was about 6 percent; the prevailing inflation at the time was 8 percent. The idea was that internal prices would rapidly go below the ceiling and be driven down according to the behavior of the ceiling.

The results. What happened—and this is the first of the problems with the scheme—was that internal prices, rather than converging to the ceiling, initially jumped and then were very slow to converge. Consumer prices never converged to this; wholesale prices almost converged for a period but then again went up. Figures were: for the first nine months, the increase in internal prices was 27 percent higher than the increase in the ceiling; for the first eighteen months, the increase was 54 percent higher than the ceiling; and for the whole twenty-seven months of the experiment, the increase was 117 percent higher than the ceiling.

The natural consequence of this different rate of growth between internal and international prices was a delayed but firm effect on the balance of payments. Of course, the gap depended on the cumulative effect of the delay in or lack of convergence, which hurts the balance of payments. The deterioration of the Argentine balance of payments is a textbook case of how the balance of payments worsens when there is an increasingly overvalued currency. The first area of the economy to decline was services and tourism; the second one was imports. Exports had performed relatively well.

During the time, there was an improvement of the terms of trade of the country. I don't think the improvement had much to do with the effects of this appreciation of the currency, because after the policy was changed, the terms of trade still continued their trend, and this does not disprove that Argentina is a small country.

But the deterioration of the current account was very steady. It became negative by the end of 1979, and in 1980 it showed a deficit of almost US$5 billion. By April 1980 the capital account also showed deterioration. So the government had to face a decision whether to continue with the program or to change it. The decision was to continue. Additional measures were taken, the more important of which was to abandon the minimum term for capital inflows, which used to be one year. One could bring money in for thirty days if one wanted. But by then the effects of the deterioration in the payments situation started to show in the confidence people had about having assets in pesos and debts in dollars. From this point on, the level of interest rates became increasingly high in real terms.

So for a very long period Argentina had an increasing deficit in the current account, an increasing indebtedness, and increasing real interest rates.

By September 1980 the succession of the government was decided. People knew that the new government was unlikely to follow the economic policy of the current government, and this added to the risk of having peso assets and dollar debts and to the effects of this risk on the interest rates. These effects were extreme toward the end of the period. If it is certain that at a given date there will be a 30 percent devaluation, then to remain in pesos assets requires an interest rate of 30 percent one month before devaluation, an interest rate of 15 percent two months before, and an interest rate of 10 percent three months before. This is a schedule that sets the minimum level of interest rates in domestic assets.

Now this, of course, happened as the final months of the tablita approached. In the past the government had reacted to this by shifting the final date, extending the tablita. So the whole system shifted, and the floor to domestic interest was postponed. But when the final date could not be postponed because of political reasons and the central bank continued with the tablita, then movement started up along the interest rate floor.

This is a sketchy description of the process. It is true that after the second quarter of 1980 monetary and fiscal variables did not accompany the process. I do not think they were important enough up to this point. There already was a 54 percent difference between the increases in domestic and international prices, and the real exchange rate had gone from an initial 96—taking 1970 as equal to 100—to a level of 70.

As to what happened later, I have some divergent evidence from that presented by Mario Blejer [see chapter 1]. I think Blejer mentioned a twelvefold increase of credit to financial institutions. Overall figures show that the behavior was not the one needed, but neither was it so dramatic a deterioration—that is, when credit to the private sector (including financial institutions) and to the public sector is included.

Benefits and costs. What were the final results of this policy that guided Argentina's economy for twenty-seven months? Clearly, there was a benefit in the decrease of the inflation rate—roughly from 150 percent to 75 percent, based on an average of the consumer price index and of the wholesale price index (of course, with a question mark about the sustainability of this policy in the face of a foreign sector deteriorating so rapidly that nobody thought the policy could be continued).

The costs were mostly in three areas, one of which—the fiscal—is probably not completely attributable to the scheme, but they were particularly heavy in the foreign sector. This first problem was a negative foreign sector current account balance of almost US$5 billion and a debt of US$2.8 billion. The change in reserves plus the change in debt gave a deterioration on the net international position of the country from December 1978 until the end of the experience in March 1981 of almost US$17 billion. This is a very important change that will condition the economic policy of the country for at least several years.

The second problem was the deterioration of the public sector, from a deficit of 4 percent of GNP in 1978 to one of 7 to 8 percent of GNP in late 1980 and early 1981. This deterioration came mostly as a result of the second package of measures, undertaken in mid-1980 but effective in

October 1980. One of these measures was to replace taxes on labor and other smaller taxes by increasing the value-added tax. The idea was that this would improve the allocation of resources and would also have some positive effects on trade. But the intention also was that the fiscal effect of these measures would be neutral. As it turned out, the effect was not at all neutral: the gain in revenues from the value-added tax was only 30 percent of the loss of revenue on the other taxes forgone. And this made for the jump in the fiscal deficit, an effect that cannot, of course, be attributed to the exercise.

The third problem was the situation of the business sector. The business sector faced very difficult times because, already in 1980, it had a problem of a decrease in the absolute amount of sales. In addition, it had problems of increasing its prices because of a delayed effect of the preannounced exchange rate schedule. Furthermore, it had the problem that wages kept increasing. A table in my paper (see table 3-1) shows the behavior of main cost components deflated by the proxy for their prices (which is a nonfarm wholesale price index). Most inputs increased much more than prices, so there was a squeeze in volumes and a squeeze on margins. The margin of contribution deteriorated or became negative. And on top of that, for the final nine months of the experiment the real interest rate was about 45 percent a year.

Since everything is substitutable, the idea was that when firms are faced with this interest rate they should be efficient, adjust their behavior to market signals, and diminish their debt. The problem is that it is not very easy to adjust when facing these conditions, and businesses were stuck with their debt. In the section of my paper entitled "The Process" I have mentioned some very simple models that show the length of life of an enterprise as a function of the debt-assets ratio and the difference between the return on assets and the real interest rate. For instance, if there is a −30 percent difference between the rate of return on a firm's assets and the cost of money, and if the initial debt-assets ratio is 2:3 (that means a debt-equity ratio of 2:1, which is usual in countries that have had negative interest rates in the past), then the firm completely loses its net worth in 1.3 years—that is, in sixteen months. It is the leverage effect working in reverse. There also have been some studies answering this question: if a firm starts from a very high debt-equity ratio and has a return on assets higher than the interest rate, how long does it take for the firm to have a normal debt-equity ratio? The period turns out to be fairly long.

Many Argentine firms lost their net worth; many more, certainly, were unable to repay their debts. Of course the financial entities did not want to make explicit this quality of their loan portfolios. So there was kind of a connivance between debtors and creditors to perpetuate the situation, and this explains why firms were willing to pay such high interest rates.

But by the end of the period the amount of this borrowing was so huge that the government faced the alternative of letting a very important part of the business sector go broke or of giving a subsidy, which of course is inflationary, to reduce the debt-equity ratio. This problem is still unresolved.

Looking at these results, I have to be candid. I cannot elliptically call the policies not successful; I must call them failures.

Causes of failure. The question is to assign to one of three different sources the cause of failure. Was it because of errors in policy implementation? At the time the scheme was introduced, paternity was acknowledged by the central bank, and some people attributed grandfatherhood to foreign sources. Now I think that, in order not to link the policy with any theory, we could call it "the orphan model," because nobody wants to have anything to do with it anymore.

So I will try to identify the elements of the orphan model as perceived in Argentina, and then it is up to others to link it with approaches and nonapproaches.

Of course there were implementation errors, and very clear ones at that. The first was to assume that the initial exchange rate was undervalued. An argument often used to show that there was still some undervaluation was that real parity had changed in the past because of the liberalization policies, and so on. This has turned out not to be true.

The second error was that as debt increased its impact on parity was not perceived. This is very important: at the end of the experiment the additional burden of the increased debt upon the current account was US\$3 billion—that is, 30 percent of exports—and this meant a clear shift in the parity level.

Third, the exchange rate depreciation schedule was unrealistic and over ambitious. In another interesting paper by Mario Blejer (Blejer and Mathieson 1981), a model shows this point to be especially critical.

Then there are the questions Rudiger Dornbusch poses [see his comments in chapter 8]— that monetary behavior, especially in the second part of the Argentine experiment, did not play by the rules. And there probably are further instances in which implementation departed from the model in smaller details.

So there certainly were aspects of implementation that did not agree with the initial model, but when one looks at the figures—I did no econometric analysis—I can assure you that the feeling is that errors in implementation do not wholly explain the failure of the experiment. This leads to the question whether the model itself might have had some elements that did not accurately portray reality.

One such element was the expectation about the "law of one price." It was expected that internal prices were going to behave according to the ceilings set by international prices. The argument about nontradables was dismissed, and it was expected that convergence was going to happen quickly. The evidence is strong that the law of one price does not work—at least in the period that is relevant for policy. The instruments must be adjusted for this fact.

Daniel Schydlowsky (1981) has made the point that it is not only nontraded goods, but also traded goods, that have a very important nontraded component. Those who had classes with Gottfried Haberler might remember that he sometimes mentioned that oranges in Germany are German, even though everybody knows there are no orange trees in Germany. But of the final price of oranges, more than half is value added in Germany.

Another element was the expectation about the "law of one interest rate," which of course did not hold either. I do not agree with the idea of saying that all the causes for the difference between domestic and international interest rates can be put in one bag called exchange risk. I think this bag must be opened to see what the components are, and I think they are not all merely exchange risks. I can give an example. The operating costs might have something to do with the difference in interest rates—and differences between operating costs inside and outside might be huge.

So interest equalization did not happen and caused the question of deterioration of the Argentine business sector. And a further element of unrealistic expectation is that the model apparently did not contemplate very clearly how noncompliance with the laws of one price and of one interest rate would feed back into the process in which required policy changes are made.

Final comments. I want to finish these comments about the model by saying that all the literature on which the model was nurtured mentions that it is important to explain the official settlements account, and that what happens to the other side is really immaterial. But what we have seen in the case of Argentina is that what happens to the other side is very important. Any elementary course in financial analysis tells you that it is very different to have an inflow with a quid pro quo and an inflow without one, and that, if debt is accumulating, this modifies the dynamics of the system and its final solution.

Moreover, it is one thing to look at the balance of payments capital movements, the net capital movements, and another thing to look at the increase in debt, because the capital movements net out the outflow of funds from the country. But of course when one has to pay the debt, one cannot simply call upon any Argentine having money abroad and tell him "bring back the dollars; we have to pay the debt." What matters in a deteriorating situation is the increase in debt and not the net balance of the capital account. And there may be very important differences.

Against this lack of attention to what is the counterpart of the official settlements account, I can make a few comments about the importance of its composition. What I have done is the following. Looking back at the balance of payments as in cash flow analysis, one sees a level of inflows composed of exports plus capital inflows, and one has some composition on how this is spent—different kinds of imports, capital outflows, and so on. Somewhere in the middle of this experiment, Argentina had a very important increase in the inflow of funds through more debt. So what I did was to extend the outflow projections as if this had not happened and then to compare the composition (the real composition) with the assumed one. This is a fairly rudimentary method, but it permits one to say something about the change in the pattern of use of foreign exchange caused by the debt increase. The resulting uses of funds in Argentina were: first, outflow of funds; second, tourist expenditures; third, unorthodox imports; fourth, arms.

Next, one may ask what is the repayment capacity generated by the use of the increased indebtedness shown by this preliminary study. The study shows that it pays to look to something else than one side of the official settlements account.

This brings me to another of my final points. This idea of looking at the official settlements account is really to say that reserve changes plus the goods balance plus the capital balance equal zero, and one theory says that reserves are a function of a few things. And if one bundles all the rest together, one does not need any explanation because this is the offset (the negative) of reserve changes.

If the composition of the rest is thought to matter, then of course, one has two things: goods and capital balances. Let us concentrate on the goods balance. Then one has two theories of the foreign sector. One does not have to explain the capital balance; it comes out of the other two. This is very elementary. But the point is that unless one assumes that the arguments in this function (the goods balance) affect only the capital balance and not at all the reserve changes, then one can accept to look only at official settlements. Now, as Harry Johnson (1976, 1977) has said, one has to have monetary arguments in explaining the rest. By the same token, one has to include the arguments of the other functions in the monetary one, unless one makes very unrealistic assumptions. I am sorry, that is elementary, but it does not seem to be applied, and unless one feeds back the arguments into the monetary explanation, something is missing.

The last comment I wanted to make has been made very forcefully by Rudiger Dornbusch [see his remarks in chapter 8], and this is the end of the story in Argentina: interest rates were so high that businesses went broke, and the government had to bail them out. In the end the government had the worst of both worlds. During a year and a half it had very high interest rates because it talked about future exchange rates instead of selling exchange at those rates, and then it had to pay anyway. So it seems that it is much better to sell the exchange forward, reduce the risk, and see what happens.

Of course, in time of difficulty this approach only solves one side—it does not solve the question of people buying foreign assets. If people do not have confidence on the asset side, they go outside, although on the liability side they hedge. But in relatively quiet times, this approach will keep down interest rates.

Leonardo Auernheimer

I would like to start at the end of José María Dagnino Pastore's exposition and say something about what the monetary approach to the balance of payments is and what, I think, it is not. In particular there are several things that the monetary approach is not, and it might be relevant to underline them.

In José María's paper [chapter 3] there are three equations said to characterize the monetary approach to the balance of payments. One, equation (3.1), was called the "law of one price," which says that the domestic price of traded goods is the world price times the exchange rate, all of this adjusted for tariffs and other transaction costs. The second, equation (3.2), is the "law of one interest rate," and the third, equation (3.3), is an expression containing a demand for money function. As far as the law of one price and the law of one interest rate are concerned, I always thought it to be well understood that those equalities are adjusted for all kinds of transaction costs and eventually for the presence of lags and—in particular in the case of the interest rate, but also in the case of commodities prices—for uncertainty about the future. I will return to this briefly later because the point is important also in the case of commodities, in a context such as in Argentina, where there was a great deal of skepticism concerning the fulfillment of the announced tariff reduction.

It is the third expression that I think characterizes the essence of the monetary approach to the balance of payments, and this is the demand for money. I cannot resist the temptation to think that, if one is forced to define the monetary approach to the balance of payments in just one sentence (and, later, perhaps add to it), the way to do it is to say that the approach is just the extension to an open economy of what monetarism is in a closed economy. One could forget about the law of one price or the law of one interest rate holding at all times (because of lags and all of that) and still have the approach. But if the assumption that there is a stable demand for money is dropped, one goes broke, in exactly the same way that monetarism goes broke in a closed economy without that assumption. Of course, many may not agree with this characterization of monetarism, and it would take another symposium to argue about it—it has already taken several conferences to do so.

A second point to be made is that the monetary approach to the balance of payments does not say which variable to control. In particular, it does not tell whether we should preannounce and control the future path of the exchange rate—the "tablita"—or whether we should float and control the rate of monetary expansion. I am emphasizing this point because the famous tablita has been taken in Argentina as the culprit behind many of the things that happened there. And one has the suspicion that perhaps some things would not have been very different with a different control variable—say, a monetary rule. For one, I think that the situation as far as the interest rate is concerned would not have been very different; we do have a lot to learn now from the U.S. experience, where there is no tablita but a monetary rule, and where real interest rates during the current stabilization attempt have been unprecedently high.

If we make an adjustment for the monstrosity of the magnitude of changes in the countries of the Southern Cone compared with the relatively smooth operation of the U.S. economy—adding or subtracting a couple of zeros—then we observe very much the same behavior in the real interest rate following a stabilization attempt, whether under the tablita or a monetary rule. Of course, perhaps a conclusion—even though it is not stated in José María's paper—is that we should abandon any kind of rule of this sort, and this is another thing to discuss. [See also comments by Guillermo Calvo and Roberto Zahler, below.] I just want to clarify that the tablita, or fixed exchange rate, is not an integral part of the monetary approach to the balance of payments. All that the monetary approach emphasizes is that one can control any nominal variable, but only one.

Another thing the monetary approach does not tell is how people form expectations. It says that expectations are very, very important, and that they are the crucial element in the demand for money, but it does not tell how expectations are formed. In fact, much of monetarism and the monetary approach to the balance of payments proceeded for a long time on the basis of a theory about how people form expectations—the adaptive form—that in 1982 is not well regarded by most monetarists.

Also, I do not think—and this probably could prompt a long discussion, but I just want to mention it—that the monetary approach says we should look at the level of reserves and explain everything from this standpoint without looking at where changes are coming from. If we did so, then we would be left in the embarrassing position Rudiger Dornbusch describes [see his comments in chapter 8], unable to explain much.

The monetary approach is an analytical framework that is based on the existence of a stable demand for money function; into this framework we can place different things and see what the results are. For example, if we consistently "sterilize", then hell is going to break loose. By the way, there is a reference in José María's paper [see the subsection "Limitations and Shortcomings of the Model"], in the manner of a criticism to the use of the monetary approach, suggesting that we cannot use the approach when the government sterilizes. This is precisely when we can use it and when the approach shows how powerful its predictions are: if we sterilize and keep increasing the money supply, then the equilibrium is going to be very short-lived.

Until now I have used a very stringent characterization of the monetary approach as an analytical framework built around the assumption that there is a stable demand for money. There are nevertheless elements that are not necessarily part of this characterization but that most monetarists believe—perhaps this is what has been called "global monetarism." One such element, to which Rudiger Dornbusch refers extensively [chapter 8], is the belief that adjustments take place in prices rather than in output. I am not quite convinced by Dornbusch's argument; of course, the approach is equally useful when real income, not prices, is the adjustment variable, but I would furthermore think that most monetarists would not necessarily reject the possibility that real income is the variable that moves. In any case—and within this description of things that strictly, according to my characterization, are not a part of the approach but that monetarists believe—I would like to emphasize two elements that happen to have been of great importance in the case of Argentina. These have become quite visible in the academic world and, I believe, are of tremendous importance in policy applications. And they ought to be mentioned here because academicians are not always wrong.

The first is the idea of rational expectations. I hesitate to mention the term because it conjures ideas about esoteric models, people using crystal balls, and so on. But if one thinks of rational expectations as the belief or the assumption that the public will use the information it has and make projections about the effects of government actions—based on the behavior of the current policy or on exogenous variables (for example, a certain preannounced rate of devaluation, or a rate of monetary expansion), rather than on, say, past values of the variable to be predicted—then such an assumption is very relevant to the case of Argentina.

The second is the idea that government, after all, does have a budget constraint. This is an idea that is creeping—perhaps too slowly, but firmly—into several different theoretical works. Of course, we always knew that governments have a budget constraint, but only now are we realizing the full implications when we analyze this constraint in conjunction with the first idea of rational expectations. These, then, are twin ideas that lead to the conclusion that people form expectations not so much about the consequences of government controlling one variable—say, in the case of the tablita, the exchange rate, or in the case of a monetary rule, the rate of monetary expansion—but about things that are one step farther back, toward the guts of the whole thing. And so the result is as if the public would know better than the government. And the question is not so much whether the public believes the government, or whether the public suspects that the government has some secret intentions it is not revealing, but whether the government is going to be able to hold the policy line.

As I mentioned before, there are some theoretical works using these twin ideas that are extremely interesting and show surprising results—Obstfeld (1981) and Sargent and Wallace (1981) are the two works that come to mind.

All of this is important not only because it tells us about the ultimate elements at which the public is looking when it forms expectations, but also because if one makes certain accounting right, then sometimes it does not make such a big difference the manner in which government finances its expenditures. In particular, it does not seem to make a lot of difference whether expenditures are financed by money creation or by borrowing. Incidentally, and pertaining to this general point, I have some quarrel with the procedure of looking—as José María does—at just the level of reserves held by the central bank and the level of total foreign indebtedness. I think that we also need to look carefully at the total assets held abroad by domestic residents, because the reasons that prompted these people to buy foreign currencies could be, if reversed, the same reasons that may well prompt them to sell them back. For purposes of evaluating total welfare, it does not make much difference whether the central bank is holding U.S. dollars or foreign bonds, or whether an Argentine resident does. If someone living in Argentina borrows US$100,000 from a bank abroad and buys a US$100,000 bond, or a house, the operation should not change things much.

The question of whether the manner in which government expenditures—or, perhaps, deficits—are financed makes any difference is important in the case of Argentina because, as we all know, preventing the level of central bank reserves from falling was accomplished for some time by direct borrowing abroad. And if we consider the public as having some idea about government's budget constraint, and if we use the 25 percent of total expenditures being financed through conventional taxes (the number that José María presented, which is very dramatic), then it should become rather obvious to the market that ultimately it is the inflation tax that will pay for the budget deficit. The government can borrow abroad but sometime will have to pay for it—the principal, or the interest, does not really matter. There may be some postponement of the problem, but in the extreme case of rational expectations the postponement cannot exist, and the effect can be immediate.

In looking at the case of Argentina I would say that there has been a fundamental incompatibility or inconsistency between the rate of preannounced devaluation, with the implicit revenues from the inflation tax attached to it, and the level of government deficit to be financed by such inflation tax. But what I find in José María's paper is that there is perhaps one—certainly not more than two or three—references to the deficit, and then only in passing. And I am also surprised that this deficit, which I would normally see as a cause of the problems with the plan, is described in the paper as one of the consequences of the plan. I would definitely tend to see the situation the other way round.

When there is a realization in the market that there is a budget deficit well above the revenue from the inflation tax implicit in the preannounced rate of devaluation—and this point was made very clearly in Argentina before the whole thing collapsed, in a piece by Calvo and Fernandez (1980)—then there is a tremendous skepticism about the survival of the whole program and, in particular, about the preannounced rate of devaluation.

There was another strong skepticism in Argentina, this one about the determination to go ahead with the tariff reform. I think that the importance of this skepticism has not been stressed enough, and that it had an important role in the case of Argentina. When we talk about the law of one price, for example, I think that much of whatever lags did exist in the domestic prices of imported goods falling in line with world prices had to do with expectations about the continuation of the opening to trade. There are costs involved in establishing import lines, for example, and few people would pay for those costs if they expected the open trade policy to collapse within six months. Uncertainty about commercial policy also had implications for the indebtedness of firms. There were many firms that under an expected continuation of the trade liberalization policy would have gone out of the market but did not do so under the strong suspicion that the policy would be reversed. Meanwhile, these firms borrowed tremendous amounts.

And since I am referring to the indebtedness of firms, of course a strong reversal of the liberalization of financial markets had been—and is—expected. When capital markets were liberalized, there was a transfer of part of the inflation tax, which before had been used to subsidize zero or negative real interest rates, from firms to the government. I have no numbers to prove this interpretation, but it would be interesting to check it. What firms expected since 1981 was a reversal of that situation—what, in an irreverant way is sometimes called "jubileo," or mass absolution. I do not expect that firms would have been in the same position of indebtedness if this expectation had not been so generalized.

The way I look at the case of Argentina is that there has been a big problem of inconsistency. Granted, there have been other problems—for example, the way in which prices of goods and services produced by the public sector have behaved—and this is pointed out in José María's paper. But, again, I think that it is this inconsistency between preannounced behavior and the budget deficit that was at the heart of the problems. One lesson to be learned is that not only should we not fool Mother Nature, but also that we cannot.

Interruptions in the policy also caused difficulties. When José María talks about costs and benefits of the stabilization program in Argentina, I think that the costs, to a large extent, are the costs of having interrupted the program at a certain point. The lengths of time involved must be kept in mind. If the end of 1978 is taken as the formal initiation of the stabilization program, the economic team that was identified with that program had a preannounced life of about twenty-six months. Roughly, I would put the effective life of the program at about sixteen or seventeen months; it was clear for about nine or ten months before the change in government—to take place in March of 1981—that the whole package of measures was going to be abandoned, and almost every candidate for finance minister was talking about an initial devaluation of 30 percent. So one certainly could not expect that the program would last for very long under those circumstances.

Speaking of lengths of time, I think that when one looks at the alternative to what can be called global monetarism or liberalization, such an alternative for Argentina is simply price and income policies. If I were not an economist involved in technical details, but just a man of the street, then I would ask whether seventeen months of effective life is a lot of time for a program that apparently at that point is giving bad results. Is this a long time compared with the time that alternative policies—price and income policies—had, which was about fifty years? When the cost of stopping inflation and removing distortions is discussed, so should the cost of solving all the problems of having created inflation and distortions in the first place, and the discussion should be labeled as such.

At a more technical level, I think that the problem of interruptions in policy deserves some thinking. Because of political considerations, an economic team has a short expected life. There are in attendance here some experts on that. The question for the economic policymaker then is which plan is best if he is going to last for two years; which plan is best if he is going to last for four years; and so on. He should try to see the relationship between his expected length of time in office and the kind of misery the economy will be left in if the plan is interrupted. With some plans—and this is true of some of the programs being examined, and I do not know how it can be avoided—it seems that an interruption in midcourse somehow leaves the situation worse off than it was before—that one cannot anymore be the same person one was before. The policymaker should look for some elements of robustness and ask the further question of where he will be left if this plan is interrupted. And the answer to such a question might well be an important consideration in choosing among some possibilities within the monetary approach—for example, whether to go with the tablita or to control the money supply.

But even in the Argentine experience, much has been gained in terms of awareness, and perhaps now will come a new cycle in policy, so that five years from now there will be another effort. But it takes a long time to change the way the public forms its expectations about government actions, especially after fifty years of a policy of controls. Some may disagree with me about the prevalence of this long policy of controls, and it is true that in Argentina, at least, there were a few periods when attempts were made to liberalize and to remove controls. But the liberalization that was intended in those periods was little more than talk—such as lowering tariffs from 500 to 300 percent—and the attempts were all very short-lived and very partial. Domestic capital markets were never free, and the general attitude was one of price and incomes policies.

Finally, I will conclude my remarks with a comment about the alleged failure of the monetary approach in the Southern Cone. José María was skeptical that some of us have not talked enough about failures, but I believe that he has been a bit too harsh on this score. Part of the responsibility for failure, I think, should be attributed to groups that started exerting political pressure on the Argentine plan as soon as the plan started to "bite." Concerning commercial policy, for example, when the plan was announced a ridiculous thing happened in Argentina— the stock market went up dramatically. The stock market represents, by and large, the market value of industrial firms whose products are going to be in trouble in a tariff reform in favor of liberalization; nevertheless, everybody in the stock market thought the reform was going to be just great for one and all. The government made an error in describing the plan. The saying was, "We are not reforming commercial policy to destroy national industry," and businessmen who confused their own efficiency—and they are very efficient—with social efficiency were all very happy. The point was not made clear that some part of Argentina's industry would be hurt, and as soon as this started to happen the political pressure became very strong.

John Williamson

I agree in substance with almost everything in José María Dagnino Pastore's paper [chapter 3] and I am merely going to stress one or two implications. I agree that the failure of the experiment in Argentina was primarily due to the naivete of the model used rather than to an inconsistency in its application. The model that underlay that program was not the monetary approach in the rather general sense that was defended above and that, for example, Frenkel and Gylfason (1980) and Gylfason and Helliwell (1981) have integrated with other approaches—an integration that Dagnino Pastore recommends in the last item of his paper's "Conclusions." The monetary approach in this general sense says that, if one wants to understand the behavior of the overall balance of payments, one had better pay some attention to what is happening in the money market. I think that is common ground. Indeed, the only intellectual puzzle I have ever had about that proposition is who is supposed to have opposed it.

The theory, as I understand it, that underlay the experiment in Argentina was a much stronger version of the monetary approach, which Marina Whitman once christened "global monetarism." This embodies three crucial assumptions, as Dagnino Pastore emphasizes. The first is perfect arbitrage in goods, or the "law of one price"; second, perfect arbitrage in securities, or the "law of one interest rate"; and third, as Rudiger Dornbusch also mentions [see his comments in chapter 8], full employment, the assumption that changes in money feed through into changes in prices rather than changes in output. This strong version of global monetarism underlay the program in Argentina, and I am prepared to defend the proposition that the Argentine experiment provides evidence that this strong form of the model is not an appropriate one.

Let me first turn to the goods market, which in some ways is the most crucial one, and the law of one price. Dagnino Pastore's paper establishes quite clearly that the law of one price did not hold and that a massive appreciation of the real exchange rate occurred during the period of the experiment. That is consistent with massive evidence from other countries, both on a casual level and from very detailed empirical work by several authors; indeed, I regard the law of one price as the theoretical economic proposition that has been most conclusively disproved by empirical evidence in the history of our discipline.

There are partial explanations of the failure of the law of one price that have to do with the particular situation in Argentina. An interesting one that was hinted at in Dagnino Pastore's presentation [above] was the "privatization" of the tariff: when the trade liberalization first started, apparently the only firms in a position to import were the firms that produced similar goods in Argentina. So, of course, these firms did not cut their prices; they simply sold foreign goods and took higher profit margins. Hence, there was not the downward pressure on prices.

In the initial stages of the program, there was also a lowering of the real interest rate as perceived by Argentines, since Argentine inflation remained high while the interest rate appeared very attractive to a foreign borrower (because there was a guarantee that future depreciation would be much lower than the rate of internal inflation). Hence there was a capital inflow, downward pressure on interest rates, monetary expansion, and an increase in demand for nontraded goods, which sustained inflation in the nontraded goods sector.

I think both of these factors—privatization of the tariff and excess demand for nontraded goods—were present in the Argentine case. But a more fundamental and more general lesson is that the idea that prices are rigidly held together in some unique equilibrium price structure is wrong. We live in a world of imperfect, not perfect, substitutability between goods. Inflation in a particular sector moderates in part in response to excess supply appearing in that sector; hence, the forces making for expansion in the nontraded goods sector enabled inflationary inertia to continue in that sector. This led to a considerable real appreciation and to what some of us judged at that time—surely rightly, with the light of hindsight—to be a massive overvaluation of the peso in 1979-80. The fundamental point is that one can expect the inflation in the nontraded goods sector to slow down only after excess supply has emerged in that sector as well as in the traded goods sector. In other words, there is no cheap way of reducing inflation through exchange rate policy. If appreciation works, it does so in the same way as other conventional anti-inflationary programs work, which is by creating excess supply to exert downward pressure on prices.

Dagnino Pastore's paper seems to me to provide additional evidence in favor of this view of the world, because relative prices changed during the Argentine experiment in exactly the way I would have predicted before I had ever heard of the law of one price ten or fifteen years ago. I would have argued that there are indeed some tradable goods that obey the law of one price— namely, those homogeneous primary commodities that are traded on essentially competitive worldwide markets (what Ronald McKinnon [1979] has called "tradables II"). But there are also differentiated manufactured products for which, even within a particular sector, there is scope for relative prices to change quite considerably without discipline from prices becoming particularly strong ("tradables I"). The different behavior of these two types of tradable goods was supported very clearly in the recent paper by Vittorio Corbo (1981). Of course, this is then taken a stage further in the nontradable sector, which includes labor and wages.

What happened in the period of the Argentine experiment is absolutely consistent with this view. Prices of tradables II did slow down, as represented by the exchange rate. At least that is the best proxy in Dagnino Pastore's paper: one may assume that prices of homogeneous primary products did indeed move in line with the exchange rate plus international inflation. The wholesale price index, which comes much closer to being dominated by tradables I (differentiated products), continued to rise faster than the exchange rate, but less fast than the consumer price index, which has a much larger component of nontradables.

Let me turn briefly to the capital account and to the law of one interest rate. I think that the model has been eviscerated in the version that is presented in Dagnino Pastore's paper. If one looks at equation (3.2) in the subsection "The Model," it now has that unexplained uncertainty term in it at the end, and that's really not what we were being told by global monetarism a few years ago. Global monetarism said that the domestic interest rate was going to be equal to the international interest rate plus a rate of depreciation and perhaps some other terms to represent transaction costs or even uncertainty, but uncertainty that was supposed to be exogenous to everything else that is going on in the economy. Essentially, that is still perfect arbitrage, and one can get the global monetarist results. But as soon as a term is put in that represents uncertainty postulated as endogenous to the system itself, then one is back in the game of using the monetary approach as one component of a general equilibrium model and is no longer thinking in terms of perfect arbitrage.

In particular, if one asks what influences uncertainty, one needs at least two elements. The first is the situation of the country's indebtedness in relation to the rest of the world, so that the more it borrows, the greater is the uncertainty whether a preannounced exchange rate will remain credible. The second is the overall credibility of the economic program. In that case, one no longer has a capital inflow that can be treated as dependent on exogenous variables in the way that global monetarist theory used to claim.

Let me turn briefly to the final aspect, the question of full employment. The question is whether changes in monetary demand will take the form of changes in prices rather than changes in output. It is interesting that in the Argentine case there was no emergence of significant unemployment until the end of the experiment. Something close to full employment was in fact preserved until early 1981. One of the possible explanations is that there was labor hoarding because of an expectation that the experiment could not last. That is consistent with the fact that in 1981 there was a breakdown of full employment, but it is not consistent with the global monetarist story.

In conclusion, I do not think that one can condemn economic liberalization per se on the basis of the Argentine experience, although I do think there perhaps is a case for urging greater caution in the speed with which such programs are implemented.

In general, I would draw the same conclusions that Rudiger Dornbusch suggests [see chapter 8]: one needs to have a balanced package, which includes not merely an attempt to grind down the rate of inflation by arbitrage through the reduction in depreciation of the exchange rate, but one also needs to encompass in the package fiscal policy and some sort of incomes policy.

José María Dagnino Pastore

The few further comments I have concern: capital outflows, opening the economy, the willingness of firms to pay high interest rates, the capital account equation, the laws of one price and one interest rate in relation to the exchange rate, and the flexibility of the monetary approach.

• The Argentine experience shows that capital outflows do not return home in substantial proportions. One must imagine some kind of asymmetric rationality, but this is what happens.

• I earlier made a comment I would like to expand about this kind of policy and the opening of the economy. One can assume better implementation of a system such as this if there is a more favorable initial situation and if one is willing to accept for a period an appreciation of the currency. Opening the economy—according to Anne Krueger's (1978) long study of ten countries and to other sources—requires a period of undervaluation or heavy export promotion because the odds when one opens are against one, not in favor. That is the main message. And this seems to go against the idea of an intermediate period during which those variables move in directions opposite to those prescribed when the opening is used for stabilization purposes.

• The next point is the question of why firms kept paying high interest. I think the situation was very rigid for enterprises. Why did they not close down? Well, if firms already had lost their net worth, for them it was no different to lose one or two times their net worth. They still had some chance of survival if they kept going. So there was a kink somewhere in the behavior.

• On the question of the capital account equation, I agree that in my paper [see equation (3.2)] I could have imposed a more rigid formulation, but I wanted the equation to reflect not only an approach from the literature, but also what was taught and said in Argentina and went into this model as expectations.

• One additional thing deserves some attention, although there is probably something on it in the literature. The law of one price has to do with the level of the exchange rate. The law of one interest rate has to do with the change in exchange rates. This difference is valuable when analyzing solutions, not for the question of stabilization but for the question of adjustment of the balance of payments. This could give some basis for justifying an anathema—to use for a while a two-tier exchange market to adjust the balance of payments situation.

• Finally, I would like to make one comment on a point Sebastian Edwards [see the section on Chile, below] and others have made. This is about the flexibility of the policy we are discussing. I think that here there is a kind of contradiction. It is endogenous to the policy to make believe that it is not flexible. So, it is not very consistent to have the policy shift later on. Once one chooses the line of committing the government to this policy, the government has to be very strong to make it believable, and then it is caged in. But this constraint is not exogenous, it is endogenous to the approach.

Guillermo A. Calvo

I am afraid that we will be going back over some of the issues that we know very well already. But I will do so in a rather stylized way. I will divide my commentary into three parts: the first will be on facts; the second will be on theories, which are more conjectural facts; and the third will make some tentative policy recommendations.

The facts. I will not review the numbers because José María Dagnino Pastore has given a good characterization [chapter 3] of what happened in the recent Argentine experiment. I will instead focus on some of the salient characteristics of the facts. The first is something that, before these experiments were launched, we probably would have hesitated to mention or admit. It is that during this period wide and highly serially correlated fluctuations in the real exchange rate seem to go beyond what can be accounted for by long-run considerations concerning, say, structural factors such as tariffs or terms of trade. For the case of Argentina, this is very well documented by a paper by Rodríguez and Sjaastad (1980). Playing with those numbers from 1980, for instance, one finds that the exchange rate appreciated. By the middle of 1980 I found that it had appreciated by about 10 to 15 percent.

This teaches that the policymaker who adopts this kind of program should in principle be prepared to tackle situations of this nature.

The second fact I would mention—one that is important and has been discussed here by several others—is the inconsistency of fiscal and monetary policy or, in this case, of fiscal and exchange rate policy. By the middle of 1980 several economists in Argentina came to the conclusion that the target set for March 1981, which was to have a constant exchange rate forever after that time, would be inconsistent with the level of the deficit as a proportion of real GNP. In fact, together with Roque Fernandez (Calvo and Fernandez 1980) I presented some rough numbers assuming that the rate of the deficit was 4 percent for 1980 and showing that it was highly unlikely that that sort of policy could be continued. It turned out, however, that after the numbers were available at the end of 1980 that the deficit was about 6 percent.

In the regular sort of macroeconomic theory on which we were all raised in the 1960s, we used not to pay too much attention to this kind of inconsistency. But "rational expectations" has changed all that. And perhaps through us the public, too, is becoming more aware of these inconsistencies. So, one does not have to make assumptions that the public has the appropriate model; it is enough that the public listens to the economists. In Argentina, there was wide agreement among economists that there was a problem in the making and that the problem would lead eventually to a devaluation.

I list that as a fact. Another fact that I observed during that period is that capital mobility, although it was not perfect, made for a rather close connection between expectations of a devaluation and the nominal rate of interest. An econometrician would have trouble finding this connection. Econometric attempts to do so have been mentioned here, but I would not know how. The reason I say this is that, while I was in Argentina, I was part of the public. We knew, for instance, that when Martínez de Hoz was going to give a speech, it would fuel expectations that he would have some news, which he eventually did not, but we all felt that maybe somebody knew something about the probability of a devaluation. Sure enough, the nominal interest rate started to rise.

That is not a puzzle in principle. What was puzzling (and I refer to this because I think it may be an interesting line for future, at least theoretical, research) is why—after the minister spoke very clearly and, at least in my mind, went back to before the time any doubts were raised—the interest rate did not fall immediately. I will have something to say about that later.

In any case, I felt then that there was a close connection between inflationary expectations and the nominal interest rate. That brings me to another issue we have been discussing, which has to do with the real interest rate. It is very important, of course, to distinguish between the ex ante and the ex post real interest rate. If everybody is expecting a devaluation, then the nominal interest rate would go up in the same proportion as the expected rate of inflation. From the viewpoint of resource allocation, such a rise could be perfectly neutral. If the process does not last very long, then the change provoked by it would not have to be large.

But if there is no devaluation ex post, then the real interest rate ex post will become positive—in fact, could become very much so. That implies there will be a transfer of resources from borrowers to lenders. Such transfer can last, of course, until some borrowers start going broke or start having problems in renewing their debt. This seems to have been an important factor in the case of Argentina, even granting that the ex ante real exchange rate did not change very much. It appears that there was a substantial decapitalization, if you wish, of the business sector. In Argentina this helped to generate a strong force to unite the industrial sector in lobbying for a substantial devaluation and for a substantial program of bailing out.

These I consider facts. But why is it that things happened as they did? Can we explain with these facts something of what happened? The lack of consistency is very clear. The question is what to do with it; to what extent does this phenomenon help us explain the central question that we must answer. That is, why did we have this appreciation of the real exchange rate? The question lies at the core, I think, of all the problems we are discussing. The natural remedy would seem to be a devaluation. Argentina tried that. What happened? Probably the real exchange rate depreciated—I think it did, the last time I looked at the numbers. But also unemployment increased from about 2 percent to 6 percent and apparently kept increasing. So, it is a mixed blessing. One solves one problem and then confronts another.

Theories. What about theories? Let me mention very tentatively one line of the thought that I have not seen exploited here in any way. In all the discussions that we have heard so far and that I have heard in other places, in connection with this problem, very few people have tried to trace the appreciation of the real exchange rate to the substantial decontrol in the banking system. Yet this is one of the most important structural changes that has occurred in Argentina, in Chile, and worldwide. It is a very complicated problem because it involves money and a change in the nature of money. It is bad enough to try to explain why money exists when there is only one currency. So, I will only raise the issue and a few of its implications.

Just to whet the intellectual appetite and to justify why I feel something should be done, imagine for a minute the very simple-minded monetary reform of lowering bank reserves. In a closed economy, lowering bank reserves through the money multiplier would simply produce, possibly, a once-and-for-all rise in the price level and nothing else. If that were done in a small open economy, and if there were controls on capital mobility, then the same upward pressure on prices would exist, but there would be tradables and nontradables. And the price of tradables can go up. So, the whole pressure would go into the nontradables sector, and there would be an appreciation not associated with any change in the amounts of private wealth or of "high-powered" money in any way. It can also be shown—I did so in another recent paper (Calvo 1980)—that one would get the same kind of effect even with perfect capital mobility because, by lowering reserves, if one postulated the model carefully and began with utility functions, for instance, it is quite natural to have a positive liquidity and utility effect even when net private wealth remains unchanged. The system is simply made more efficient and given more money. If money does anything good in that economy, it will increase utility, which might increase expenditure, and so on.

These are very simplistic implications because monetary reform does much more. It places savers and investors closer together. Savers become more conscious of the rate of return on investment, and so on. It is a major change, and one can already see that part of the appreciation can be explained by these kinds of policies.

There is another effect that I also would mention. It has to do with the fact that the availability of closer competitors to high-powered money might tend to reduce the interest elasticity of the demand for high-powered money. That is something that, if one fiddles around with it, will come up very easily. It has not been exploited. Jacob A. Frenkel, Roque B. Fernandez, and myself are analyzing this effect to understand the implications (Calvo and Fernandez 1983). If one can affect the elasticity of the demand for money, then monetary policy clearly could, in principle, become very effective in affecting the interest rate. Small changes, shocks in the demand and supply for money, might be reflected in big changes in the interest rate.

Another of the puzzles in Chile and Argentina is not only that the real interest rate is high, but that it is so volatile. This may be partially explained by our previous remarks; for, if we have a competitive system that makes the demand for money very inelastic with respect to the interest rate, we may have built this type of volality into the system.

An additional effect is that there seems to be a connection—mentioned by several people here—between the degree of international capital mobility and the appreciation of the real exchange rate. I know that Arnold Harberger will have something to say about that [see his comments in chapter 8], so I will pass up this issue.

But let me stop here on theories and mention very briefly the policy recommendations that come to mind. Again, these are very tentative. If I were asked to bring about a stabilization program on the basis of, say, a constant or predetermined rate of devaluation that is given me, and if I also am told that the policymaker does not like the real exchange rate to depart very much from what is accounted for by "basic forces" in the economy, then I would start first with (a) trade liberalization. Next, I would begin the (b) slow and steady removal of capital controls. And last I would (c) decontrol the banking system.

Why (b) after (a)? Because the models we have available suggest very strongly that capital mobility facilitates the overshooting. If, instead, capital mobility is imperfect, one could better control the behavior of the real exchange rate through monetary policy.

Finally, why (c) after (b)—why decontrol the banking system only after removing capital controls? Because if one lowers the reserve ratio, for instance, the interest rates on deposits will be relatively high, or at least higher, and this will make it attractive for very short-term capital to come in. The high liquidity of those assets, however, would also facilitate capital outflows. Therefore, the economy would be subject to fluctuations that have originated abroad. It is as if the country's money became international reserves. The country is subject to all the problems that larger countries suffer when there is a portfolio shift against or in favor of their money.

One last point that has some theoretical interest beyond this discussion is the problem of why interest rates are so high and remain so high.

In line with what we have been saying here, let us suppose that a fixed exchange rate system is in place, but that there is some inconsistency somewhere in the system—the fiscal policy is out of line, there is some political problem, or the like. Suppose that everybody feels that, if the policymakers are pressed hard enough by circumstances, they may devalue the currency. Now, imagine that there is imperfect capital mobility, and all of a sudden there is a shock in the supply of money that raises the interest rate. A situation like that, without any information, presents a Lucas-type signal extraction problem. One does not know what actually happened. One knows that the interest rate went up but not whether it is a purely monetary phenomenon or whether it happened because some insiders in the economy found out that the probability of devaluation had increased. As a result, it would be rational to assign part of the rise in the interest rate to the fact that maybe one does not have full, or the right, information.

If everybody felt that way, then contracts would be made at a higher interest rate. Now, if nothing happens from then on, presumably that interest rate will go down and will go to full equilibrium. But we are talking about economies that are buffeted all the time, and I can envision the possibility of this phenomenon continuing for a significant period of time.

The point I want to make is that, at the very least, this kind of reasoning explains not necessarily the magnitude, but the persistence, of the rise of high nominal and (if there is no devaluation) also high real rates of interest.

Vito Tanzi

I wish to say a few things about the fiscal deficit because everyone has mentioned that it played an important role but then has gone on to talk about something else. It seems to me that in Argentina this was the major reason that the stabilization attempt failed. I was involved in the stabilization program of Argentina between March-April 1976 and the end of 1977. I have not followed the situation in Argentina since then, but I want to convey my impressions as I had them at the end of 1977.

The situation then was the following. The deficit, which had been about 14 percent of GNP in 1976, was falling rapidly by 1977. As I think José María Dagnino Pastore has said [see his first set of comments above, under "Background"], it came down to about 4 percent in 1977, which was the best year.

Why did it come down? That, I think, is a very important question for understanding why the program failed. The deficit came down for a variety of reasons. First, because inflation was coming down fast, and tax payments were made with average delays that I had estimated at around four to five months. This means that each peso that should be collected today instead gets collected four or five months in the future. If an inflation rate of 10 percent per month is compounded five times, it is easy to get a fall in real revenues. So the large reduction in tax revenue in 1976 was largely the result of accelerating inflation, and the large increase in revenue in 1977 was largely the result of decelerating inflation. It was not an exogenous increase in expenditure or an exogenous fall in taxes that caused the large deficit in 1976. That deficit was itself to a large extent inflation induced. In other words, it became endogenous. It was a function of inflation, while at the same time it caused inflation. Therefore, when the inflation rate came down, as it did in 1977, tax revenue inevitably started going up in real terms.

The second reason was that temporary emergency taxes were introduced. All of them were introduced with a specific time limitation, mostly one year, eighteen months, or two years. It thus was clear that, when those taxes expired, revenue would fall. The third and very important reason for the fall in the deficit (by perhaps 4 or 5 percentage points of GNP) was the reduction in real wages in the public sector. Nobody has mentioned here that wages were cut by perhaps

50 percent of their 1975 levels in real terms. And this, by the way, might help to explain why there was no unemployment for a while and why unemployment finally rose later when wages caught up. It was inevitable that, once wages caught up to their previous level, the deficit would go up from 4 or 5 percent in 1977 to 8 or 9 percent.

There were also some permanent adjustments in the tax system that helped to improve the situation in 1977, but these were less important.

To introduce a concept that I have not seen used in the literature, there is a "core level" of the fiscal deficit in an economy. This core level depends on "permanent" expenditure and "permanent" income of the government. We talk about permanent income of the individual, but we never talk about the equivalent for government. One cannot measure the impact of the deficit on an economy by looking at the size of the deficit at a single moment in time. One has to project two or three years in the future and say, under normal circumstances, what the expenditures will be, what the taxes will be.

Under normal circumstances, what would happen in Argentina is that, inevitably, all the improvements in 1977 of a temporary nature would disappear by 1979—and that is exactly what happened. So I think we should pay far more attention to the dynamics of the fiscal deficit and why it changed and perhaps a little less attention to other considerations.

Joseph Grunwald

The discussion so far has concerned short-run effects. I think it is established that either the monetary approach has not worked because of specific circumstances or that it intrinsically cannot work in industrializing countries. We have not said anything about some long-term aspects or discussed policies from a long-term perspective. First of all, as Mario Blejer has mentioned [see chapter 1] producers in Argentina became importers. This was not necessarily a sound development. The oligopolistic situation that existed under import substitution was not eliminated. It shifted to importers, who maintained control over the market.

And I ask myself: with these policies in the Southern Cone, can one really discriminate between the efficient and the inefficient import substituters? The assumption underlying these policies is that the system works with minimal imperfections so that the liberalization policies will force out the inefficient producers and will not affect the efficient ones. Therefore, in the long run, the economy will be healthier. This is not the case, given the imperfections of the Southern Cone economies.

The question here concerns the effects on long-run industrialization. Have these policies, based on the monetary approach and sometimes impetuous liberalization, prejudiced the level of industrialization in these countries? I think nobody will argue that import-substituting industrialization has been an efficient process—but have not the corrective policies gone too far, too fast? By not being able to discriminate between efficient and inefficient producers, have not these policies also deindustrialized efficient producers, so that eventually these economies will have to start afresh on a costly industrialization process in the future?

CHILE

Vittorio Corbo

First I will summarize the issues of the Chilean experience, some of which were raised in Mario Blejer's exposition [see chapter 1]. I will then elaborate these issues (deterioration of the real exchange rate, increased capital inflows and expenditures, the relative price between tradables and nontradables, domestic and international inflation and interest rates) in the context of macroeconomic developments in Chile. Finally, I will draw some conclusions about the management of economic liberalization and stabilization programs.

Summary of the issues. One point no one has mentioned is that in the Chilean case we have observed substantial deterioration in the real exchange rate in the past year and a half—where I am defining the real exchange rate price of tradables relative to nontradables. The deterioration of the real exchange rate in late 1979 and 1980 was very much a consequence of backward wage indexation, as Rudiger Dornbusch mentions [see his comments in chapter 8]. However, the deterioration in the, say, four or five quarters before May 1982 was accompanied by a large recession, thanks to the substantial increase in net capital inflows. The tremendous spread between the domestic and foreign rates of interest meant that the capital inflow went up from around US$2 billion in 1979 to US$3 billion in 1980 and close to US$5 billion in 1981. The absorption of the capital inflow created a deficit in the current account in 1981 of around 15 percent of GDP. In previous years the deficit had been 4 or 5 percent of GDP, so the deficit in the current account as a percentage of GDP went up over 9 percentage points in one year. How was that digested by the system? The drop in interest rates in 1980 created a tremendous expansion in aggregate demand; the increase in the demand for tradables increased the deficit in the current account; and the increase in the demand for nontradables pushed their prices upward. Thus, the capital inflow was absorbed into the system with domestic inflation above international levels, and the Chilean economy ended up with a booming nontradables sector and a large deterioration of the real exchange rate, especially in the last two quarters of 1981. This deterioration was the way of absorbing the US$5 billion in capital inflows.

This deterioration in the real exchange rate was not a consequence of the U.S. dollar's appreciation in international markets. The dollar's appreciation under an exchange rate for the peso fixed with respect to the dollar affected only the nominal price of tradables. Thus, in 1981 the nominal price of importables was below the one observed at the end of 1980, and the same thing happened for exportables. The price of tradables in nominal terms was a little lower in 1981 than in 1980, and the deterioration of the real exchange rate came mainly from a large increase in the price of nontradables, which increased almost 20 percent in 1981. The weighted average for the inflation rate in that year was therefore around 9 percent.

If my story is correct, all this was the adjustment made possible by the quantum increase in capital inflows that was triggered by the large interest rate differential following the fixing of the exchange rate. The real exchange rate moved toward a new equilibrium compatible with this new level of capital inflow. But then there was the problem of the tremendous loss in competitiveness, which has real effects, especially if the 1981 levels of capital inflows were thought to be unsustainable. The question that arises from my previous analysis is the optimum borrowing strategy for a country. People at the Central Bank of Chile were very concerned in 1978 and 1979 with the consequences of the opening up of the capital account. There was a lot of pressure on them to open the capital account because of the tremendous difference between domestic interest rates and international interest rates. The thinking was mostly in terms of models in which foreign and domestic assets are perfect substitutes. I think these two assets are far from being perfect substitutes. In major part, the domestic credit is commercial credit, and the intermediation is very expensive. Domestic credit is a domestic asset with very low substitutability for foreign assets—especially in a system such as Chile's, in which commercial banks are not allowed to take exchange rate risks. Thus, when these banks borrow in dollars they can only lend in dollars.

As a consequence of all the pressures from both private and government sources, the central bank accelerated the opening of the capital account, but this accelerated opening up created an additional increase in capital inflow that had to be absorbed with a further deterioration of the real exchange rate, or it postponed the recuperation of competitiveness, or both.

Thus, the substantial increase in capital inflow has much to do with the deterioration of the real exchange rate in 1981. I do not believe, as Larry Sjaastad does [see chapter 5], that the deterioration is due to a stroke of bad luck in the form of the appreciation of the U.S. dollar. The appreciation of the dollar directly affected the rate of inflation, but only indirectly affected the exchange rate. If the U.S. dollar had not appreciated, Chile would have experienced much higher inflation, but the real exchange rate had to deteriorate anyway for the Chilean economy to absorb the capital inflow.

The issues in macroeconomic perspective. In my remaining remarks I will concentrate on some of the macroeconomic developments from around 1979 until May 1982. I think there is much to be learned from the Chilean experience in this respect. It is not that other aspects of liberalization and stabilization are unimportant, but I think most economists would agree on the importance of trade and internal market liberalization, especially when the economy in question has known widespread internal price controls and substantial variance in the rate of protection that cannot be justified by any economic argument. With respect to trade liberalization, there can be some disagreement about the speed at which to open up the economy—whether to eliminate first quantitative restrictions or tariffs; how small should the spread be in the final tariff system—but there is no doubt that the chaotic tariff structure of the pre-reform period had to be changed to one with less tariff dispersion. There could also be arguments to counteract some of the side effects of trade liberalization on income distribution. Sebastian Edwards, the next commentator, will look into some of the issues relating to the commodity liberalization process, so I will set that issue aside.

The Chilean experience has been very successful from the point of view of reducing the rate of inflation—inflation was around 1,000 percent in 1973 and 1974, and it was reduced to around 30 percent in 1980 and to below 10 percent in 1981. The reduction from 1,000 percent to 20 or 30 percent a year is a tremendous improvement, and it is something that we would all agree is a sign of success. I am more concerned, however, with some of the recent macroeconomic developments in the Chilean economy.

There are many such developments at the same time in Chile. The only way to analyze all of them would be to have some kind of general equilibrium model. But the number and simultaneity of these changes makes it impossible to estimate a stable structure for such a model. So, one has to be very careful with the interpretations. I am going to give some of the expected implications of some of the changes that have taken place in the last few years, but it is an impossible task for me to identify which of these changes have been the most important.

Among the recent developments in the Chilean economy, I think one of the most important is that, after a long period of an active "crawling peg" from 1973 until February 1978, the exchange rate started to be used as a stabilization device. This process culminated in June 1979 when the exchange rate was fixed in nominal terms with respect to the U.S. dollar. This was done at a time when Chilean inflation ws substantially above international levels. Why was this done? One must be honest and go back to read some of the evidence of the period before February 1978. At that time the authorities bought the idea that the "law of one price" applied even in the short run, and that all goods were tradables. People believed in one way or another that fixing the exchange rate implied a very rapid convergence of the domestic rate of inflation with the international rate of inflation. Furthermore, the only way the fixed rate would be feasible in the long run was if the domestic inflation rate would drop sharply after the fixing of the exchange rate to a level close to the international inflation rate. One way or another, through strong production and consumption substitution between tradables and nontradables, it was thought that the law of one price would be valid not only in the long run but also in the short run.

At the time that the exchange rate was fixed, the monthly inflation rate was around 3 percent.

Furthermore, after the exchange rate was fixed, wage indexation was confirmed in the new labor law, although it had existed also for the previous five years. Thus, the evolution of the real exchange rate that followed was due in large part (besides the evolution in the international prices of tradables) to the dynamics of the prices of nontradable commodities. Yet, the evolution of the price of nontradables was closely related to the evolution of wages based on backward indexation with a decreasing inflation rate. At that time, as I have mentioned, domestic inflation in Chile was substantially above international levels. So, especially after June 1979, there was a deterioration in the real exchange rate that was a direct consequence of the fixing of the exchange rate and was independent of the evolution of capital inflows and other macro-economic variables.

The deterioration of the real exchange rate was initially just a consequence of the price dynamic. If the fixing of the exchange rate had been the only change, then there would have developed a loss of competitiveness and then a recession. However, a second effect took place that validated this lower real exchange rate and made it possible that the lower real exchange rate (resulting from the fixing of the exchange rate) could now be closer to the equilibrium value. This change was the substantial increase in net capital inflows.

One consequence of fixing the exchange rate was that the ex post real interest rate for dollar-denominated loans was highly negative from the third quarter of 1979 until the last quarter of 1980. Why? Largely because Chilean domestic inflation did not converge with international inflation for quite a long time. If a Chilean got a loan in U.S. dollars, the rate of interest was -27 percent in the fourth quarter of 1979; the interest rate for such loans continued to be negative for all of 1980. At the same time, the real interest rate for peso-denominated loans was as high as 22 percent in the first quarter of 1980.

So, there was a substantial difference between borrowing in the domestic market and borrowing in the international market. Obviously, this would create a portfolio substitution and push down the average real interest rates, and real interest rates decreased substantially after the fixing of the exchange rate. The real interest rate was accommodated (was financed) through capital inflows—substantial capital inflows of around US\$3 billion in 1980 and US\$4.8 billion in 1981.

This decrease in the real interest rate created a substantial expansion in aggregate expenditures in 1980 and 1981. Of this substantial expansion, part went to tradables and created a deficit in the current account. But the demand for nontradables also increased and created pressures on the price of nontradables. Given the decrease in the real interest rate, the prices of nontradables had to improve anyway, and this improvement validated the decrease in the real exchange rate that followed the fixing of the exchange rate. What this meant is that the Chilean economy did not have the recession in late 1979 and 1980 because the decreasing real interest rate had created a substantial increase in expenditure, which in turn required a lower real exchange rate to equilibrate the market for nontradables.

Both supply and demand changes can account for the substantial increase in capital inflow. On the demand side, the large spread between real interest rates for peso loans and for dollar loans increased the demand for the latter. On the supply side, reduction in barriers to capital inflows, together with a more favorable attitude toward Chile by the international banking community, accounted for an increase in the supply of capital to Chile. Thus, on top of the loss of competitiveness from fixing the exchange rate, it is entirely possible that a further loss was called for by the large capital inflows, or at least that the drop in the real exchange rate of 1979-80 was now an equilibrium value.

The loss of competitiveness from the third quarter of 1979 on can be seen in table T4-1. In column (1) I have given the price of importables (PM) divided by the price of nontradables (PN1). In column (2) is the price of exportables (PX), excluding copper, divided by PN1. Column (3) shows a geometric average of PX and PM, with weights of 0.50 for each.

Table 4-1. Real Exchange Rates in Chile, 1975-81

Year and quarter	PM/PN1 (1)	PX/PN1 (2)	PT/PN1 (3)	PM/PN12 (4)	PX/PN12 (5)	PT/PN12 (6)	PT/W (7)	PX/PM (8)
1975								
I	1.639	1.664	1.650	1.541	1.565	1.553	2.165	1.014
II	1.662	1.689	1.675	1.545	1.571	1.559	2.487	1.015
III	1.702	1.707	1.703	1.579	1.585	1.582	2.201	1.003
IV	1.751	1.779	1.762	1.629	1.654	1.641	2.203	1.015
1976								
I	1.731	1.775	1.751	1.595	1.637	1.616	2.214	1.025
II	1.528	1.524	1.525	1.407	1.404	1.405	1.922	0.996
III	1.339	1.371	1.355	1.280	1.311	1.297	1.628	1.022
IV	1.177	1.278	1.226	1.173	1.272	1.222	1.422	1.084
1977								
I	1.095	1.151	1.122	1.103	1.161	1.132	1.249	1.051
II	0.903	0.992	0.946	0.940	1.031	0.984	1.117	1.095
III	0.910	0.940	0.924	0.961	0.994	0.977	1.048	1.032
IV	0.952	0.968	0.960	1.014	1.030	1.022	1.169	1.015
1978								
I	1.016	0.967	0.990	1.057	1.008	1.033	1.104	0.951
II	1.015	0.907	0.959	1.048	0.937	0.991	1.076	0.892
III	0.998	0.875	0.934	1.042	0.914	0.975	1.045	0.876
IV	0.998	0.899	0.946	1.032	0.930	0.980	1.063	0.899
1979								
I	0.987	0.925	0.954	1.012	0.950	0.981	1.002	0.937
II	1.000	1.000	1.000	1.000	1.000	1.000	1.000	1.000
III	1.082	1.186	1.132	1.025	1.124	1.073	1.050	1.095
IV	0.984	1.103	1.041	0.946	1.063	1.003	1.030	1.121
1980								
I	0.939	1.118	1.025	0.897	1.070	0.980	0.920	1.191
II	0.925	1.092	1.003	0.880	1.039	0.957	0.864	1.178
III	0.916	1.018	0.965	0.872	0.969	0.919	0.831	1.110
IV	0.874	0.917	0.894	0.831	0.873	0.851	0.736	1.049
1981								
I	0.846	0.844	0.843	0.812	0.812	0.812	0.686	0.998
II	0.784	0.775	0.779	0.767	0.761	0.764	0.630	0.989
III	0.725	0.709	0.716	0.724	0.709	0.716	0.571	0.978
IV	0.703	0.679	0.691	0.716	0.693	0.705	0.561	0.966

Note: Second quarter of 1979 = 1.0. The nominal exchange rate is defined as the number of units of domestic currency required to purchase one unit of foreign exchange. Variables are defined as follows:

PN1 = Price index for nontradables obtained from the Cortazar-Marshall consumer price index based on the equation estimated in Corbo (1981).

PN12 = Aggregate of PN1 and price of differentiated tradables (Corbo 1981).

PX = Export price index in pesos, measured as a Divisia index of the major Chilean exports.

PM = Import price index in pesos, obtained as Divisia index of the exchange-rate-adjusted industrial components of the wholesale price index for Argentina, Brazil, United States, Japan, and Germany, using the structure of imports from each of those countries as a weighting base. The index is also adjusted for average customs duties.

W = Nominal manufacturing wage rate.

PT = Geometric average of PX and PM, with weights of 0.50 for each.

Source: Corbo (1982).

The price of importables is a Divisia price index of the price of manufacturing exports (adjusted for the exchange rate) of Argentina, Brazil, Germany, the United States, and Japan, weighted by the current share of the imports of these five countries into Chile. For the price of exports, again I use a Divisia price index of the price of the eight major exporting commodities of Chile, excluding copper. PN1, the price of nontradables, is a subcomponent of the consumer price index.

Column (4) shows a weighted average of the price of importables and the price of exportables. In column (5), the only change from the previous column is that I have included a more comprehensive definition of nontradables; the column shows an aggregate of pure nontradables plus differentiated tradables. The same has been done in columns (6) and (7).

Column (7) shows the wage-deflated price of tradables, which experienced tremendous decrease after indexation was introduced and also after the inflation rate decreased following the fixing of the exchange rate. In a system with backward inflation, when inflation decreases, the indexation mechanism pushes up the real wage. Real wages in the last quarter of 1981 were over 60 percent above what they were at the beginning of 1975.

The wage measure that I have used is a measure of labor cost. Therefore, this is the wage index adjusted by the change in social security taxation. I had to make this adjustment because there was a major change in social security legislation throughout the period. Social security taxes in Chile are much lower today than they were at the beginning of the period.

Column (8) measures the terms of trade (PX divided by PM), which showed a loss toward the end of the period but a large gain in 1980.

Larry Sjaastad points out that W/PN1 [column (7)] divided by PT/PN1 [column (3)] gives W/PT, the ratio of the real wage to the price of tradables, and that this figure rose from 2.099 in the last quarter of 1979 to 3.863 in the last quarter of 1981, roughly doubling. He asks whether I find this plausible. Not only is it plausible, but it reflects the major recession in the tradables sector in Chile today. (Wages in the manufacturing sector account for no more than 20 percent, sometimes less, of costs; the rest goes to raw materials and capital cost, with value added at around 50 percent of output).

What can we conclude from this evidence? We see an important loss of competitiveness when the data of 1979 are compared with the latter part of the period. This loss of competitiveness is as much as 30 percent if one considers the real exchange rate of importables. There are different ways of defining the real exchange rate, but all the measures point to a deterioration of the real exchange rate after the second quarter of 1979. I also have done some computations with other aggregations—for example, a neo-Keynesian one in which the price of the domestic commodities is in relation to the price of the output of the rest of the world, and the same commodity is compared in both markets. That measure also shows a substantial real appreciation in 1980 and 1981.

The point one should keep in mind is that, from 1979 to 1980 and even in 1981, the drop in the real exchange rate was accommodated with an increase in capital inflows. This movement, which was initially a movement away from equilibrium, was accommodated later with the decrease in the real interest rate. In this period, as shown in Corbo (1981), a devaluation with the same level of capital inflows would not affect competitiveness and would only affect the rate of inflation. This was so because the Chilean economy was close to an equilibrium situation.

On top of these internal developments of the Chilean economy, the impact of the international recession, at least from the point of view of output losses, must be taken into account. In 1981, Chile suffered an important loss of income as a consequence of the deterioration in the commodity terms of trade and a substantial increase in the international interest rate. This loss of income was of the order of US$1.2 billion. The aggregate loss from the effects of the terms of trade and the interest rate was of the order of 3.4 percent of 1981 GDP. This contributed, other things being equal, to a larger current account deficit in 1981.

Thus, at the end of 1981 Chile faced a substantial loss of competitiveness over the past year and a half and a large current account deficit of around 15 percent of GDP. What happened in 1981? Toward the end of 1981, net capital inflow from the rest of the world started to decrease drastically. At the same time, the central bank had to increase domestic credit to rescue light financial institutions; thus, the risk of devaluation increased. The net effect of these two developments was an increase in the real interest rate toward the last quarter of 1981.

Capital inflows were US$1 billion in the third quarter of 1981. They went down to US$580 million in the last quarter of 1981 and to US$300 million in the first quarter of 1982. As a consequence, the interest rate of both peso and dollar loans increased substantially, especially the former. The real annual interest rate of peso loans, as I mentioned before, is over 50 percent in May 1982. The increase in real interest rate causes substantial decrease in expenditures. So now the mechanism has to work in reverse—the Chilean economy needs an appreciation of the real exchange rate. When expenditures are cut, part of this expenditure cut falls on tradables, and that will help the adjustment because it will reduce the current account deficit. Unfortunately, part of the expenditure cut falls also on nontradables, and, if the prices of nontradables are inflexible downward, that creates unemployment. The cut in expenditures has already been produced in Chile. The commercial account that had a deficit of close to US$2 billion in 1981 is today almost balanced on a monthly basis. There has been a substantial decrease in expenditures, especially in the sectors that usually suffer the most when the real interest rate increases—the construction sector and the sector that produces durable goods.

The construction sector has been the most heavily affected because toward the end of 1979 and the beginning of 1980, when the interest rate was very low, there was a tremendous expansion in this sector, an expansion that had not yet been absorbed in the economy. But now, with high interest rates, the construction sector has a substantial accumulation of inventories. Houses are not selling. Real estate prices have dropped substantially, maybe 25 or 30 percent in real terms.

As I said, the mechanism must now work in reverse—a depreciation of the peso (an increase in the real exchange rate) is called for. In the previous situation, the appreciation of the peso was achieved under a fixed exchange rate regime, with domestic inflation above international inflation. With a fixed exchange rate, the depreciation of the peso requires a domestic inflation rate below the international rate. With the price of tradables constant in nominal terms, there must be a substantial decrease in the price of nontradables to accomplish the exchange rate depreciation. If the loss of competitiveness is of the order of 25 percent, this will require a substantial reduction in the price of nontradables.

The problem is that, as we all know, the prices of nontradables are very inflexible downward. Under these circumstances, it is very difficult to produce the required improvement in relative prices of tradables. It is even more difficult in Chile because of the compulsory backward indexation of wages. As long as there is wage indexation, it is difficult to achieve improvement in relative price. We all can see that the unemployment rate has gone up substantially. In March 1982, the unemployment rate was 19.1 percent in Santiago, up around 8 percentage points from the September 1981 figure, and the average for the whole country was 18.4 percent.

Conclusions. The problems of Chile in 1982 are not so much the results of failed trade liberalization policies but of inadequate macroeconomic management. The problem facing the country is how to produce an improvement in relative prices. As was said earlier, this is a problem that started with the fixing of the exchange rate and was compounded by the drastic opening up of the capital account. When the interest rate decreased, to have a fixed exchange rate did not hurt because the drop in relative price of tradables was accommodated by the system. But because capital inflows have been reduced and the real interest rate has gone up, there must be an improvement in the relative prices of tradables. With the fixed exchange rate, the only way to do this (especially when the rest of the world has low inflation) is to cut the prices of nontradables—even when the prices of these goods are inflexible downward (very strongly so, as Chile has shown). How to "oil" this improvement in relative prices?

There is no doubt that Chile should devalue. However, one will need to develop a system that should neutralize the impact upon expectation of an official devaluation. If one devalues once, people will think that one will devalue again tomorrow. If the capital account is closed, then there is a very simple decision—to change the exchange rate. But with an open capital account, the effect of devaluation on expectations must be considered. One way to do so might be to develop a future market in such a way that people could cover themselves for the risk of future devaluations. Another solution might be a "tablita" that people think is feasible in the near term, maybe a two-year tablita with some large immediate devaluation and a small devaluation over the following two years. Such a devaluation would work now because it would start from a situation of disequilibrium, with relative prices of tradables below equilibrium for the new level of capital inflows.

The goal is a system people will believe in. But I think Chile has shown that the "pure" system of waiting for nontradable prices to decrease will not really work—that mechanism has not worked in any country in the world before, and it has even less chance of working in a system with 100-percent-plus backward wage indexation.

Sebastian Edwards

I will divide my presentation on the Chilean experience in four parts. Throughout I will try to focus on the implications of this case. First I will discuss the process of trade liberalization and its possible effects on employment. Next I will consider the real exchange rate, and here my remarks might overlap with what Vittorio Corbo has said [see the preceding subsection]. Then I will comment on the puzzle of the real interest rate, and, finally, I will offer some brief conclusions.

Trade liberalization and employment. Between 1975 and 1979, Chile reduced its tariff from an average of about 100 percent, with a high degree of dispersion, to what basically is a uniform 10 percent tariff. The main objective the government was pursuing by this policy was to improve efficiency and to generate a reallocation of resources according to comparative advantages. At the time, this process of trade liberalization was not seen as a stabilization tool.

A problem that has not been sufficiently analyzed—and one that I think is important for the inferences we can draw from the Chilean case—is to what extent this quite rapid reduction in tariffs had an effect on the Chilean employment problem, which in turn is related to the problem of the difference between the short- and long-run effects of liberalization processes. It is very hard to know exactly what happened in Chile at that time, since a number of other policies were also taking effect. In 1976, for example, there were approximately 600,000 unemployed in Chile, about 17 percent of the labor force. And this figure excludes people working in the minimum employment program. This (1976) was the first year that the tariff reduction process was serious, with tariffs being reduced to an average of approximately 24 percent.

The question then is, to what extent can the tariff reduction program be blamed for the unemployment? The answer is not easy, since at the same time tariffs were being reduced the stabilization program was having some negative effects on the employment level. The reduction of the public sector, which accounted for at least 100,000 unemployed, was also taking place. However, despite this inherent problem of trying to attribute, as it were, different levels of unemployment to different causes, I think that it is very important for future liberalization attempts to make a distinction between the short- and long-run effects of liberalization in the real sector in Chile.

We all know from trade theory that, in the long run in a developing country that presumably exports labor-intensive goods and imports capital-intensive goods, a tariff reduction will move resources away from imports, and that this shift will have a positive effect on wages: there will be an increase in real wages. In the short run, however, things can be very different. In particular, and just as an example, if one assumes that there are some problems in the mobility of factors of production, and if capital is sector specific in the short run, to maintain full employment we know that real wages, at least in terms of one good, will tend to go down.

The problem that arises then is, to what extent will wages, if they are left on their own, indeed adjust downward to accommodate this tariff reduction process at a level of employment that is, if not full, the same level as before? In the Chilean economy at this time it was very difficult for a reduction of real wages to take place. The reason was that—if not by law, at least in fact—there was 100 percent wage indexation. There was also a minimum wage that increased 22 percent in real terms between 1975 and 1977. So, the question now is, to what extent can we attribute part of the unemployment problem in Chile to the facts that (1) tariffs were reduced very quickly; (2) there are some rigidities in the short run, mainly factors that cannot move instantaneously; and (3) wages are rigid downward, at least in the short run.

Some rough calculations I have done (Edwards 1982a) show that in the Chilean case the effect on unemployment of these particular factors can be anything between 2 to 4 percentage points. Although that is not much compared with the 17 percent unemployment of 1976, it is large enough to make one worry about what the dynamic processes of trade liberalization should be and, specifically, about how fast tariffs should be reduced.

In this respect, I believe that future experiments of the kind should try to couple tariff reductions with wage policy that would be more effective in impeding increases in the level of unemployment. In addition, it may be advisable to implement the process of tariff reduction in a staged fashion—preannouncing very clearly different stages, and making sure that these negative, short-run employment effects are minimized.

In the case of Chile, as I said, rough calculations show that between 2 and 4 percentage points of the unemployment level of 1976/77 can be explained or can be attributed to this trade liberalization process. The industries that were most affected were foodstuffs, textiles, and metallurgical industries. The reduction in unemployment in those industries was in the range of 80,000 to 90,000 people.

In the long run, in contrast, the Chilean economy—in particular, the industrial sector—responded surprisingly well to the trade liberalization process. What we actually saw was an adjustment process in which, from a very high degree of inefficiency, a number of firms moved to a degree of world competitiveness. Although at the beginning we observed in Chile something similar to what happened in Argentina, in that producers became importers, new importers quickly came into business. The level of competition in the long run did indeed prevail.

In summary of this first part, I think that the Chilean experience provides an interesting case study that should be pursued. More research is called for with respect to the difference between the short- and long-run effects of trade liberalization on employment. The main conclusion that will emerge, I think, is that the existence of rigidities in the short run can cause significant unemployment effects. I think this has fairly important implications, as research by Neary (1982) indicates.

Trade liberalization and the real exchange rate. In this second part of my exposition, I would like to talk a little about the real exchange rate. Between June 1979 and May 1982, there was substantial real appreciation of the peso. Depending on the figures one considers, this appreciation was between 15 and 30 percent. That the government decided to peg the peso to the U.S. dollar in June 1979, and that the dollar has appreciated in the world market, accounts for between 9 and 11 percent of this real appreciation, depending on the basket of currencies one considers. The question that we should ask ourselves—and one that has been asked in this symposium—is, to what extent is this appreciation an equilibrium phenomenon? Does a process of liberalization require a real appreciation of the exchange rate?

We know that the effect a real liberalization has on the real exchange rate is not clear. However, some arguments have been mentioned. One is the Balassa effect, which was particularly popular in Chile in late 1980 and early 1981 as an explanation of the real appreciation. If one takes plausible values of different parameters, calculations that I have made (Edwards 1982b) show that the Balassa effect does not explain more than 3 to 4 points of the real appreciation. There definitely is a Balassa effect, and countries that grow faster would have a tendency for the relative price of tradables and nontradables to decline. But in the Chilean case this accounted for at most 4 percentage points; there still are 26 more points to explain.

We then move to another plausible explanation—the effect of capital inflows. An economy with many restrictions to capital inflows suddenly had at least some of them lifted. What do we observe? The economy now has the possibility of increasing expenditure substantially above income. The mechanism through which this happens, as has been suggested, is the reduction in real interest rates, which in the case of Chile were 4.75 percent in real terms in 1980, substantially low for Chile. So, there was a huge increase in capital inflows that amounted to US$5 billion in 1981, almost 15 percent of GNP. Part of this increase in expenditure went to nontradables, and part went to tradables. But the part that went to nontradables applied pressure to the relative price of nontradables, generating a real appreciation.

Thus, in some sense it might be argued that a process of liberalization of the capital account has to cause a real appreciation of the exchange rate. However, to understand fully the case of Chile, we must go further and ask if the level of capital inflow of 1981 was an equilibrium level. The answer, clearly, is that it was not. Fifteen percent of GNP as a capital inflow cannot be sustained by any country, and particularly not by Chile, where in 1981 foreign indebtedness increased by 61 percent, to reach more than 50 percent of GNP.

Once we answer this question and say that a capital inflow of 15 percent of GNP cannot be a long-run value for this variable, then we must ask what will happen next. At some stage we have to come back, if not to the old level of capital inflow, to a new and higher postliberalization level of inflow—one, however, that will be substantially below 15 percent. And this is, I think, what we can observe in May 1982 in Chile. Interest rates are going up so this reduction in expenditure can take place.

Again, the problem is that part of this reduction in expenditure has to fall on nontradables, that the relative price of nontradables will have to go down. But in most cases the prices of nontradables are rigid to going down. Furthermore, in Chile the wage law makes this particularly difficult, since for all practical purposes wages in real terms constantly have to grow over time.

Now the question is, what can be done to ease this transition? Of course, if the price of nontradables cannot go down, the adjustment is going to take place through their quantities. And that is exactly what is happening in Chile. There are projections that 1982 GNP will decrease between 9 and 12 percent. We just heard from Mr. Vittorio Corbo that unemployment reached 18 percent nationwide and 19.1 percent in Santiago in the first quarter of 1982.

In some respects, however, this reduction in the level of real activity can be avoided or at least minimized. Since the nominal price of nontradables cannot go down, the adjustment could come through an increase in the price of tradables through a devaluation. Now, the problem with this is related to what has been said here earlier. For political reasons, the Chilean government largely ruled out devaluation as a policy for 1982. Also, at this time the existence of wage indexation laws in Chile would partially reduce the degree of effectiveness of a devaluation.

Liberalization and the real interest rate. Let me now make just a few remarks about real interest rates. Interest rate arbitrage in Chile has not taken place, and no one expected that it would take place. The basic reason it has not is that the capital account in Chile is not open and has never been open. There are important restrictions to capital flows. Short-term capital flows are not allowed. The shortest term of a capital inflow is two years, and for all practical purposes most capital inflows have had a sixty-six-month maturity. The barriers to capital inflows are that the capital can only come into the country at certain maturities. There can be loans. A Chilean bank can get a foreign loan, but the loan has to be at least at two years' maturity. Then, the bank can loan these funds internally for at least ninety days. After the ninety days, the bank has to reloan the funds; only after two years can the capital inflow go back to its source.

This introduces what I think is an important point: that the expectation of devaluation that is incorporated in any decision of borrowing in Chile is not an expectation of devaluation in the very short run. It is diffused through a longer period of time. So, even if the expectation of devaluation is not very high, the variance associated with this expectation is. And this makes the devaluation also very high.

Conclusions. I agree with the comment Larry Sjaastad has made to me. As always, several things were going on in the economy at the same time—inflows of capital only at certain maturities, lack of interest rate arbitrage, high real interest rates, and expectations of devaluation. As he mentions, most of the US$5 billion in capital inflows came during the first half of 1981, when the demand for credit had grown many times. At that same time, people in Chile started to realize that the situation with the exchange rate was unsustainable. Thus, expectations of devaluation developed toward the second half of 1981. These expectations started to become more and more important as 1981 evolved.

So, on the one hand there were capital inflows, on the other there was a rapidly growing expectation of devaluation. In 1981 the economists in Chile were revising their expectations constantly. They started the year assuming that the current account deficit would be US$2 billion, and they ended up with US$5 billion.

This brings us again to the problem, mentioned earlier by Mario Blejer [see chapter 1], of the flexibility of policy [see also comment on this issue in chapter 8]. We must leave options open to be able to handle situations like the one in Chile in 1982. It is, I think, a little strange to hear economists, when they talk about the present Chilean case, arguing on how devaluation can be done without the public realizing that it is devaluation.

Vittorio Corbo has mentioned [above] that a future market might be one way to neutralize the expectation of devaluation when the capital account has been opened, and Pablo Spiller [see his comments below] discusses the Uruguayan experience with a futures market in U.S. dollars. With respect to a forward market, the experience of Portugal might be interesting to look at. In 1977 the Portuguese opened a forward window that had the characteristics Spiller describes—people had to pay for forward delivery in a discount fashion. The payment had an interest rate. To take delivery in the forward market, the same restrictions for buying on a spot market applied. Something of this sort might work in a country that does not have full capital openness, such as Chile.

Rolf Lüders

I thought it would be interesting to look at the problems of economic liberalization and stabilization from the other side, from the point of view of people who are riding this roller coaster, people such as we in Chile. What I thought I would do is tell you a little about how a relatively large group—one of those oligopolistic groups some of you worry about—adjusted to this model.

I will start at the point at which the recovery took place, which was probably somewhere around 1976, and divide the subsequent time into two periods—1976 through 1981, and the end of 1981 to May 1982.

At the beginning of 1976, I think most Chilean businessmen had about the same expectations. We anticipated a very fast increase in GNP, and a rapidly falling local interest rate. We also expected a dramatic structural variation because of the change in customs duties and a more or less constant real exchange rate. And we expected wages to go up more or less in line with per capita GNP.

What did we do, given these expectations? Our group in Chile was managing probably around fifty or sixty companies (about twenty-five of those were in the financial area; the rest were in the industrial, mining, agricultural, and trade areas). Using some examples, I am going to describe our activities, dividing my analysis between existing companies and companies we created and general adjustment strategies in the Chilean case.

Existing companies and adjustment, 1976-81. As an example of an existing company in the export activity, where we thought we would have a comparative advantage, I will mention Inforsa (wood products). What did we do in Inforsa? We invested a lot of money, something like US$40 million, in a newsprint machine, US$180 million in a cardboard box factory (jointly with a foreign group), and about another US$40 million in a woodboard factory. This was clearly an area in which we thought there was a comparative advantage and in which we were expanding quite rapidly.

Another existing activity we had was a factory that manufactured large electrical home appliances. That was formerly a highly protected sector, but one in which custom duties were also reduced to 10 percent. Nevertheless, in Chile we had the natural protection of transport costs. What did we do here? First, we merged our factory with four or five other factories, out of the seven or eight that operated in Chile. In May 1982 there were only three left, ours being one of them. We increased output per worker very rapidly, mainly by reducing the number of workers employed. And this was possible because people were working harder in Chile, perhaps as a result of a generally more competitive climate. Investments in that electric appliance factory were minimal, perhaps even less than depreciation funds. Nevertheless, productivity in the industry increased rapidly, from about US$11.0 (1980 dollars) per person (a relatively stable average of past performance) to US$47.0 per person in 1981.

In this industry we did what John Williamson perhaps criticizes [see his comments above and in chapter 8]. We produced in Chile only those goods we were efficient at and for which a large domestic market was available, and we imported the rest of the products in this line. Profits earned from our importing activities were kept low because, as soon as we tried to raise our prices, someone else imported the products directly. Arbitrage enforced the "law of one price" for this product.

We invested in another industry, a motor compressor factory (specifically, for refrigerators). We were producing them for the Andean Common Market; that is, for the whole west coast of Latin America. Once the economy opened up and Chile withdrew from the Andean Market, we were not able to produce the compressors at a profit. We had to close down and sell the machinery to a foreign country (Brazil).

I have mentioned three examples that show the sort of adjustment that took place in the country. The net result, I would say, was an expansion in production.

Created companies and adjustment, 1976-81. With respect to companies we created, we expanded very fast in the financial area and did very poorly with some companies in the tradables sector.

Another adjustment we had to make was to the high interest rates. As has been mentioned, interest rates were extremely high between 1974 and 1976. Since foreign funds were cheaper than domestic sources, we arbitraged. We went out to get money abroad, opening up offices in New York and London and so on, to be in contact with foreign financiers and to get money into the country. We also bought a bank in Panama, and another in Uruguay. As a result, our group brought in substantial amounts of foreign resources, and this was also done by other major groups. Nevertheless, as also has been mentioned, our efforts were not enough to make domestic interest rates equalize with foreign interest rates.

The overall result of our actions was that during 1976-81 the group increased output by a factor of three, in part because we bought companies that were government owned, and we doubled employment. We financed this expansion process by substantially increasing our debt level, forced by low profits as a proportion of equity. Most of the debt was foreign but part was in local currency. Of this domestic debt, a portion was in consumer-price-indexed interest rates, with low real rates, but was in local nonreadjustable terms and therefore accrued high interest rates.

This fact brings us back to the problem José María Dagnino Pastore has mentioned [see chapter 3 and his comments on Argentina above]. When interest rates shot up again in 1981, we of course faced the same problems of most Chilean companies, which were the effects of high interest on the debt-profit and debt-equity levels.

Adjustment strategies in the Chilean case, end 1981–May 1982. Let me now have a look at how accurately we forecasted the developments in the Chilean economy. As said, we believed that GNP would grow rapidly, and it did. We also expected a big structural change in the Chilean economy, and this took place. We further anticipated that the real exchange rate would stay more or less constant, but, as you know, it dropped dramatically. We expected wages to move more or less in line with GNP per capita, but they went up substantially with respect to our expectations.

So, in Chile we came to the end of 1981 and to the beginning of 1982 with these problems: high interest rates, low exchange rate, and high wages. No matter what vehicle or theoretical model one might have in mind, I would guess that one could not expect the real exchange rate to remain at its May 1982 value, and then one must expect an internal price and wage adjustment process to take place in order to produce an increase in the real exchange rate.

We also expect the interest rate to stay high. When I say high, I mean a 25 percent real interest rate or higher over a period of a few years. Based on that assumption, our group is adjusting its business activities. We are changing our liability structure wherever we can toward cheaper credit sources. We are trying to adjust employment to the expected level of output, which, as you all know, has fallen dramatically. A drop in GNP of 3 to 4 percent has been mentioned. Right now we expect that the fall will probably be slightly greater. So, we are adjusting our employment level to that drop in output.

We are reducing salary levels wherever we can—mainly at the professional level and not so much at the general workers' level. Here I raise a point that is important for the discussions of this symposium. It is very different when this problem is seen from a macroeconomic viewpoint than when it is seen from a company's point of view. From the macro point of view, it is obvious that salaries are one way of adjusting. But for only one company to adjust salaries has little effect because wages are not a very important cost element of any one particular company—normally, other inputs a company purchases make up for a substantial part of costs. Of course, in turn these inputs have wages as costs of production. Therefore, even if at the macroeconomic level wages are half of GNP, at the level of any one industrial company wages are usually not very important. If a firm is one of the few to reduce wages, the only thing it gains, really, is the animosity of its laborers. Companies therefore tend to avoid wage reduction.

Another way in which we are adjusting is by selling assets, to kill short-term debt and to avoid what I would now call the "Dagnino Pastore problem." The only way out is to sell assets, even if one loses money in the short term. I suppose that is the way the whole system tends to adjust.

If we now accept this record of personal experience, it becomes obvious that the problem with the automatic adjustment, which is implicit in the model we have applied in Chile, is basically one of wage flexibility and asset price flexibility. Wage flexibility has been frequently discussed, and I will only add that time and historical elements are very important. Even in Chile, we probably would have been more likely to adjust our wage levels faster if we had had forty years of social market economy instead of forty years of our type of interventionist economy.

If this transition is to be made—from an economy in which for a long period of time the government has decided everything to a market economy—I think the change will probably have to be slower or more managed if a successful "automatic" adjustment experience is to be realized.

Another problem in Chile's adjustment is asset prices. I am surprised we have not talked more about asset prices [see later comments by Zahler (below), Teitel (chapter 6), and Dornbusch, Williamson, Corbo, and Harberger (chapter 8)]. In Chile, asset prices probably went up in real terms eight times or so from the 1970s to the 1980s. Anyone who visits Santiago knows that houses there cost about two or three times as much as here in Washington, and so on. It is obvious that these prices eventually will have to come down. But the problem is that those assets were purchased by most owners when their prices were at a peak, and the purchase was financed with debt. So, if those prices are forced down, either companies or the owners of these assets must incur losses and eventually go broke. Nobody is willing to pay that price easily, especially because it strongly affects the whole financial system, and this system becomes an ally of the asset holder.

My guess is that one of the main reasons that interest rates in Chile are so high has little to do with devaluation expectations or any other explanation and more to do with people clinging to their assets and trying to avoid losses. Unfortunately, banks finance this process because they are afraid they themselves will go broke if they let their creditor companies go broke. Unless we address this problem, I think we are not addressing the real problem of high interest rates, at least not in Chile. I do not know what happens in other countries, but from what Dagnino Pastore has told us, I believe the problem in Argentina is very similar.

Linda M. Koenig

I would like to clarify a point made by Vittorio Corbo [see his comments above]. Then I would like to comment on the interest rate question.

Mr. Corbo spoke of a loss of competitiveness, since the fixing of the peso in mid-1979, of as much as 30 percent. That loss is very difficult to measure. But, assuming that Mr. Corbo's is the correct figure, I would like to point out that it would still mean that prices in Chile must increase by 30 percent less than prices in the rest of the world, not necessarily that they must decline by 30 percent. Of course it is true that, if this lesser increase were to occur over a five-year period, we might well conclude that that period was too long for such an adjustment to be sustainable.

I want to make this point because Mr. Corbo has also said that inflation had been positive in Chile so far in 1982. Although that is true, it is also true that inflation was only 0.2 percent over the first five months of 1982. I think that it will prove to be substantially less than inflation in the rest of the world. So, perhaps within two years or three, it is possible that the 30 percent loss of competitiveness can be regained.

On the problem of the interest rate, I have some question in my own mind as to how high interest rates in Chile actually have been in the past. I will leave aside the most recent six to nine months, in which I think we can agree that interest rates have been extremely high. In fact, they have gone up in nominal as well as in real terms. But if we look at interest rates in Chile over the longer run, the first thing we observe is that half of the stock of credit is in U.S. dollars. That is the stock of credit extended by the Chilean financial system; it does not even include the credit that is coming into Chile to the largest companies, which can borrow directly from U.S. banks. So, half of the stock of credit which is being intermediated through the Chilean financial system is denominated in dollars. This credit is being lent out at spreads ranging anywhere from 1.0 to 1.5 percent over LIBOR [London interbank offered rate] to as high as, say, 5 to 7 percent over LIBOR. These spreads, I think, generally reflect the situation of the individual borrower rather than that of the country as a whole.

If we then leave the dollar-denominated part of credit aside, we have the other half to examine. The other half of Chilean credit is going, let us say, to the less creditworthy part of the borrowing universe. Furthermore, a great deal of this credit—most of it—is at very short term. When one speaks with Chilean firms about the structure of their borrowing requirements, one discovers that, in most cases, these firms are making negligible use of short-term credit. Obviously, they do everything possible to avoid using it.

If we put all this together now and come back to the statement that firms are under-capitalized, that they have tended to overborrow in the past—and if we generalize that to say that most firms have overborrowed and that there may be firms in the picture that should not even have existed or should not have received credit—then I think the level of interest rates for peso loans that one observes in Chile, while high, is not altogether surprising. I do not think this level should be taken as a proxy for average interest rates.

URUGUAY

Pablo T. Spiller

I do not intend to give a full description of what happened in Uruguay, but to deal instead with one issue that has been discussed several times in this symposium. That is, the capital or even the goods markets in the three countries of the Southern Cone do not work competitively. Hence, either or both the "law of one price" or the "law of one interest rate" may not work.

Although it seems that the law of one price did work for Uruguay, at least until 1981, I think that the law of one interest rate did not work, except since the beginning of 1982. To that I will return later.

Several reasons that the law of one interest rate may not have been working have been provided in our discussion: expectations of future devaluation, premium rates, and so on. I would like to examine what the actual degree of competitiveness in the Uruguayan banking sector may imply for this issue. In this context, I can contribute some findings, from a paper Edgardo Favaro and I have just finished (Spiller and Favaro 1982) concerning the degree of competition in the Uruguayan banking sector, the effects some of the regulatory changes since 1977 have had in promoting competition in that sector, and the effects of competition on the behavior of interest rates.

Competition in the Uruguayan commercial banking sector. The Uruguayan commercial banking sector comprises one large public bank, the Banco República, and twenty-one private banks. This number of private banks in existence has been the same since 1965; since that time, no entry to the banking sector has been allowed unless a new bank buys some other existing bank.

In addition, the Uruguayan financial system includes what are called "banking houses." Banking houses are different from banks in that they are allowed to raise deposits from domestic residents. In 1977, however, the Central Bank of Uruguay allowed these institutions to raise funds in pesos from nonresidents. Since then, the relevance of these banking houses has systematically increased, both in raising funds and in making loans.

On the one hand, then, the system has strong barriers to entry. On the other, there are other institutional factors in the system that may promote the implicit or explicit development of cartel relationships. Among these factors is the easy access to information on competitors' behavior (the central bank distributes such information). Also, the overall number of bank branches is held constant.

In the study we have finished (Spiller and Favaro 1982) we were able to identify the kinds of conjectures that banks in the industry had about the reaction of their competitors. We were able to reject competitive assumptions. Both Cournot and Bertrand expectations were rejected. We were unable, however, to reject a model that assumes implicit collusion among the four largest firms. Interestingly, the public firm, the Banco República, was among these leading firms.

First, in particular we found that each of the four leading firms expected very strong retaliatory measures by the other three if it tried to expand its market share. Second, we found that the small firms also expected some retaliation, by the leading firms against the small firms' expansion. In contrast, the large firms expected the small firms to accommodate the large firms' attempts to expand. We who study industrial organization describe this type of industry as a Von Stackelberg industry, where there is a leader in the sector and followers. That type of industry will not resemble a competitive industry.

This degree of interaction changed around 1978. After 1978, the four leading financial firms still reacted to any intent by the others to increase output, but the degree of interaction was strongly reduced. For example, before June 1978 each one of the leading private banks expected the others to increase their output by 1.6 percentage points to any percentage point increase of its own; that is, any one leading bank expected to lose market share if it tried to increase its own output. After June 1978, the reaction expected from the other banks was cut in half, to less than a percentage point, 0.8.

The main finding of our work, then, was that allowing the opening of the banking houses significantly increased the level of competition in the sector. That is not to say that after 1978 the Uruguayan banking system became a competitive sector, but that the degree of competition and its efficiency seem to have increased significantly. The effects of the 1977 regulatory changes can be seen in the behavior of what I call, using industrial organization terms, the price-cost margin. I define the price-cost margin as the interest charged, minus the interest paid on deposits, divided by the interest charged. The price-cost margin before 1977 was about 50 percent; by the end of 1980 it was below 20 percent. It had a downward drift, with variations, with a substantial cut by the end of 1977.

There is another number worth looking at. It is the variance of interest rates among banks. This variance among banks increased dramatically after 1978; before, it had been quite small. I see in the behavior of the variance of the interest rate a proof that there is a much higher degree of competition in the commercial banking sector. Before 1978 the cartel was stable, with a common interest rate.

Macroeconomic implications of competition. What then are the macroeconomic implications of promoting competition? Let me first discuss the level of the real interest rate in Uruguay. Until 1976, the banking sector was constrained by a relatively low maximum rate of interest. Hence, it is difficult to tell what the real interest rate actually was at the time. However, since that restriction was lifted, the real rate, or what we observe, became positive. Moreover, if we look in dollar terms at the most frequently charged peso interest rate, it had a premium of around 20 percentage points above the London interbank offered rate [LIBOR]. Although it can be argued that 20 percentage points just compensates for the risk of devaluation, I think that this is not the whole story, in particular because of two pieces of additional evidence.

First is the issue of exchange insurance, what Rudiger Dornbusch proposes [see his comments, and those of José María Dagnino Pastore, in chapter 8]. There were two periods in

Uruguay when exchange insurance was introduced—one in 1980 and another in effect today. In 1980 it was "free insurance," which meant one could, in effect, buy any amount of future U.S. dollars one wanted at the "tablita" rate without paying for it. There was no really strong effect on interest rates.

The second round of exchange insurance was introduced in December of 1981, when the central bank decided that the interest rates were terribly high. The central bank asked the Banco República to sell future dollars. Sometime by the end of 1980 they eliminated the free insurance after some US$1.5 billion had been sold. In December 1981 they introduced futures again, but this time one had to pay for them. That did not have a strong effect on the level of interest rates either. It is difficult, then, to base the explanation of the high level of interest rates on the premium for devaluation risk. [See Sebastian Edwards's comments on Chile, above.]

The second issue is that the term structure did not show any immediate devaluation coming through.

If we can say that part of the reason for high interest rates is that the banking sector does not behave very competitively, then what are the policy implications? To find out, I tried a very pedestrian test of the law of one interest rate by regressing interest rates on interest in pesos and on interest in LIBOR and the devaluation rate, and it did not work very well.

But one of the results was that an increase in the rate of devaluation over the next three months increased (on average) the rate of interest on a three-month deposit by only 0.24 percentage points. That says that, at least in that period, if one tried to reduce the interest rate by reducing the rate of devaluation, it would not have been very helpful. At the beginning of this presentation I mentioned that interest parity had been achieved since the beginning of 1982. It occurred in the following way: when the central bank realized that exchange insurance did not affect the interest rate, the Banco República started charging less for its loans and paying less on its deposits. We cannot forget that the Banco República has more or less 30 percent of the Uruguayan market. When the Banco República started paying 10 percentage points less than it was paying before and started charging less than it was charging before (it set a maximum, I think, of 37 percent on time deposits and 50 percent on loans), the market achieved interest parity. Although I do not want to say that this is the way interest parity should be achieved in every country, it seems that in Uruguay this policy may have been much more effective than trying to reduce the interest rate by reducing the rate of devaluation. In that sense, I agree with Rudiger Dornbusch that a mix of policies must be used in markets where one can expect noncompetitive behavior. Some kind of enforcing rules may be very fruitful.

A REGIONAL VIEW

Roberto Zahler

At this stage I think that almost all of the main economic events that have happened in Chile, Argentina, and Uruguay have been covered in one way or another by the different discussants, so I believe that a formal comparison between the three cases may not prove very useful. For example, I would say that the Argentine experience has been very different from the Chilean and the Uruguayan, mainly because the fiscal and public enterprise deficit was not able to be controlled in Argentina. But then I would have to add that Uruguay and Chile were experiencing in 1982 a very similar situation to the Argentine one, in the sense that the public sector budget went into deficit, banks were having great difficulty in obtaining the repayment of loans, and bankruptcies had started and threatened to go out of control. Even though it appears that the magnitude was not the same, there was a clear tendency for the same type of problems as in Argentina to appear in Chile and Uruguay.

Therefore, I will try to emphasize certain issues—some that are common, and some that are specific to certain countries—whose analysis and discussion may contribute to a better understanding of some of the problems that have been found in the recent actual implementation of economic stabilization and liberalization policies in the Southern Cone.

The monetary approach and its applications. I agree with Mario Blejer [see chapter 1] that liberalization and stabilization are two very different kinds of policies. Whereas liberalization policies have to do mainly with resource allocation and, therefore, with a particular approach to long-run development strategies, stabilization policies are generally related to restoring basic macroeconomic equilibriums. The monetary approach to the balance of payments, however, is a theoretical construction (a theoretical approach) for understanding the overall change in gross international reserves. As such, and appropriately focused, it may give strong insights to and predictions of not only the balance of payments, but also the general macroeconomic evolution of a particular economy—whether "liberalized" or not, whether inflationary or not.

What policymakers and countries outside the bounds of the discussion here are interested in—besides a fundamental question regarding the prospects of growth and development of economies following stabilization-liberalization policies, a topic that will not be covered in this symposium—are the dynamics, the adjustment process, the time path of key macroeconomic variables. Theory, and the literature in general, has not dealt with this aspect in a systematic fashion; the Southern Cone experience is very rich and may give interesting insights that can contribute to a better understanding of the problems under analysis.

First one must consider the initial conditions that characterized the political and economic circumstances of the three countries: profound political changes and important macroeconomic disequilibriums and, therefore, the need for implementing macroeconomic policies of some kind in which demand management (through fiscal, monetary, and exchange rate policies) would play a central role. But many different policies—with different objectives, magnitudes, speeds, and sequences—were implemented, and this makes a reasonable evaluation of them extremely difficult, especially when one tries to correlate effects and causes appropriately.

Perhaps the most important confusion in the analysis of the Southern Cone economic policies is related to the general lack of distinction made between "structural" reforms, which have been occurring with different force in the three countries, and those related to the "functioning" of the economic system. Among the former type of changes one can mention the attempts to reduce and reorient the size and role of government, the privatization of public enterprises, changes in the wealth distribution and the social security system, labor market reforms, and the like. But trade and financial reforms, reductions in the size of some government-induced distortions, a more important role for the competitive market, and relative prices as resource allocation mechanisms are, in a certain sense, of a qualitatively different nature.

I would say that the structural changes that have occurred in one way or another in these three countries are perhaps one of the issues most discussed among the people who analyze these experiments, and these changes are not strictly related (although obviously they have some connection) to stabilization policies, financial reforms (both on the domestic front and in the international capital movements), trade reforms, and so on.

The sequence of economic liberalization and stabilization. Therefore, I think that the task of separating one policy change from another is extraordinarily difficult and equally important. For example, one of the issues that Guillermo Calvo has mentioned [above] has to do with the sequence of opening up the commercial and capital markets. This is an area where theory has said very little and where experience is also very scant. Casual observation would indicate, for example, that Chile liberalized its trade account quickly and its capital account relatively slowly, whereas the reverse was true for Argentina and Uruguay. Some people even believe that the failure of Argentina's economic program was basically due to the incorrect sequencing of the opening-up process. It has been argued that, when capital flows are allowed to move more freely first, "too much capital" comes in, and without an adequate trade liberalization policy the excess supply of money keeps fueling inflation at very high rates. As a matter of fact, it is clear that, for this to happen, the "sequencing" is not enough in itself and must be accompanied by specific exchange rate and domestic credit policies. But, as has been mentioned here earlier, there seems to be general agreement that the main cause of the Argentine failure was the country's inability to control the public sector deficit. This deficit, together with the financial bankruptcies, were things that did not happen in Uruguay and, until recently, in Chile, and perhaps together they— not necessarily the sequencing of financial and trade liberalization—were the main cause of the failure of the Argentine economic policy.

Regarding the sequencing of trade and financial liberalization, if a choice is to be made as to which should come first, I think that the sequence of opening up trade first and liberalizing capital afterward may be the correct one. But I would like to insist on a point I will elaborate below [see "On the law of one interest rate"] regarding the imperfections of the capital markets. Both the international and domestic financial markets are in no sense perfect; in particular, the access to these markets is extremely differentiated. Therefore, if it is decided to make the capital account liberalization slow, or to undertake it after the commercial opening up has been implemented, or both, it has to be done in a thoughtful way and must be complemented by appropriate monetary and credit policies. This is particularly important if it is decided to avoid some of the undesirable side effects that may accompany the delay in opening up the capital account—mainly the possibility of generating, through the interest rate differential and the import of capital, huge transfers of resources from the government, medium and small enterprises, and consumers to those economic agents who have easy access to foreign financial credit.

In any case, analysis of the sequence of trade and financial reforms deserves much more attention than has been given until now, and it may prove very enlightening for future experiences in the region.

Economic interdependence. Another technical point that is important to consider is that people tend to think that when an economy is relatively closed, then the spillover of the excess supply of money goes primarily into domestic goods or financial markets. Here we need to understand that an economy can be integrated with the world economy even though it may have high trade barriers (as long as there is no "water in the tariffs"). Obviously, the more open an economy, the higher its degree of integration with the international economy. The point I would like to emphasize about the spillover of the excess supply of money is that its impact on tradables and nontradables or the financial markets has to do more with the degree of integration than with the degree of openness to the world economy.

Unemployment. The experience of the Southern Cone countries has also been very different in relation to the unemployment situation. Particularly interesting is the case of Chile, which shows a very high level of unemployment, in both absolute and relative terms, compared with its historical record. How much of that can be explained by trade opening up or by the lack of dynamism in intra- and intersectoral labor mobility? Or is the high unemployment the outcome of a sustained process of privatization of public enterprises that has not been accompanied by new private sector real investment? Or could it be a consequence of labor market legislation? Again, one or a combination of these causes should explain the situation, but we have very little empirical analysis on how much unemployment is explained by each of them.

Domestic saving. A third element in this multiplicity of policies is related to the liberalization of domestic financial markets and its effects on national saving. There seems to be a high degree of correlation between such liberalization in the three countries and a lowering in domestic saving. Of course, this does not mean that liberalizing capital markets must necessarily lead to a reduction in domestic saving. As is well known, one must distinguish between financial and total saving; furthermore, other policies that stimulated inflows of international capital and consumption expenditure may have been the main cause of the domestic savings reduction observed in the region.

One can see from the foregoing that it is very difficult to isolate the specific causes of certain outcomes, but that it is very important to do so because negative effects may be erroneously attributed to otherwise well-conceived and technically sound reforms—something we as analysts should definitely try to avoid. I would like to mention two more issues—export promotion and the current account of the balance of payments—in relation to the opening-up process.

Export promotion. As Mario Blejer has said [see chapter 1], the main objective of liberalization policy is to shift from inward-oriented development strategies to outward-looking ones, thus to eliminate distortions, to improve resource allocation, and to induce more rapid economic growth. But here the question arises whether it is true that in practice trade liberalization has been accompanied by export promotion. The way this policy was generally implemented in the three countries points in the direction of a "neutral" policy rather than to one of export promotion. It was neutral in the sense that comparative advantages and a lower general homogeneous tariff would decide how many resources would be assigned to tradables and how many to nontradable goods production. Nevertheless, one of the most important lessons that we can learn from the experience of these three countries is that the degree to which export promotion will be induced depends critically on what is going on with the capital account and with the real exchange rate.

When domestic capital markets were liberalized in the three countries, nominal interest rates became very high. When the exchange rate policy pursued was guided by stabilization objectives—as it was, perhaps, to a certain extent understandably, because of the inflationary history of the Southern Cone—a U.S. dollar-denominated interest rate differential was created with respect to international rates, and this differential naturally induced domestic agents to get indebted internationally. This policy-induced demand for foreign financing, together with the extraordinary affluence of private international liquidity in the second half of the last decade, explains why so much financial credit came into these countries, credit that reinforced the tendency for a timid and conservative exchange rate policy. In other words, since there seemed to be no foreign exchange bottleneck because of the international capital inflows, these countries tended to substitute foreign indebtedness for export promotion, which in turn reinforced the overvaluation of the domestic currency, generating large current account deficits mainly through increased imports. In effect, opening up in the Southern Cone was identified more with imports liberalization and foreign indebtedness than with export promotion.

Therefore, for commercial opening up to be associated with a dynamic exportables sector, it has to be implemented with account taken of its interrelations with financial and exchange rate policies.

The current account. An issue closely connected with liberalization and export promotion has to do with the relation between the capital and the current account of the balance of payments. Does the current account matter? I think experience shows that the current account matters very much. First of all, a crucial point is that foreign saving may complement or substitute for domestic saving. This can also be seen as a question of how much of the current account deficit is being invested in the country, or, put another way, of how much is the real future burden of the foreign debt. This is another subject that merits more discussion, especially in relation to foreign capital inflow and domestic bank management. In the three countries, particularly in Argentina and Chile, there has been a large inflow of capital and very little consideration, it seems (either from foreign banks or, especially, from domestic banks), of the way in which these funds have been used.

Many people believe that, as long as the private sector gets indebted, then nothing really important may happen in these countries. Why? Because that indebtedness would essentially be a transaction between two private partners, and there would be no important consequences of an eventual default. I consider this to be a naive position. The recent experiences of Argentina and Chile show not only that the private banks and firms may be extremely inefficient in their loan and expenditure decisions but, further, that the governments have not been willing to allow private financial enterprises to go bankrupt because of the impact on the domestic economy as a whole and the potential effect such bankruptcies could have on the countries' creditworthiness and future access to international capital markets. It seems to me that there should be no a priori prejudice regarding who gets indebted (private or public sector); the crucial elements are how that debt is being used and the social profitability of those funds.

The law of one price. At this point I would like to comment, from another perspective, on an issue that has often been mentioned: the "law of one price." We all know that the law of one price refers mainly to levels and not to rates of change. Nevertheless, it seems that policymakers in the Southern Cone have sometimes assumed that, as long as the nominal exchange rate is fixed or there is a "tablita," then domestic inflation will reproduce the international inflation plus the eventual devaluation associated with the predetermined path of the exchange rate. Here experience shows that, when an exchange rate policy is initiated with the idea of targeting domestic inflation to international inflation, the price level of the country may differ from the price level in the rest of the world—or that, because of lags in the adjustment process, domestic inflation for some time may exceed international inflation, and the country can end up with a price level higher than the price level of the rest of the world.

To restore equilibrium, given the exchange rate path, will require not only expenditure-reducing but also expenditure-switching policies—in particular, a change in relative prices in favor of tradable goods. For this to happen, the domestic price of nontradables (assuming a fixed nominal exchange rate) will have to change at a lower rate than the relevant international inflation. Given that international inflation today is going down, the need for domestic inflation to be smaller than world inflation may mean that the prices of nontradable goods, wages, or both will have to fall in absolute terms. Naturally this may be a process very costly in unemployment and losses of production—a situation that clearly can be seen in the present Uruguayan and Chilean experience. Furthermore, if domestic inflation needs to be near zero or negative to restore the equilibrium between foreign and domestic price levels, this makes it more difficult for real interest rates to go down to more reasonable levels; such difficulty therefore reduces the profitability of investment and the prospects of recovery.

The law of one interest rate. In relation to the preceding point, I would like to add something on interest rate parity, or the "law of one interest rate." The experience of the Southern Cone shows that, for some reason(s), it takes an extremely long period of time for domestic interest rates, appropriately defined, to equal the international rates. One has to realize that small countries do not face a horizontal supply of foreign financial capital, but rather an upward-sloping one, because of the behavior of international banks (as regards exposure, country risk analysis, and so forth). Furthermore, the imperfections of both the domestic and the international financial markets may be of great importance. In particular, it seems that the capital market's segmentation, the differentiated access to the international financial markets, the oligopolistic nature of the domestic banking industry, the existence of nontradable domestic assets, and the expectations of devaluation all contribute to explaining not only the difference between domestic and foreign interest rates, but also the extremely high spreads between loan and deposit rates and the big differences between the cost of loans denominated in U.S. dollars and those denominated in local currency. Furthermore, the demand for credit tends to be quite inelastic and shifts outward because of the behavior of banks and firms regarding future economic events. Given that there seems to be a tendency for the process of capital account liberalization to be slower than that of trade reform, attention has to be given to the way in which the financial liberalization is implemented. One has to realize that, in addition to the factors just mentioned, the relatively slow financial opening up will by itself create the interest rate differential. Therefore, care has to be taken to ensure that the central bank (and not enterprises with easy access to international capital markets), through appropriate credit and monetary policy, will make the monopoly profit on the "imports" of financial capital.

Enough has been said here on high interest rates and investment; I would only like to mention that the three countries provide experiences in which wages and exchange rates have been, in a sense, controlled subject to intervention. The only macroeconomic price that was allowed to move almost totally freely was the interest rate. Therefore, it is not at all surprising to see, given the inconsistency of some of the exchange rate and wage policies, the extreme volatility of interest rates in the region.

The flexibility of policy. Regarding the macroeconomic adjustment mechanisms, I believe that the experience of the three countries shows that more flexibility is needed. Policymakers need to have certain policy instruments at their disposal, even though they may decide not to use them. This is not a matter of principle; it is just a matter of technical instruments. I think automaticity and nonintervention by themselves have proven to be extremely dangerous and costly when important changes must be faced in, let us say, the world economy or the structure of the domestic economy.

The question of flexibility has been phrased as the traditional choice between "rules versus discretion" [see Mr. Calvo's comments above]. I believe that this is not the best way to approach the problem, since one needs to know and to analyze specifically what types of rules are being designed and what kind of flexibility, if any, is incorporated in those rules.

People tend to think that "rules" imply impersonality or nondiscretionality. In reality the issue is much more complex—not only because of the "initial conditions" with which different economic agents enter to play the "economic game," but also because there may be de facto discretionality (for example, the differentiated access to international financial markets generated by some types of market segmentation). Furthermore, if in situations such as the Chilean or Uruguayan ones today one rules out a (more pronounced rate of) devaluation—as well as any type of government intervention, incomes policies, or the like—what one is in fact postulating is a firm belief in automaticity, in itself a specific kind of extremely rigid "rule."

Asset prices. Another way of seeing the most important recent problems of the Uruguayan and the Chilean economies is that there has been an overshooting in the prices of real and financial capital. Obviously, these asset prices will have to go down sooner or later, one way or another.

In the case of the Chilean economy, the prices of land, buildings, machinery, enterprises, and so forth have increased to extremely high and, in the long run, unsustainable levels. The value of the Chilean capital stock has been enormously inflated in the past years. This may have been caused by diverse factors—mainly by the maintenance of a high and unrealistic exchange rate, by overly optimistic expectations of future earnings and economic growth that evidently could not be realized, and, last but not least, by the highly artificial increase in the values of shares and capital stock of financial and productive firms owned by a few major economic groups.

An attempt to solve some of the macroeconomic problems is being made through reductions in aggregate expenditure and, very slowly, through a change in relative prices of tradable and nontradable goods by way of what have been called "automatic adjustment mechanisms." Even though expenditure reducing and expenditure switching are necessary ingredients of the policy package, it seems to me that little attention has been given to the capital loss that the country as a whole will have to incur. The questions here are the magnitude of the capital loss and who will take it. Until May 1982, at least in the Chilean case, depositors and foreign banks have not taken the capital loss. That is one thing that is sure. The capital loss has been absorbed by the shareholders of some banks and "financieras" that were subject to government intervention and by many nonbank enterprises; but it has mainly been absorbed by the country as a whole through the transfers of resources from the government to these financial enterprises.

One of the big economic and political problems that Chile will have to face in the near future is the effect of both the magnitude of this capital loss and of the way in which the capital loss will be distributed among different sectors and groups of the Chilean society. More generally, for the Southern Cone as a whole, I think these will end up being crucial issues in the final evaluation of the policy packages that have been implemented in these countries. If in fact the people and firms that made the wrong decisions are the ones that suffer the losses, as "the gospel" would recommend [see Arnold Harberger's comments in chapter 8, the subsection "On Asset Prices"], that would indeed be coherent with the global strategy. The problem in Chile is that people may begin to lose faith in the gospel, for until May 1982, at least, neither the foreign banks nor the domestic savers (both of whom supposedly made the "mistake" of investing their funds in some banks) have suffered. The government has intervened and backed, as a lender of last resort, those financial institutions that were near bankruptcy.

Finally, on this point it appears that the whole process of selling assets is not so simple and may have important repercussions in these economies. Given the recession in 1982, who is going to buy the assets? The little experience we have shows, in the case of the Chilean banks, that they are being sold to foreigners. Very probably the same would hold true for a majority of assets, and I think that this possible denationalization is an issue that has to be considered most seriously.

The fixed exchange rate. It seems to me that some type of "crawling peg" mechanism, or tablita, is preferable to fixing the nominal exchange rate at a constant value. The reason is that the policymaker then has much more flexibility and a greater number of instruments available in facing unexpected external or internal shocks. If one fixes the nominal exchange rate—or if one sets a long time span before one can alter the rate of future changes of the exchange rate—the adjustment mechanisms will work mainly through changes in the prices of nontradable goods and through quantity changes, the latter naturally including labor unemployment and variations in general economic activity.

Devaluation. Regarding the effectiveness of a devaluation, I would like to iterate that effectiveness is not independent of the economic conditions faced by an economy when the devaluation may take place. For example, I do not think that a devaluation in Chile in mid-1982—in a country with recession, with inventories accumulating, with 19 percent unemployment, and with relative prices clearly out of equilibrium—would instantaneously express itself in a similar rate of inflation. It all depends on how the devaluation is done and on what other policies accompany it.

A well-designed devaluation scheme would contribute to solve the price disequilibrium between tradable and nontradable goods. Furthermore, a little inflation, which undoubtedly would accompany a devaluation, might help to reduce the real interest rate and might contribute further, in this way, to put the price system back on an equilibrium path.

Alternative policies. Finally, I would like to comment briefly on what Professors Harberger [chapter 8] and Sjastaad [chapter 5] mention in relation to the recent Chilean economic experience—that it could, according to them, be qualified as a success, or even as too much of a success.

I think that when one makes a judgment such as that one must distinguish between means and ends and, among the latter, specify the relative weights one assigns. In this sense, if one considers traditional objectives of economic policy, such as growth, employment, stabilization, and the like, one realizes that the control of inflation is, together with greater control of the public sector budget, perhaps the single accomplishment that could be qualified as successful. But when one considers other indicators, such as unemployment figures, foreign debt, investment and growth, and changes in income and wealth distribution, I think it is extremely doubtful for one to evaluate the results of economic policy in that country as successful. Some people may say that more time must be allowed for the effects of these policies to be evident. That may be true, and no one can be sure today of the results some five or ten years from now, but I consider it a highly questionable assertion, to say the least, to affirm that these results, as of May 1982, constitute a big success.

Moreover, in relation to the Chilean economy—which today faces, in my opinion, the three main problems of a severe recession, relative prices out of line, and large financial difficulties (the last of these associated with what has been called the asset price bubble or the capital loss problem)—it seems to me that when people look for new policy measures to implement it is difficult to find them, given the restrictions that the same economic policy has imposed on itself. If one is afraid of flexibility and does not want to devalue; if one does not want to modify, even temporarily, the tariff policy; if one does not want to change the controls on the inflow of capital; if one does not want to have more state intervention as a way, for example, to deal with unemployment; if one does not want to do any of these things and just wants to rely on automaticity—which is implicitly, I think, what we have heard in this symposium—then one in effect has decided simply to wait and hope for the best.

REFERENCES

Blejer, Mario I., and Donald J. Mathieson. 1981. "The Preannouncement of Exchange Rate Changes as a Stabilization Instrument." _IMF Staff Papers,_ vol. 28, no. 4 (October).

Calvo, Guillermo A. 1980. "Apertura financiera, paridad móvil y tipo de cambio real." In _Ensayos Económicos_ no. 16, pp. 53-72. Buenos Aires: Banco Central de la República Argentina, December.

Calvo, Guillermo A., and Roque B. Fernandez. 1980. "Pauta cambiaria y deficit fiscal." _Ambito Financiero_ (July 16). Reprinted in Roque B. Fernandez and Carlos A. Rodríguez, eds., _Inflación y estabilidad._ Buenos Aires: Ediciones Macchi, 1982.

_____. 1983. "Competitive Banks and the Inflation Tax." _Economic Letters_ (forthcoming).

Corbo, Vittorio. 1981. "Inflation in an Open Economy: The Case of Chile." Paper presented at the Second Regional Meeting of the Econometric Society, Río de Janeiro. _Cuadernos de Economía_ (Santiago), vol. 19, no. 56 (April 1982).

_____. 1982. "Chile: An Overview of Macro Developments." Processed.

Edwards, Sebastian. 1982a. "Trade Liberalization, Minimum Wages, and Employment in the Short Run: Some Reflections Based on the Chilean Experience." Department of Economics Working Paper no. 230. Los Angeles: University of California, February.

_____. 1982b. "Diferenciales de progreso tecnológico y diferenciales de inflación." _Cuadernos de Economía_ (Santiago), vol. 19, no. 56 (April), pp. 87-92.

Frenkel, Jacob A., and Thorvaldur Gylfason. 1980. "A Synthesis of Monetary and Keynesian Approaches to Short-Run Balance-of-Payments Theory." _Economics Journal,_ vol. 90 (September), pp. 582-92.

Gylfason, Thorvaldur, and J. F. Helliwell. 1981. "A Synthesis of Keynesian, Monetary, and Portfolio Approaches to Flexible Exchange Rates." In Economic Studies Seminar Paper no. 180, pp. 1-37. Stockholm: Institute for International Economic Studies, University of Stockholm, October.

Johnson, Harry G. 1976. "The Monetary Approach to Balance of Payments Theory." In Jacob A. Frenkel and Harry G. Johnson, eds., The Monetary Approach to the Balance of Payments, ch. 6. Toronto: University of Toronto Press; London: Allen and Unwin.

_____. 1977. "The Monetary Approach to Balance of Payments Theory and Policy: Explanation and Policy Implications." Econometrica, no. 44, pp. 217-29.

Krueger, Anne O. 1978. Foreign Trade and Economic Development: Liberalization Attempts and Consequences. Cambridge, Mass.: Ballinger/National Bureau of Economic Research.

McKinnon, Ronald I. 1979. Money in International Exchange. New York: Oxford University Press.

Neary, J. Peter. 1982. "Intersectoral Capital Mobility, Wage Stickiness, and the Case for Adjustment Assistance." In Jagdish N. Bhagwati, ed., Import Competition and Response. Chicago: University of Chicago Press, pp. 39-67.

Obstfeld, Maurice. 1981. "Capital Mobility and Devaluation in an Optimizing Model with Rational Expectations." American Economic Review, Papers and Proceedings, vol. 71, no. 2 (May), pp. 217-21.

Rodríguez, Carlos A., and Larry A. Sjaastad. 1980. El atraso cambiario en la Argentina: ¿Mito o realidad? Ensayos Económicos no. 13. Buenos Aires: Banco Central de la República Argentina, March.

Sargent, Thomas J., and Neil Wallace. 1981. "Some Unpleasant Monetarist Arithmetic." Federal Reserve Bank of Minneapolis Quarterly Review (Fall), pp. 1-17.

Schydlowsky, Daniel M. 1981. "Alternative Approaches to Short-Term Economic Management in Developing Countries." In Tony Killick, ed., Adjustment and Financing in the Developing World. Washington, D.C.: International Monetary Fund.

Spiller, Pablo T., and Edgardo Favaro. 1982. "The Effects of Entry Regulations on Oligopolistic Interaction: The Uruguayan Banking Sector." Philadelphia: Department of Economics, University of Pennsylvania, November. Processed.

PART III

Evaluation
and Lessons from Experience

5

Liberalization and Stabilization Experiences in the Southern Cone

Larry A. Sjaastad

During the 1970s, all three Southern Cone countries—Argentina, Chile, and Uruguay—initiated major economic liberalization and stabilization programs. In Chile and Argentina, the programs followed virtually unprecedented political turmoil (from which Uruguay did not entirely escape) that resulted in new governments willing to experiment with market-oriented economic models in sharp contrast with the paternalistic, interventionist economic policies of the past. In all three countries, liberalization was most pronounced in the financial and foreign trade sectors, although other markets were affected as well. The Chilean program was the most coherent and comprehensive of the three: tariffs were reduced to a uniform 10 percent; interest rates were completely deregulated; the fiscal system was overhauled; the social security system was completely changed; and so on. In Argentina, the reforms were primarily in the foreign exchange and financial markets; although relatively ambitious plans for trade liberalization were announced (and partially executed), the reforms were not as pervasive as in Chile. Reforms in Uruguay were similar to those in Argentina, but they were not carried out within the framework of a more or less formal plan as in Argentina. This paper will focus principally upon the stabilization programs, although the other reforms will not be completely ignored.

In the months after the symposium of May 1982, major changes in economic policy have occurred throughout the Southern Cone, changes that would have substantially affected the discussion. Chile abandoned the fixed exchange rate system shortly after the June 1982 devaluation but has since settled on an indexed peg to the U.S. dollar accompanied by severe exchange control. From mid-June 1982 to late January 1983, the cumulative devaluation in Chile had been 100 percent at the official rate, compared with 170 percent depreciation in the "parallel" market. Fearing collapse of the Chilean financial system, the authorities intervened in all major private financial institutions, some of which are in the process of liquidation.

The fall of the Galtieri government in Argentina in June 1982 led to a major change of policy, one that was intended to improve the asset position of the financial system but one that has been extremely inflationary. In Uruguay the economic team was replaced, and the peso was floated in late November 1982, largely in response to the serious deterioration of the fiscal situation (the deficit in 1982 was 10 percent of GDP). By late January 1983, the Uruguayan peso had depreciated by more than 100 percent since the float began.

Along with unemployment, foreign debt service has become a critical problem in the Southern Cone, as it has in Brazil and Mexico. Clearly these events would have drastically altered the nature and emphasis of the discussions at the May symposium. But that symposium occurred prior to these events; hence this paper—which is an enlargement of the author's comments at the time—will retain the orientation of those comments rather than try to evaluate the significance of the more recent developments.

The stabilization programs of the three countries were quite similar in that they each used the exchange rate as the central mechanism for reducing the rate of inflation, but the programs were quite different (particularly in outcome) in the manner in which fiscal problems were handled. Chile, which pioneered the "mini-devaluation" policy in the middle 1960s, was the first to introduce the exchange rate table (or "tablita") in January 1978. Uruguay followed later that year, and Argentina introduced its first tablita in January 1979. In all three countries, the table was pegged to the U.S. dollar, and the policies did succeed in sharply reducing the rate of internal inflation. In July 1979, the Chilean authorities replaced the exchange rate table with a fixed exchange rate regime, which was also the Argentine policy target for early 1981 (one that was disrupted by the minor but unscheduled Argentine devaluation in early February 1981). The Chilean program was to last four and one-half years (until June 1982), whereas the Argentine program was clearly abandoned in March 1981 after only a little over two years. The Uruguayan program endured for four years—until the float in November 1982. In all cases, the programs ended with massive devaluations (or depreciations, in the case of the floats).

This paper will attempt to analyze the strengths and weaknesses of the stabilization policies in each of the three countries. The emphasis will be on Argentina and Chile, however, because the Uruguayan stabilization program was still in effect at the time of the symposium. The paper will focus on five areas: country differences in initial conditions and the implementation of supportive policies; the general stabilization model; the outcome in Argentina and in Chile; and, finally, the lessons to be learned and the implications for future policy.

BACKGROUND

Argentina and Chile experienced record rates of inflation during the decade of the 1970s, rates that approach 1,000 percent a year. In both countries the cause of the inflation was a large fiscal deficit financed by the central bank, and in each case the specter of hyperinflation was avoided only by drastic (and timely) reductions in public sector spending. Although fiscal reforms were obviously necessary to reduce inflation, it does not follow that they, in themselves, would be sufficient to do so. Thus, both Argentina and Chile faced the additional task of bringing the rate of inflation to tolerable levels (more correctly, to levels consistent with the residual fiscal deficits). Moreover, political considerations dictated that these stabilization processes be effected without significant losses of real output. Indeed, Chile encountered this final stage of stabilization while confronted with a very low level of economic activity and correspondingly high unemployment, and Argentina was still in the grip of the severe recession of 1978.

In addition, both countries were committed to major reforms intended to liberalize their economic systems; Chile was more advanced in this respect than was Argentina, owing to the fact that the Chilean coup d'etat occurred some thirty months prior to a similar event in Argentina. Thus, the stabilization programs had to be consistent with the spirit and philosophy of new economic policies in general, a consideration that ruled out direct controls.

Both countries chose to retain the essence of their existing exchange rate regimes, but to modify them so as to exploit the process of expectation formation with regard to inflation. One supposes that this approach was adopted in Chile and Argentina—and also in Uruguay, although that country had far less inflation than the other two—because it was thought to be consistent with the growing openness of these economies and because it required but a minor change in existing institutional arrangements concerning the foreign exchange market.

Thus, in December 1977 a new exchange rate policy was unveiled in Chile, whereby a diminishing rate of devaluation (with respect to the U.S. dollar) was preannounced. One year later, essentially the same policy was incorporated by Martínez de Hoz in his "Plan del 20 de Diciembre" for Argentina. Meanwhile, in late 1978, Uruguay also introduced the preannounced exchange rate table (the tablita).

In a sense, the exchange rate tables were a natural evolution of the mini-devaluation policies with which all three countries had had considerable experience. What was involved was merely a formalization of the mini-devaluations, but with the important difference that the rate of devaluation was intended to affect the rate of inflation, rather than vice versa (as was the case with the former policy). Thus, the exchange rate tables were intended to convey key information concerning the expected evolution of the price level in the future rather than merely to provide a more or less stable "real" exchange rate.

All three countries continued the link to the U.S. dollar, a choice that subsequently caused much mischief. However, that choice again was a natural one because the currencies of Argentina, Chile, and Uruguay had always been tied to the U.S. dollar, even after the collapse of the Bretton Woods system in the 1971-73 period. At the time, that choice seemed logical also because the dollar had been depreciating regularly against other key currencies since 1971. For countries with an apparent inflationary bias, tying to a depreciating currency seemed quite reasonable. It was, of course, the subsequent appreciations of the dollar in late 1980 and early 1981 that brought much of the grief that Chile and Uruguay have recently experienced [see "The Role of External Shocks," below].

There were, however, major differences between Chile and Uruguay on the one hand and Argentina on the other, particularly with respect to fiscal policy. Chile had, in 1975, largely eliminated her fiscal deficit through a sharp reduction in expenditure and a subsequent tax reform. The fiscal problem in Uruguay—although never completely eliminated—was never as severe as in Argentina and Chile, and, with modest reforms since 1974, it remained manageable until 1982, when it exploded to 10 percent of GDP. Argentina, however, began her stabilization program with a large fiscal deficit, and plans to reduce or eliminate that deficit were repeatedly frustrated. The failure to eliminate that deficit (and the certainty of the expectation that it would ultimately be monetized by the central bank) eroded the credibility of the stabilization program long before it had a chance to succeed.

THE MODEL FOR ECONOMIC STABILIZATION

For an economy in which all goods are traded internationally, it is widely held that the internal rate of inflation is determined by the external inflation and by changes in the exchange rate. This proposition is merely an extension of the "law of one price." To the extent that this law holds at every moment in time, the price level is completely determined, as is its rate of change. In such an economy, exchange rate policy is obviously sufficient to determine the rate of inflation, and there can be little question about the efficacy of that policy as a stabilization tool.

The presence of "home," or nontraded, goods complicates the analysis because the exchange rate can affect the price of these goods only indirectly—through substitution effects, through expectations, or through both. The general idea is that—under normal assumptions concerning preferences and production possibilities, and given the state of overall demand relative to production—there is but one price of home goods, relative to that of traded goods, which will clear the home goods market. Letting the nominal internal price of traded goods be determined by external prices and the exchange rate, then, determines the <u>equilibrium</u> nominal price for home goods, and hence the equilibrium price level.[1] <u>Changes in the income-expenditure relationship</u> will alter that equilibrium nominal price for home goods. For example, an increase in overall demand relative to output will also increase the demand for home goods, and equilibrium in that market can be restored only by a rise in the price of home goods relative to those of tradables.

Exchange rate movements may influence the price of traded goods in at least two ways. The first, and more vulgar of the two, is by direct arbitrage between home and traded goods markets. A devaluation, for example, is often thought to provoke a rise in the price of nontraded goods by direct substitution effects: demand is shifted toward the now relatively cheaper nontraded goods, and supply is shifted toward the now relatively higher-priced traded goods. The resulting excess demand for home goods drives up their price.

A second, and perhaps more relevant, channel of influence is by way of expectations. Once economic agents understand—or infer—that the equilibrium relationship between the prices of home and traded goods is neither random nor arbitrarily determined, a change in the price of traded goods will cause these agents to revise their expectations concerning the equilibrium price of home goods. Under such circumstances, an excess demand for (supply of) home goods will not be required to drive up (down) the price of home goods; the change will occur spontaneously, as it were.

Although the exchange-rate-based approach to stabilization pursued by Chile and Uruguay beginning in 1978 and by Argentina during 1979-80 could be expected to influence the trajectory of inflation under either of the above interpretations concerning the channels through which that policy operates, the second interpretation lends a greater air of both sophistication and credibility to that approach. Indeed, if the rate of inflation could be forced down only by generating an excess supply of home goods—and the attendant increase in unemployment—the policy of a declining rate of devaluation would presumably have met with formidable political opposition. Under the second interpretation, however, no such excess supply of home goods is _essential_ to the stabilization process. Indeed, in principle there is no reason why the rates of inflation _and_ unemployment cannot decline simultaneously so long as the rate of devaluation is announced for a considerable period in advance. The preannouncement effect was, of course, the cornerstone of the policy in all three countries of the Southern Cone.

OUTCOME: THE ARGENTINE EXPERIENCE

The Argentine exchange-rate-based stabilization program began in January 1979 and continued until early February 1981, when the exchange rate table was broken with an unscheduled devaluation of 10 percent. The exchange rate table was the centerpiece of the Plan del 20 de Diciembre, which has been analyzed in depth by Rodríguez (1979). Because the early results of the stabilization program were evaluated by Rodríguez and Sjaastad (1979), what follows in this section will be essentially an updating of that study.

Immediately before implementation of the Plan del 20 de Diciembre, the rate of inflation in Argentina was about 150 percent a year (measured by the wholesale price index, WPI), and the rate of devaluation was about 80 percent but quite unstable. The stabilization program reduced the rate of devaluation slightly to an initial level of about 5 percent a month. At that time, the exchange rate table was announced through the month of August 1979, with a diminishing rate of devaluation. For the first eight months of the program, the cumulative devaluation was at an annual rate of 60 percent—a rate implying that, if the price level were to respond to the program, the rate of inflation would be cut approximately in half over an eight-month period. Subsequently, the exchange rate table was repeatedly extended, always with a diminishing rate of devaluation. As of mid-1980, it was anticipated by the central bank that a zero rate of devaluation would be reached in February 1981.

As is well known, the Argentine stabilization plan did not succeed, although the rate of inflation was substantially reduced by the end of 1980. The minor devaluation in February 1981 destroyed the credibility of the exchange rate table and led to two major devaluations (in March and May 1981) and to the abandonment of the fixed exchange rate in June 1981. From February to June 1981, the Argentine "commercial" peso, which remained "fixed," was devalued by about 125 percent. The "financial" peso, which began to float in June 1981, was devalued by the market by an additional 70 percent immediately after the float. By mid-1981, the rate of inflation had returned to the levels of 1978, and the stabilization plan had become a dead letter.

Shortly after the stabilization program was initiated in early 1979, there began to be a public discussion of the "atraso cambiario" (exchange rate lag) in Argentina. Indeed, it was that discussion that prompted the Rodríguez-Sjaastad study (1979). That study determined that, as of the first quarter of 1979, there was very little disequilibrium relative to 1970, which was a "normal" year in Argentina. Although accumulated inflation was far in excess of accumulated devaluation during the period after the coup d'etat, much of the rise in the price level was found to be the consequence of real changes—hence, changes in the equilibrium relationship between the exchange rate and the price level. These changes took the form of elimination of very large export taxes, imposition of a value-added tax that struck imports and exempted exports, and the like. After taking those effects into account, Sjaastad and Rodríguez (1979) concluded that the exchange rate disequilibrium was only of the order of 10 percent during the first quarter of 1979.

The Sjaastad-Rodríguez results have been extended through 1980, and the results are presented in table 5-1. The variables P_m, P_x, and P_h are, respectively, indexes of the internal prices of importables, exportables, and nontraded ("home") goods.[2] The P_t variable, which refers to an index for traded goods, is a geometrically weighted average of P_m and P_x.[3] The penultimate column of table 5-1 indicates the departure of P_h from its predicted equilibrium value (that is, P_t), assuming that the ratio P_h/P_t was in equilibrium (and indexed to unity) during the first quarter of 1978. The final column indicates the degree of disequilibrium assuming that 1970 was a year of full equilibrium. The results indicate that a significant disequilibrium had developed by the end of 1979, the prices of home goods being 15 to 20 percent higher than their equilibrium value, and that the disequilibrium worsened during the course of 1980.

Table 5-1. Wholesale Prices and Relative Price Variability
in Argentina, 1978-80

Year and quarter	P_m	P_x	P_h	P_t[a]	$(P_h - P_t)/P_h$ (percent)	
					1978 (first quarter) base	1970 base
1978						
I	100.0	100.0	100.0	100.0	0.0	−5.2
II	114.5	128.2	127.0	122.4	3.7	−1.5
III	124.3	158.4	152.6	143.3	6.5	1.3
IV	140.9	209.6	191.6	178.0	7.6	2.4
1979						
I	165.7	256.1	250.7	214.0	17.1	11.9
II	209.1	320.0	317.0	268.5	18.1	12.9
III	262.7	451.4	408.5	361.2	13.1	7.9
IV	294.6	474.7	471.9	390.0	21.0	15.8
1980						
I	341.3	510.6	532.9	432.5	23.2	18.0
II	378.5	592.3	609.0	492.5	23.7	18.5
III	421.5	673.5	685.8	555.1	23.5	18.3
Oct.	462.7	678.2	763.7	581.3	31.4	26.2

Note: Figures are three-month averages. See text for definition of prices (P).

Source: All basic price data obtained from Boletín Estadístico Trimestral (Buenos Aires: Instituto Nacional de Estadística y Censo [INDEC]), various issues.

a. Defined as $(P_m)^{0.412}(P_x)^{0.588}$.

Table 5-2. Price Level and Exchange Rate in Argentina, 1978-80

	Wholesale price index (WPI)[a]			Exchange rate[b]		
		Rate of inflation (percent)		Pesos per	Rate of change (percent)	
Date	Level	Quarterly[c]	Annual[d]	U.S. dollar	Quarterly[c]	Annual[d]
1978						
March	100.0	27	147	721.0	21	114
June	124.6	25	157	788.5	9	102
Sept.	151.5	22	145	866.5	10	98
Dec.	191.2	26	142	1,003.5	16	168
1979						
March	246.7	29	147	1,156.5	15	60
June	316.4	28	154	1,316.5	14	67
Sept.	410.5	30	171	1,472.5	12	70
Dec.	439.9	7	130	1,618.5	10	61
1980						
March	496.2	13	101	1,747.5	8	51
June	582.8	17	84	1,854.5	6	41
Sept.	635.2	9	55	1,933.5	4	31
Dec.	692.7	9	57	1,992.5	3	23

a. Source: Boletín Estadístico Trimestral (Buenos Aires: INDEC), various issues.
b. Source: International Financial Statistics (Washington, D.C.: International Monetary Fund). End of month.
c. Change from end of previous quarter.
d. Change from end of quarter twelve months earlier.

The results also indicate that the distortion in relative prices began to emerge before the stabilization program began. Although the disequilibrium in 1978 was negligible (using 1970 as the reference point), the upward trend in P_h/P_t began in early 1978 and accelerated once the stabilization program was put into effect. Indeed, the rate of inflation during the first three quarters of 1979 was higher than during any quarter of 1978, measured by the WPI. Clearly, the exchange-rate-based stabilization policy did not have the desired initial effect in Argentina. The relevant data on inflation and devaluation for the stabilization period are presented in table 5-2.

The Argentine stabilization program lasted twenty-five months, but it was clearly doomed to failure well before it was abandoned in early 1981. Although no comprehensive study of that experiment is yet available, certainly three factors contributed significantly to its lack of success: the manner in which the tablita was introduced, the fiscal deficits, and political uncertainty.

Introduction of the Plan del 20 de Diciembre

From table 5-2 it is evident that the rate of devaluation at the time the stabilization plan was implemented was far below the actual rate of inflation and well below the prior rate of devaluation. Moreover, the reduced rate of devaluation was accompanied by a removal of many restrictions on capital movements, but trade liberalization came only later. The result was that Argentine goods initially faced little foreign competition in the domestic market, but that the implementation of the Plan had an immediate effect on domestic interest rates. Monthly interest rate data are presented in table 5-3; the final column of that table indicates the peso lending rates from the viewpoint of foreign capital. Note that during 1978 the "arbitrage"

Table 5-3. Nominal and Real Interest Rates and Rate of Inflation by Month
in Argentina, 1978-80

Date	Nominal interest rate[a]	Rate of inflation[b]	Real interest rate[c]	Arbitrage interest rate[d]
1978				
Jan.	13.2	11.3	1.7	5.9
Feb.	11.0	6.5	4.3	4.2
March	8.9	8.1	0.7	2.9
April	8.0	9.2	− 1.1	2.4
May	8.1	9.2	− 1.0	4.1
June	8.3	5.9	2.3	6.8
July	7.9	5.5	2.3	6.2
Aug.	7.7	6.8	0.8	5.1
Sept.	7.2	5.9	1.2	3.4
Oct.	7.4	9.0	− 1.5	3.2
Nov.	7.4	8.5	− 1.0	1.9
Dec.	7.7	8.0	− 0.3	2.7
1979				
Jan.	7.4	11.3	− 3.5	2.2
Feb.	7.1	8.4	− 1.2	2.3
March	7.1	8.9	− 1.7	2.4
April	7.1	6.6	0.5	2.5
May	6.9	8.8	− 1.7	2.4
June	6.9	9.4	− 2.3	2.5
July	7.6	7.0	0.6	3.5
Aug.	8.0	12.6	− 3.8	4.1
Sept.	8.1	5.7	2.3	4.4
Oct.	8.1	3.9	4.1	4.7
Nov.	7.0	3.3	3.6	3.7
Dec.	6.9	3.5	3.3	3.8
1980				
Jan.	6.7	4.3	2.3	3.8
Feb.	6.0	4.5	1.4	3.3
March	5.6	4.8	0.8	3.1
April	5.3	3.7	1.5	3.0
May	5.4	4.5	0.9	3.3
June	6.4	6.6	− 0.2	4.4
July	7.2	3.3	3.8	5.5
Aug.	6.2	3.2	2.9	4.7
Sept.	5.6	3.0	2.5	4.3

Note: Rates obtained from Frenkel (1981).
a. In percent monthly. The rate presented is the twenty-nine day prime lending rate.
b. In percent monthly. Rate is that of nonagricultural wholesale prices.
c. Defined as $(i - \pi)/(1 + \pi)$, where π is the inflation rate.
d. Defined as the nominal rate of interest minus the rate of devaluation, both in monthly rates.

interest rate had been, on the average, quite high and volatile. That rate stabilized immediately after the implementation of the Plan del 20 de Diciembre and remained low until mid-1979. The internal real interest rate, defined as the prime twenty-nine-day lending rate minus the rate of change of nonagricultural wholesale prices (which is quite similar to P_h, defined above for table 5-1), also had been highly variable but positive on the average during 1978—the average of the twelve monthly rates was 0.7 percent. With the implementation of the Plan, nominal interest rates fell somewhat, and inflation increased so that real interest rates became quite significantly negative. On the average, the thirty-day real lending rate was − 1.5 percent during the first six months of 1979.

From table 5-3 it is clear that there was a change in mid-1979, when internal interest rates rose significantly with respect to the rate of devaluation. It was at this point that the atraso cambiario began to be widely discussed, and hence it is plausible to suppose that the rise in interest rates was because of an increase in the perceived risk of devaluation.

These observations have statistical support. The following tabulation indicates the mean arbitrage interest rate, the standard deviation of that rate, and the standard deviation of the mean for 1978-80:

	Mean	Standard error	Standard error of the mean
1978	4.07	1.61	0.464
1979	3.21	0.92	0.265
1980	3.93	0.85	0.283
Jan.–June 1979	2.38	0.12	0.048
July 1979–Sept. 1980	3.97	0.70	0.181

The t-ratio for the difference between the 1978 and January-June mean interest rates is 3.67—highly significant. The same ratio for January-June 1979 against that for July 1979-September 1980 is 8.51. The arbitrage rate during the first six months of the plan was not only highly stable but also significantly below the rates immediately before and following.

These findings suggest the following explanation for the failure of the Plan in Argentina to reduce the rate of inflation immediately. The initial effect of the Plan was to reduce the risk associated with short-term foreign borrowing; reduced risk then led to a reduction in nominal interest rates such that real interest rates for nontraded goods became negative. This in turn provoked a wave of speculative demand for nontraded goods, thereby augmenting inflationary pressures. This process continued for about six months, until the banks and the public began to fear that the process would lead to devaluation; fear of devaluation triggered an increase in domestic interest rates such that the real interest rate became positive. Positive real interest rates, of course, eliminated the speculative demand for home goods, and the inflation collapsed in the last quarter. The fear of devaluation remained, however, and the "arbitraged" real interest rate never returned to the level of the first semester of 1979.

In summary, the failure of the Argentine Plan to bring about an early reduction in the rate of inflation—despite the evidence from interest rate behavior indicating that the exchange rate policy was treated with credibility—may well have its roots in the opening of the Argentine capital market when the Plan was implemented.[4]

Fiscal Deficits in Argentina

Until 1977, the Argentine deficit was financed principally by internal inflation, but from that year forward a substantial part was financed by foreign borrowing, a practice that made possible the acquisition of large amounts of international reserves by the central bank.[5] Paradoxically, those reserves, accumulated via deficit finance, in turn made it possible to sustain the Plan del 20 de Diciembre for a considerable period of time, but there can be no doubt that the persistent fiscal deficit played a key role in the ultimate demise of the Plan. The fiscal deficit eroded the credibility of the Plan because permanent reliance on foreign finance of the deficit was regarded as implausible if not impossible, and because the low rates of inflation implied by a stable exchange rate (the final objective of the Plan) would not generate enough "inflation tax" to finance the fiscal deficit.

In 1977 the Argentine authorities adopted a rather peculiar arrangement regarding reserve requirements for commercial banks, the intent of which was to prevent the large "spreads" between borrowing and lending rates that had characterized the Chilean financial system after the fiscal reform there of 1975. Under that arrangement, the Central Bank of Argentina paid interest on reserves corresponding to time deposits but charged interest on that part of demand deposits not held as reserves. The interest rate used for this purpose was approximately equal to the interest rate paid on time deposits, which in turn was about equal to the rate of inflation. The Argentine authorities simultaneously imposed a uniform reserve requirement, presumably to prevent changes in the composition of the demand for money from affecting the demand for base money. The net effect of this arrangement was to convert the Argentine financial system into the equivalent of one with a zero reserve requirement on time deposits and a 100 percent reserve requirement on demand deposits. Reserves held against time deposits cost the banks nothing, and the return to banks from attracting demand deposits was approximately zero. This development effectively transformed the base for the inflation tax into M_1 rather than the monetry base.[6] The arrangement did succeed in avoiding a large spread between borrowing and lending rates in the financial system, but it also resulted in a contraction of M_1. The result was that inflation of about 100 percent a year was required to generate sufficient revenue to service a fiscal deficit of 5 percent of GDP. Given that the Argentine authorities demonstrated no ability to reduce the deficit below that level, it became increasingly clear—particularly during the course of 1980—that the fixed exchange rate target was totally incompatible with that deficit. A fixed exchange rate would result in a rate of inflation no greater than 20 percent, whereas the existing deficit required a rate of inflation five times greater. Although external finance of the fiscal deficit was feasible in the short run, it was widely held that the inflation tax was the only long-run solution.[7] This inconsistency between exchange rate policy and fiscal policy strengthened the conviction that the exchange rate table would ultimately be violated, a conviction that was clearly expressed in the capital market.

As was noted above, the enormous accumulation of reserves by the Argentine central bank was made possible only by the external finance of the fiscal deficit. The ongoing inflation propelled the demand for nominal cash balances, and hence monetary base, even higher. Because the supply of base was not being met by central bank purchases of domestic assets (that is, treasury paper), monetary equilibrium required that the central bank accumulate foreign assets. These assets, which reached about US$10 billion by the end of the 1979, created the illusion on the part of the authorities that the exchange rate table could be defended indefinitely, although in fact it was the imminent prospect of total illiquidity that forced the monetary authorities to float the peso in June 1981.

Political Uncertainty in Argentina

Uncertainty about the continuity of exchange rate policy in Argentina became extreme during the second half of 1980—not only because of the growing threat of a run against the peso that could force a devaluation, but also because of the change of government programmed for March 1981. The prolonged silence of General Viola, after being designated as president-elect in early October 1980, contributed enormously to that uncertainty. By the end of 1980 it was no longer questioned that the exchange rate table would be broken. It was merely a matter of how large the devaluation would be, and when it would occur.

OUTCOME: THE CHILEAN EXPERIENCE

The Chilean stabilization experiment resulted in a fixed exchange rate after nineteen months of decelerating devaluation (and inflation), and that rate remained fixed for just short of three years, until the June 1982 devaluation. What shall be argued here is that the Chilean difficulties, which began in 1981, did not arise from the same elements as those in Argentina but, rather, for the most part from external shocks.

The introduction of the exchange rate table in Chile began in a very tentative manner on December 3, 1977, when the exchange rate was announced for the following two months, the

Table 5-4. Price Level and Exchange Rate in Chile, 1975-81

| | | WPI[a] | | Exchange rate[b] | | |
| | | Rate of inflation (percent) | | Pesos per | Rate of change (percent) | |
Date	Level	Quarterly[c]	Annual[d]	U.S. dollar	Quarterly[c]	Annual[d]
1975						
March	100.0	60	497	2.79	72	477
June	178.5	77	553	4.58	64	532
Sept.	247.0	40	484	6.19	36	506
Dec.	320.2	30	411	8.25	33	410
1976						
March	444.4	39	344	10.96	30	286
June	624.2	40	254	13.54	26	196
Sept.	754.7	21	206	14.33	6[e]	132
Dec.	805.4	7	152	17.03	19	106
1977						
March	1,013.0	26	128	18.38	8[e]	71
June	1,145.0	13	83	20.23	10	49
Sept.	1,246.0	5	65	23.86	18	66
Dec.	1,331.0	7	65	27.59	16	62
1978						
March	1,473.0	11	45	29.86	8	63
June	1,617.0	10	41	31.83	7	57
Sept.	1,770.0	9	42	33.05	4	38
Dec.	1,846.0	4	39	33.84	2	23
1979						
March	2,026.0	10	38	35.24	4	18
June	2,307.0	14	43	36.76	4	16
Sept.	2,850.0	24	61	39.00	6[f]	18
Dec.	2,922.0	3	58	39.00	—	15
1980						
March	3,142.0	8	55	39.00	—	11
June	3,356.0	7	45	39.00	—	6
Sept.	3,622.0	8	27	39.00	—	—
Dec.	3,744.0	3	28	39.00	—	—
1981						
March	3,736.0	0	19	39.00	—	—
June	3,700.0	−1	10	39.00	—	—
Sept.	3,700.0	0	2	39.00	—	—
Dec.	3,597.0	−3	−4	39.00	—	—

— Not applicable.

a. Source: Boletín Mensual (Santiago: Banco Central de Chile), various issues.

b. Source: Indicadores Económicos 1960-80 (Santiago: Banco Central de Chile, April 1981). Monthly averages of bank rate.

c. Change from end of previous quarter.

d. Change from end of quarter twelve months earlier.

e. Revaluation occurred during quarter ending in this month.

f. The actual devaluation during the third quarter of 1979 was zero because the exchange rate was fixed at 39 at the end of June 1979.

average rate of devaluation being 2.7 percent a month. The Chilean rate of devaluation had been approximately the same as that in Argentina when the program was begun there, but in contrast the rate of inflation was only half that of Argentina (see table 5-4 and compare with table 5-2). Nevertheless, the introduction of the exchange rate table involved a 50 percent reduction in the rate of devaluation in Chile.

On February 3, 1978, the table was extended to the end of that year, but again with a declining rate of devaluation that averaged 1.5 percent a month for the eleven-month period. At the end of 1978, the table was extended to December 1979, with a declining rate of devaluation that, on average, was to be 1.1 percent a month. In June of 1979, however, the rate was fixed at 39 pesos to the U.S. dollar—the level that was to be reached at the end of December—and it was announced that there would be no further devaluations.

A mere glance at table 5-4 indicates that the rate of devaluation had been falling rather consistently since 1975, with the exception of two quarters during which there were stepwise revaluations against the dollar. It is also evident that the rate of inflation (measured by wholesale prices) also fell steadily from 1975 until 1979, at which point the rate of inflation increased sharply, only to fall to virtually zero in 1981. The rate of inflation was, however, rather

Table 5-5. Selected Price Indexes and Relative Price Variability in Chile, 1975-81

Year and quarter	P_m	P_x	P_h	P_t[a]	$(P_h - P_t)/P_h$ (percent)
1975					
I	100.0	100.0	100.0	100.0	0
II	162.4	174.1	175.4	167.6	5
III	225.2	267.8	245.3	243.5	1
IV	288.2	329.7	311.6	306.2	2
1976					
I	435.1	445.6	413.4	439.8	−6
II	576.8	582.4	575.4	579.3	−1
III	627.5	684.5	709.4	652.5	9
IV	700.3	830.2	862.0	756.0	14
1977					
I	937.8	967.3	1,029.0	950.5	8
II	1,156.0	1,021.0	1,192.0	1,093.0	9
III	1,246.0	1,136.0	1,344.0	1,195.0	13
IV	1,336.0	1,282.0	1,505.0	1,311.0	15
1978					
I	1,442.0	1,473.0	1,654.0	1,456.0	14
II	1,573.0	1,594.0	1,781.0	1,583.0	13
III	1,638.0	1,744.0	1,914.0	1,685.0	14
IV	1,652.0	1,845.0	2,054.0	1,737.0	18
1979					
I	1,785.0	2,203.0	2,197.0	1,962.0	12
II	1,940.0	2,564.0	2,378.0	2,199.0	8
III	2,454.0	3,140.0	2,628.0	2,742.0	−4
IV	2,755.0	3,417.0	2,814.0	3,035.0	−7
1980					
I	2,999.0	3,711.0	3,029.0	3,301.0	−8
II	3,004.0	4,442.0	3,293.0	3,582.0	−8
III	3,126.0	4,532.0	3,455.0	3,695.0	−8
IV	3,175.0	4,751.0	3,693.0	3,806.0	−7
1981					
I	3,293.0	5,064.0	3,883.0	3,997.0	−3
II	3,230.0	5,409.0	4,103.0	4,073.0	1
III	3,164.0	5,459.0	4,276.0	4,040.0	6
IV	3,159.0	5,389.0	4,435.0	4,020.0	9

Note: Figures are three-month averages. See text for definition of prices (P).
Source: All basic data obtained from Boletin Mensual (Santiago: Banco Central de Chile), various issues.
a. Defined as $(P_m)^{0.55}(P_x)^{0.45}$.

consistently above the rate of devaluation—more so than would superficially appear to be explained by external inflation—particularly in 1979 and 1980. Indeed, from the first quarter of 1975 to June 1981, the WPI in Chile had risen thirty-six times (and the consumer price index, CPI, forty-three times), whereas the exchange rate was up only fourteen times. While much of the inflation and devaluation occurred before the introduction of the exchange rate table, a similar pattern emerged for the most recent period. From December 1977 through June 1981, the WPI rose by 180 percent, the CPI by 250 percent, and the exchange rate by a mere 41 percent. The apparent paradox is explained by a sharp rise in the external prices of Chilean traded goods. Table 5-5 contains data on various price indicators for the stabilization period, including importables (P_m, taken directly from the WPI) and exportables (P_x, defined as mining products in the WPI). Both indexes refer to internal prices; hence, they reflect the combined effect of devaluation and external inflation. The internal price of importables rose by 140 percent from December 1977 to June 1981, and that of exportables by 320 percent—whereas the devaluation was merely 41 percent. The implication is that the external (U.S. dollar) price of Chilean imports had, by June 1981, risen by about 70 percent, and that of exports by about 200 percent, since the end of 1977. This implication is roughly confirmed by independent data supplied by the United Nations Economic Commission for Latin America (ECLA).[8]

The Chilean program was successful in achieving a stable exchange rate for nearly three years, but rapidly rising external prices continued the Chilean inflation well into 1980. Indeed, internal wholesale prices rose by 45 percent, and the CPI by 38 percent, during the first year of the fixed exchange rate. That situation continued until late 1980, when the recovery of the U.S. dollar led to an actual fall in the external (dollar) prices of Chilean traded goods. During 1981, consumer prices rose by only 9 percent, and wholesale prices declined slightly. In the first half of 1982, the deflationary forces were even stronger, and consumer prices actually declined. It is widely alleged that relative prices changed drastically (in favor of nontraded goods) and that real wages rose from 10 to 20 percent.

Some data on changes in Chilean relative prices are presented in table 5-6. The observed changes come from the combined effects of external events (particularly the sharp decline in the dollar prices of copper and agricultural products) and increases in the nominal wage. Table

Table 5-6. Real and Nominal Wage and Salary Index in Chile, July 1978 to December 1981
(July 1978 = 100)

Date	W[a]	W/CPI[b]	(W/P_m)	(W/P_a)	(W/P_i)
July 1978	100.0	100.0	100.0	100.0	100.0
July 1979	146.7	110.6	104.2	96.3	87.7
Dec. 1979	179.4	116.6	102.1	103.4	94.9
June 1980	202.0	114.7	106.2	104.4	90.7
Dec. 1980	245.0	121.3	124.0	110.5	96.8
June 1981	263.3	123.6	132.4	128.1	104.2
Dec. 1981	295.4	133.5	148.7	156.0	117.8
Percent changes					
July 1979/1978	46.7	10.6	4.2	−3.7	−12.3
July 1980/June 1979	37.7	3.3	1.9	8.4	3.5
June 1981/1980	30.3	7.7	24.7	22.7	14.9
Dec. 1980/1979	36.6	4.0	21.4	6.9	2.0
Dec. 1981/1980	20.6	10.1	19.9	41.2	21.7

Note: See text for definition of prices (P).
Source: Boletín Mensual (Santiago: Banco Central de Chile), various issues.
a. Wage and salary index.
b. CPI is the consumer price index.

5-6 shows that nominal wages and salaries rose during 1981 by 10 percent relative to consumer prices and by substantially more relative to wholesale prices. During the same period, wages and salaries rose by 20 percent relative to import prices (P_m, WPI), more than 40 percent with respect to agricultural prices (P_a, WPI), and 22 percent relative to industrial products (P_i, WPI).

Much of the rise in real wages derives from the practice in Chile of indexing nominal wages to the CPI. As a result, when inflation declines—as it did during 1981—wage adjustments persist at a rate governed by the rate of inflation in the previous period. The Chilean wage policy, of course, in reality constitutes a second numeraire (the first being the exchange rate). As long as the two numeraires are consistent (as they were during the 1978-80 period), there is no problem. The sharp decline in the inflation rate during 1981, however, exposed the inconsistency. It is the rise in real wages that is most frequently cited as the motivation for the devaluation of June 1982.

The Role of External Shocks

The Chilean devaluation of June 1982 indicates a clear break with earlier policy in that unemployment was viewed as a greater problem than inflation. Indeed, at the time of the devaluation the inflation rate was negative, but the unemployment rate was approaching 20 percent. The key question is the extent to which the fixed exchange rate contributed to the unemployment during 1981-82, despite evidence that during the earlier period (1978-80) unemployment was falling along with the rate of inflation. To this writer, the answer seems to lie not so much in the exchange rate regime itself as in the behavior of the U.S. dollar. The sharp recovery of the dollar (against other major currencies) in late 1980 and early 1981 had three important consequences for Chile.

First, the (external) terms of trade turned against Chile because the revaluation of the U.S. dollar caused the dollar prices of many commodities to fall (while commodity prices in other major currencies, such as the deutsche mark, rose). Particularly important in this process were the prices of copper and several agricultural products. It is worthy of note that this process began well ahead of the so-called world recession; indeed, the world was not aware of that recession until the second half of 1981, whereas the Chileans were discussing it as early as April 1981. There was no world recession until the last four months of 1981, but there was dollar deflation from the early months of 1981 because of the effect, on dollar prices, of the dollar's appreciation. The dollar deflation has struck much of the world with a high degree of uniformity. The same complaints that are heard from the agricultural sector in Chile are heard in Uruguay, in Iowa, and in Peru. Thus, the Chilean phenomenon is not unique; rather it is but one manifestation of a worldwide phenomenon.

Second, with the recovery of the U.S. dollar came not only a change in the structure of external prices (adverse, as it were, for Chile), but also a sharp reduction in the rate of increase in dollar prices of Chilean traded goods. This led to an abrupt decline in Chile's rate of inflation from 30 percent in 1980 to 9 percent during 1981, and to actual deflation as measured by the WPI. Simultaneously (and by no accident), dollar interest rates rose, thereby offsetting the (weak) tendency for peso interest rates to decline as barriers to international capital movements in Chile were gradually dismantled. Thus, Chilean nominal interest rates remained roughly stable, with a fall in the rate of inflation of about 30 percentage points. The result was a rise of nearly 30 percentage points in the overall real interest rate, and an even greater rise in sectors such as mining and agriculture. This rise in real interest rates severely depressed the overall economy and crippled certain sectors such as construction. Expenditure fell, leading to a reversal of the enormous current account deficit of 1980 and the first half of 1981 and to an actual surplus by mid-1982.

The third effect of the dollar appreciation was on real wages in Chile. As argued above, it is the strength of the dollar that removed inflation from the Chilean scene, and that change, coupled with Chilean wage indexation policy, induced the sharp increase in real wages described above.

There is little that needs be said about the change in the Chilean terms of trade. Because Chile has no policy instruments with which to deal with that change, it must be treated as simply an unfortunate fact. Similarly, no further attention will be given to the real wage phenomenon, except to repeat that it is only remotely linked to the exchange rate and stabilization policy and that its inconsistency with that policy had to surface at some time. The remainder of this section will focus on the problem of the real interest rate, a problem that, in the opinion of this writer, is quantitatively much more important than the issue of the real wage.

The Chilean Interest Rate Problem

Peso interest rates in Chile have been extremely high in relation to those on dollar deposits (and the London interbank offered rate, LIBOR). The "spread" between LIBOR and peso interest rates has fluctuated considerably but has exhibited no decisive trend since the peso was fixed to the U.S. dollar at the end of June 1979. As shown in table 5-7, the average spread between the bank deposit rate and LIBOR from July 1979 to June 1982 averaged 1.5 percent a month, or about 20 percent a year.[9] The result is that Chilean peso interest rates were, in nominal terms, more than twice the dollar interest rates in Chile as well as in the rest of the world.

There are several aspects of this interest rate spread that are puzzling. First, the spread declined only slightly despite the substantial reduction of controls on international capital movements. Second, the spread was only weakly related to international capital movements.[10] Third, the spread can hardly be explained by devaluation risk, since there is a widespread consensus that no such risk existed during the second half of 1979 and most of 1980. Nevertheless, the spread was, if anything, higher during the second semester of 1979 than during the corresponding semester of 1981.[11] Fourth, the spread persisted despite extraordinary expansions in the volume of peso deposits and loans.

The spread contributed to extremely high real rates of interest on peso-denominated assets. Table 5-8 contains the average monthly short-term real bank deposit rates, expressed on an annual basis. The adjustment from nominal to real terms is made on the basis of the CPI. These real rates exhibit extreme volatility from month to month as well as from year to year. The rates were quite high relative to world real rates during 1977 and 1978, but fell sharply in 1979 and 1980 to about 5 percent on an annual basis, only to rise again in late 1980 and to remain high in June 1982. One explanation for this behavior is the following. During 1977 and 1978, the Chilean capital market was well insulated from the world market by capital market controls and uncertainty about the exchange rate. After the fixed exchange rate was adopted in July 1979, the stability of the spread indicates a growing integration of the Chilean capital market with the exterior. That is, Chilean nominal rates began to reflect external rates plus a relatively stable spread, resulting in a nominal deposit rate in Chile of the order of magnitude of 30 to 35 percent a year. The real rates were much lower (about 5 percent on an annual basis) during 1979 and 1980, however, because of the relatively high rate of inflation in Chile. As was argued above, the high rate of inflation in Chile during those years is explained by rising U.S. dollar prices of Chilean tradables. The Chilean inflation of roughly 30 percent during 1979 and 1980 occurred because the dollar prices of Chilean tradables were rising at that rate, despite the fact that the rate of inflation in the United States was much lower. Thus, the spread was not damaging to Chile because it was compensated for by a fortuitous set of external events. Indeed, the high nominal rates failed to attract much comment during those years.

That happy state of affairs ended abruptly with the appreciation of the dollar in late 1980 and early 1981. That appreciation—roughly 30 percent against the other major "hard" currencies of the world—caused dollar prices of most commodities to actually fall and commodity prices in

Table 5-7. Average Monthly Spread between Bank Deposit Rates in Chile and London
Interbank Offered Rate (LIBOR), 1976-82

Month	1975	1976	1977	1978	1979	1980	1981	1982
Jan.	−7.69	−1.66	1.77	2.50	2.05	2.67	1.48	2.02
Feb.	−6.92	−0.23	0.35	1.34	0.48	2.27	2.07	1.49
March	−10.62	2.77	9.96	0.11	0.48	1.87	1.98	1.17
April	−11.87	2.66	3.01	0.28	0.28	1.18	1.58	0.92
May	−0.51	2.42	0.94	1.54	1.06	1.39	1.28	1.28
June	1.69	2.91	−0.12	0.96	0.97	1.49	1.88	
July	−1.79	13.37	0.37	0.97	−3.60	1.49	1.87	—
Aug.	3.23	2.15	−0.78	1.66	1.98	1.49	1.28	—
Sept.	2.01	1.19	−4.25	2.45	1.88	1.29	0.89	—
Oct.	−2.31	1.57	1.32	2.95	1.58	1.09	1.28	—
Nov.	−1.87	1.66	1.61	2.45	1.88	1.09	1.29	—
Dec.	−1.40	2.90	−1.89	2.84	2.57	1.58	2.18	—
Annual average	−3.17	2.64	1.02	1.67	0.97 (1.39)[a]	1.49	1.59	1.36

— Not applicable.

Note: Average monthly spread calculated as $(1+i_t)/[(1+i_t^*)(1+e_t)]-1$, where i_t is the domestic deposit rate (for pesos), i_t^* is LIBOR, and e_t is the rate of devaluation for month t.

Source: Boletín Mensual (Santiago: Banco Central de Chile), various issues.

a. Excludes observation for July, when there was a 6 percent unscheduled devaluation.

Table 5-8. Chilean Short-term Bank Deposit Rates on Annual Basis
in Real Terms, 1977-82

Month	1977	1978	1979	1980	1981	1982
Jan.	24.60	63.08	24.60	22.42	15.66	34.49
Feb.	13.80	30.45	16.35	22.56	44.25	52.51
March	0.96	0.96	0.84	4.41	32.30	26.08
April	11.75	9.12	1.45	0.48	20.13	30.30
May	17.46	33.08	9.12	0.24	18.02	40.92
June	17.74	17.04	9.77	4.78	44.75	34.72
July	7.06	8.21	− 5.04	3.78	36.55	—
Aug.	13.22	12.01	−18.40	2.18	20.41	—
Sept.	12.42	17.32	−10.50	2.18	17.74	—
Oct.	17.32	37.03	5.16	−7.86	30.91	—
Nov.	57.17	41.42	12.68	−3.77	29.84	—
Dec.	40.92	44.75	18.86	13.49	38.80	—
Annual average	19.54	26.20	5.41	5.41	29.11	36.50

— Not applicable.

Note: Nominal rates are converted to real terms by removing the rate of inflation as measured by the CPI.

Source: Boletín Mensual (Santiago: Banco Central de Chile), various issues.

deutsche marks, Swiss francs, and like currencies to rise sharply. Because the Chilean peso was pegged to the dollar, the external inflation effectively disappeared, and real interest rates once again rose to reflect the spread. Thus, the great boom in construction and investment induced in Chile by the abnormally low interest rates of 1979 and 1980 was totally reversed by the reemergence of the high real rates that had characterized the earlier period.

The rise in real interest rates from 5 percent a year to levels in excess of 30 percent was undoubtedly much more damaging to the Chilean economy than the rise in real wages or the "twist" in relative prices during 1981. In many activities, the cost structure is such that, although a rise of 10 percent in real wages can be absorbed, a 500 percent increase in the user cost of capital simply cannot. The surge in unemployment during 1981—particularly in the construction sector—clearly reflects this phenomenon.

A serious implication of the above analysis is that 1981 and 1982 are "normal" years for Chilean real interest rates; the external inflation that saved Chile during 1979 and 1980 simply could not continue. Chile's external inflation of 1981 was quite consistent with that of the United States, and that rate of inflation can be expected to prevail in the long run. Put another way, Chile's high rate of inflation during 1979 and 1980 was because of changes in external relative prices, and such changes are rarely sustained for any significant period of time.

The message that emerges from this analysis is that recovery of the Chilean economy is unlikely unless the spread between Chilean and external interest rates can be reduced or eliminated. There can be but little hope that the June 1982 devaluation will significantly lower that spread (and, hence, real interest rates in Chile). Indeed, just the opposite may occur. If that devaluation leads to expectations of further devaluations, banks will have to increase their deposit rates to induce depositors to continue holding Chilean pesos.[12]

The key question is the cause of the large and fairly stable spread between domestic and foreign interest rates in Chile. As noted above, that spread was not affected systematically by either international capital movements (inflow of U.S. dollars) or by the volume of peso assets and loans (which increased in real terms by more than 200 percent from the end of 1978 to June 1982). That neither massive inflows of dollars (such as occurred during 1980 and the first semester of 1981) nor massive increases in peso credit served to reduce significantly and systematically either the spread or Chilean nominal interest rates suggests that the spread reflects underlying costs of arbitrage, costs that have been relatively stable over the past few years.

One reason that arbitrage costs might be high in Chile is that the commercial banks cannot arbitrage directly—they are not permitted to take positions in foreign currency and hence cannot, for example, borrow dollars in London to lend pesos in Santiago. Rather, a series of transactions is required: Chilean banks borrow dollars abroad and must lend the proceeds (after meeting reserve requirements) in dollars in Chile. Some nonbank Chilean entity will then convert the dollars into pesos and lend the pesos. The last step, of course, will in practice entail depositing the pesos in a Chilean bank or "financiera," which will then lend the proceeds to another Chilean entity. Because each of these transactions involves costs and the risk of default, the arbitrage process is inefficient compared with a situation in which the banks are permitted to arbitrage directly.

The possibility that the costs of international arbitrage are very high for Chile is suggested by the large spread between borrowing and lending rates in Chilean financial institutions. Data from the central bank indicate that from mid-1979 to mid-1982 the average was two-thirds of 1 percent a month. If one takes this spread as a measure of the real-resource-plus-risk cost of financial intermediation in Chile, one has a lower bound for the expected spread between LIBOR and the Chilean deposit rate. The reason is that international arbitrage, as restricted in Chile, involves some of the same operations (for example, lending to Chilean nonbank entities) as does domestic intermediation. That the actual spread between LIBOR and the Chilean bank deposit rate has been much higher may be explained by the additional transactions associated with arbitrage.[13]

The implication of the foregoing is simple. If international arbitrage currently involves very high costs because of the large number of transactions involved, a Chilean banker might very well be indifferent between paying up to 3 percent a month to obtain domestic funds, on the one hand, and paying 1.5 percent a month for dollars abroad, on the other, if his additional costs in connection with the latter transaction amount to the equivalent of another 1.5 percent per month. This conclusion appears quite plausible in view of an additional constraint on international arbitrage: banks can borrow "financial" dollars abroad only for a term of two years or more, which means that they must take a long exposure in dollars relative to the short-term lending in pesos, to which the spreads described above refer.

If it is the case that the international spread has its explanation in the high costs of arbitrage, then the solution is quite straightforward: permit the banks to take positions in foreign currencies and, hence, to arbitrage directly.

SOME LESSONS AND IMPLICATIONS FOR POLICY

There is a long-established tendency among many Latin American economists to search for explanations for Latin American economic phenomena in some "uniqueness" of the region. Often it is thought that the incentive system does not work in Latin America, that there is widespread market "failure," that policies that work in other countries will not work in Latin America, and so forth. This tendency, much stronger in the 1950s and 1960s, has only partially disappeared, and it is particularly evident in popular and semipopular discussions, especially so in Argentina. When it became clear, for example, that the Argentine Plan del 20 de Diciembre would not succeed, more frequently than not people questioned the model rather than the manner in which it was applied. Indeed, the "new" economic policy of Argentina of July 1982 appears to attribute past failures to excessively liberal (and monetarist) policies—even though those policies were neither liberal (by international standards) nor monetarist—since a fixed exchange rate regime coupled with a capital market open to the exterior effectively eliminates traditional monetary policy.

Much of the blame for the singular failure of the policy in Argentina and for the recurrence of difficulties in Chile and Uruguay has been placed on the fixed exchange rate regime itself, as if such a regime is some "unnatural" order. This occurs despite evidence that such regimes have existed successfully in many parts of the world, and for extended periods, in the past.[14] If a fixed rate regime were inherently unworkable, certainly the world would not have had to await the Southern Cone experiments for a demonstration.

As has been argued above, the Southern Cone policies of the past half-decade failed or encountered difficulties largely because of other policies incompatible with the fixed rate regime, external instability, or a combination of these. There is the question, of course, whether an alternative exchange rate regime would have served the Southern Cone countries better in the face of that external instability.

The growing literature on the characteristics of alternative exchange rate regimes in the face of domestic and external "shocks" is best described as inconclusive. There is a rather clear consensus, however, that when the shocks are monetary and of internal origin, a fixed exchange rate regime is preferable because of the endogeneity of the money supply under that regime. When the shocks are external, the simple models that have been developed do not lead to unambiguous conclusions, particularly for a small country living in a world of floating exchange rates among the major currencies. Under certain strong restrictions, it can be shown that a floating rate is superior in that it leads to less variability of real output in the face of external monetary shocks.

Discussions of the advantages of fixed versus flexible exchange rate regimes frequently neglect the important point that—in the absence of controls on capital movements, exchange controls, or both—both money and credit are endogenous under a fixed exchange rate regime. The result is that monetary and credit policy can be exercised only in the very short run, whereas full specification of monetary policy is essential to evaluation of the behavior of a flexible rate regime. Without that specification, it is impossible to predict whether a fixed rate regime will provide more stability of real output than will flexible rates. Unfortunately, it is extremely difficult to provide such a specification in practice.

There are two considerations, however, about which there can be little doubt. A flexible rate regime permits the monetary authorities at least to appear to escape responsibility for the behavior of the exchange rate, and a fixed rate regime (in the absence of capital and exchange controls) denies the authorities any lasting control over monetary and financial magnitudes.[15] If the monetary authorities cannot be counted on to behave responsibly, obviously a fixed rate is preferable because the mistakes in the conduct of the central bank will quickly be reflected in the behavior of international reserves. Alternatively, if the authorities wish to be able to disassociate themselves from their actual policy, a flexible rate regime might be preferred. These, of course, are essentially political rather than economic considerations.

Although the debate over the convenience of a fixed versus flexible exchange rate for a small country in a world of floating rates has not come to a decisive conclusion, it is clear that, if the choice be a fixed rate regime, the currency against which the country fixes matters a great deal. The decision in the Southern Cone first to peg and ultimately to fix against the U.S. dollar during the second half of the 1970s was a natural one from any historical perspective—after all, Argentina, Chile, and Uruguay had done so in one way or another for most of this century, and the choice of any currency against which to peg except the dollar would have met with skepticism. In addition, the dollar had been depreciating steadily during the 1970s, which made the dollar a natural candidate in a country whose historical experience was that of inflation rather than deflation. The change in U.S. monetary policy in October 1979, however, undermined what had been a logical choice. When the dollar began to appreciate strongly one year later, difficulties in Chile and Uruguay were not long in coming. The deflationary pressures that accompanied that appreciation would have been far less had the peso been fixed against the IMF's Special Drawing Right (SDR) or even a simple basket of "hard" currencies, such as 50 percent dollars and 50 percent deutsche marks. This observation, of course, does little more than reveal the marked superiority of hindsight.

There are important lessons from the Southern Cone experience. Although it may be too early to appreciate all of them, a tentative list follows.

- The discipline of a fixed exchange rate regime can and did reduce the rate of inflation in all three countries of the Southern Cone. Indeed, in the case of Chile and Uruguay the policy resulted in strong deflationary pressures. In the case of Argentina, internal inconsistencies in the implementation of the policy were sufficient to condemn it to failure.

- Fixed exchange rates and international capital mobility are not sufficient to guarantee "low" real interest rates. Real interest rates in Argentina rose sharply in late 1979 (and again in the first semester of 1980, with the wave of bank failures) and remained high. Real interest rates rose in Chile and Uruguay with the deflationary pressures associated with appreciation of the U.S. dollar in 1980-81. In all three cases, real interest rates were much higher than in the "dollar bloc" area (the United States and countries pegging to the dollar).

- Fixed exchange rates are inconsistent with large and persistent fiscal deficits because those deficits are themselves associated—in the mind of the public—with inflationary finance.

- Fixed exchange rates are inconsistent with additional numeraires, such as the wage indexation policy in Chile.

- In a world of floating rates among the major currencies, it matters a great deal against which currency a small country pegs. Although the U.S. dollar seemed a reasonable choice in the late 1970s, its subsequent recovery placed unbearable deflationary pressures on many economies. Pegging against a basket of major currencies would, in retrospect, have been better.

- Integration of internal with external capital markets requires that local financial institutions be in good health. If not, domestic financial weakness can have a devastating effect on domestic interest rates when uncertainty causes individuals to attempt to flee the domestic currency.

- As an economy becomes more open, careful attention must be paid to external developments. In many cases, domestic policy simply cannot cope with problems of external origin (for example, adverse changes in the terms of trade), and it is a mistake to attempt policies doomed to failure at the outset.

The reader will quickly note that few of these lessons are new. But because humans are condemned to relearn old lessons continually, there is no risk in repeating them.

NOTES

1. Formal models that lead to this result abound. See, for example, Rodríguez and Sjaastad (1979), Rodríguez (1981b), Sjaastad (1980a, 1981).

2. The price indexes are subcategories of the WPI of Argentina. P_x is defined as the price index of agricultural exportables, P_m as the import price index, and P_h as national goods of a nonagricultural origin. See Rodríguez and Sjaastad (1979) for further details.

3. The weights are based on the elasticity of P_h with respect to P_m, which is estimated at 0.412 (Sjaastad 1980b).

4. A difficulty with this interpretation of interest rate and inflation behavior in Argentina is that Uruguay pursued a similar exchange rate policy, with an open capital market and levels of protection similar to those of Argentina, but did not experience the change of relative prices that occurred in Argentina. Interest rate "spreads" with respect to external rates, however, were very high (for reasons that are poorly understood), sufficiently so that Uruguayan internal real interest rates were always positive after the adoption of the exchange rate table.

5. According to the 1979 International Monetary Fund annual report on Argentina, the public sector deficit in Argentina fell from 16 percent of GDP in 1975 to 9.5 percent in 1976 and remained at nearly 6 percent during 1977 and 1978 (IMF 1979). Data for subsequent years are not available, but it is unlikely that the deficit fell to less than 5 percent of GDP. In contrast, the budget deficit in Chilean pesos was eliminated in 1975, and since 1979 the combined peso and dollar budget has been in surplus.

6. Let B be the monetary base, D the amount of demand deposits, T the volume of time deposits, C the amount of currency, z the uniform reserve requirement, i the interest paid on reserves held against time deposits and charges against lending from demand deposits, and F the net revenue of the central bank. Then:

$$B = C + z(D + T)$$
$$F = \dot{B} + i(M_1 - C - zD) - i(zT).$$

Setting $i = \pi$ (the rate of inflation) and $\dot{B} = \pi B$, we obtain:

$$F = \pi B + \pi(M_1 - B)$$
$$= \pi M_1.$$

7. In the open debate of this issue in the Argentine press during 1980, not even the government challenged the view that the deficit would ultimately have to be monetized.

8. The unit value estimates of ECLA for both Chilean imports and exports rose 58 percent from 1977 to 1980 (annual averages). The annual average exchange rate rose by 73 percent from 1977 to 1980, which would imply an increase in the internal price of tradables of 163 percent for the 1977-80 period. The increase in the index of internal prices of imports was exactly 163 percent for the same period; however, that of exports was much higher—296 percent. There seems to be no obvious explanation for the discrepancy in the case of export prices.

9. There is also the spread between deposit and lending rates, which has been nearly two-thirds of 1 percent a month during most of the period since the peso was fixed to the dollar (July 1979 until June 1982). The lending rate is clearly an ex ante rate, and we have no observations on the ex post rate. For that reason, all comparison will be with the deposit rate.

10. The period from July 1979 through March 1982 was divided into two subperiods because the method of reporting net foreign assets was changed at the end of 1980. Until that point, short-term foreign currency liabilities of the central bank were included in the series. The capital inflow was measured as the change in the net foreign liabilities of the monetary system, on a monthly basis, and the spread is as reported in table 5-7. For the period August 1979 to

December 1980, the correlation coefficient between capital inflows and the spread was -0.53, which is marginally significant. For the period January 1981 through March 1982, that coefficient was merely -0.122, which is not significantly different from zero at even the 10 percent level. Although the results indicate that during the first period (when short-term central bank foreign borrowing was included in the series) there was a weak inverse correlation between capital inflows and the spread, that relationship does not appear during the second subperiod. The explanation may lie either in the removal of capital controls or in the change in the manner of reporting net foreign assets.

11. It is possible that an increase in the devaluation risk was exactly offset by the reduction in controls on international capital movements. Because of the implied colinearity, it is impossible to test this hypothesis.

12. Although Chile has experienced literally hundreds of devaluations, we have relatively little experience in Chile—or in other countries, for that matter—with devaluation in the context of an open capital account. In the face of controls on international capital movements, a devaluation does not lead to a flight from the currency simply because the public does not have the option to substitute foreign exchange for domestic currency (except through the black market). Devaluation in the context of a free capital market, however, is quite another thing. The only recent experience, other than that of Chile of June 1982, is the devaluation of early February 1981 in Argentina. That devaluation was quite similar to the Chilean devaluation of June 1982 because it violated a long-established exchange rate table. Just before the February 1981 devaluation, nominal deposit rates in Argentina were about 6 percent per month; they rose to about 15 percent per month immediately following the devaluation.

13. Preliminary investigation indicates that the two spreads are virtually uncorrelated for the period August 1979 through March 1982. The correlation coefficient is -0.05.

14. Experience during the twentieth century with floating exchange rates among major currencies is limited to the 1930s and the current period, which began in early 1973. Some countries, most notably Canada, have floated their currencies on other occasions, but these experiences have been quite short lived and isolated. The nineteenth century, of course, was dominated by the gold standard and, hence, by implicit fixed exchange rates.

15. Monetary authorities obviously can influence the behavior of a floating exchange rate even if they abstain from interventions in the foreign exchange market. The reason for this is because interventions in the domestic credit market (for example, rediscounts and open market operations) are very good substitutes for buying and selling foreign exchange. But by refraining from intervention in the foreign exchange market, the monetary authorities can create the appearance that they are noninterventionist.

REFERENCES

Frenkel, Roberto. 1981. "La apertura financiera externa: El caso argentino." Paper presented at the International Seminar on External Finance and Its Impact on Latin American Economies. Santiago: Corporación de Investigaciones Económicas para Latinoamerica (CIEPLAN), March.

International Monetary Fund (IMF). 1979. "Argentina—Recent Economic Developments." Washington, D.C. (June 27).

Rodríguez, Carlos A. 1979. El plan argentino de estabilización del 20 de Diciembre. Documento de Trabajo no. 5. Buenos Aires: Centro de Estúdios Macroeconómicos de la Argentina (CEMA), July.

_____. 1981a. "Commercial Policy and Income Distribution." Paper prepared for the Conference on the Free Trade Movement in Latin America, Hamburg, June 21-24. Processed.

_____. 1981b. "Política comercial y salarios reales." In Sjaastad and Douglas 1981.

Rodríguez, Carlos A., and Larry A. Sjaastad. 1979. El atraso cambiario en Argentina: ¿Mito o realidad? Documento de Trabajo no. 2. Buenos Aires: CEMA, June.

_____. 1980. El atraso cambiario en la Argentina: ¿Mito o realidad? Ensayos Económicos no. 13. Buenos Aires: Banco Central de la República Argentina, March.

Sjaastad, Larry A. 1980a. "Commercial Policy, 'True' Tariffs, and Relative Prices." In John Black and Brian Hindlin, eds., Current Issues in Commercial Policy and Diplomacy. New York: St. Martins, 1980.

_____. 1980b. "Commercial Policy Reform in Argentina: Implications and Consequences." Buenos Aires: CEMA, December. Processed.

_____. 1981. "Protección y el volumen de comercio en Chile: La evidencia." In Sjaastad and Douglas 1981.

Sjaastad, Larry A., and Kenneth Clements. 1981. "The Incidence of Protection: Theory and Evidence." Paper prepared for the Conference on the Free Trade Movement in Latin America, Hamburg, June 21-24. Processed.

Sjaastad, Larry A., and Hernán Cortés Douglas, eds. 1981. La economía política de la reforma comercial en Chile. Cuadernos de Economía (Santiago), vols. 54-55 (August-December).

6

The Nature, Costs, and Benefits of Economic Stabilization-Liberalization Programs in the Southern Cone

Simón Teitel

My contribution includes general comments about the nature, background, and regional context of the stabilization (with adjustment and liberalization) programs adopted in the Southern Cone countries in recent years; comments about the costs and benefits of the programs implemented; and concluding remarks.

THE NATURE OF RECENT ECONOMIC POLICY

I tend to agree with Mario Blejer [chapter 1] that the experience under review is a very mixed one, and that it does not constitute a good test of any theoretical approach in particular, the monetary approach to the balance of payments not excluded. Economic life is such that things are done simultaneously and not in isolation; the long run is but a sequence of short runs; and the like. Moreover, the policy experiments of the Southern Cone countries being examined in this symposium were carried out under very particular conditions normally absent in democratic societies. Thus, not only the success but even the viability of such programs must be put in an appropriate perspective.

The programs have generally included, in different degrees: liberalization of the markets for capital and labor; reductions in the level of trade tariffs and other obstacles to international trade; the reduction—also in varying degree—of the fiscal deficit; and the establishment of uniform and stable rates of exchange.

It has already been discussed that—depending on the point in time, the policy constraints, the various objectives, and so forth—different mixtures of economic liberalization (that is, opening up the economy to international trade and financial transactions) and stabilization were followed. The interaction of the stabilization programs with the liberalization policies has been critically important. This importance has been highlighted not only with respect to the policy mix (how much international trade liberalization in relation to financial liberalization), but also with respect to the appropriate sequence of policies to follow (whether to open up first to trade or to capital flows). It is also important to consider at what point in the business cycle the liberalization process is initiated, since this could constrain the extent to which liberalization will be accomplished.

THE BACKGROUND AND REGIONAL CONTEXT

There is a background to the policies under review that we tend to forget. The events we are examining are largely a reaction to what happened in the 1950s and 1960s in the economies of the Southern Cone countries. These countries were then engaged, to various degrees, in socioeconomic programs intended to improve the distribution of income. A common feature of these programs was that they lacked adequate budgetary provisions for their financing. As a result, to carry out such socially inspired legislation governments become the employers of last resort and central banks the lenders of last resort. Thus, a common result of these earlier policies was the monetizing of fiscal deficits.

The process that took place in the 1950s and 1960s in the Southern Cone countries led by its own dynamics to monetary expansion, inflation, and increases in social and political tension. We have seen that, almost independently of the oil shock in 1973-74, the internal situation of these countries brought about various episodes of hyperinflation that resulted in the adoption of import controls, multiple rates of exchange, and a host of other measures.

The reaction to this state of affairs—as embodied in the various stabilization-liberalization programs—was that the authorities, while initially professing to fight inflation, also took the opportunity to liberalize and to "privatize" the economy. It is fair to say that Chile is the country that—in the period under review—has carried out the most profound internal and external liberalization while largely eliminating the government deficit and succeeding in drastically reducing the rate of inflation.

For the region, the 1970s were characterized, on the average, by a substantial process of revaluation of the real rate of exchange. For Latin America as a whole, the rate of exchange was revalued at an annual rate of approximately 2.3 percent between 1970 and 1980—that is, a cumulative revaluation of approximately 25 percent. (These are regional figures, and they do not apply to any particular Southern Cone country.)

If we try to explain the change in the rate of exchange—and this is, of course, a very naive exercise because many other effects mentioned at this symposium must also be operating—by trying to relate it to the terms of trade and to the inflow of capital, we see that, for the region as a whole, a substantial proportion of the variation in the exchange rate during this period can be explained by changes in these two variables. In 1980 U.S. dollars, for each billion dollars of capital inflow from abroad, the exchange rate of the region was revalued by 0.76, taking the 1970 rate of exchange level as 100; for each point of increase in the terms of trade, the rate of exchange was revalued by 0.45. (Inter-American Development Bank 1982)

Compared with other countries in the region during the 1970s, Argentina and Uruguay were at the top in terms of the appreciation of the rate of exchange. Looking at the effect of the two variables (inflow of foreign capital and terms of trade), we see that, for both Argentina and Uruguay, only the inflow of capital was significant in accounting for changes in the rate of exchange.

Chile was the only country in the region that effectively devalued, with respect to 1970. This process has recently changed, and the need for substantial devaluation has increased because of the very negative impact of declining terms of trade (largely the result of falling copper prices and the increase in the price of oil).

Having looked at the background and the regional context with particular regard for the exchange rate and the possible causes for its appreciation, I turn now to how I perceive some of the costs and benefits of these policies.

COSTS AND BENEFITS OF RECENT ECONOMIC POLICY

Most analysts agree that the populist economic policies carried out previously in the Southern Cone countries were characterized by all sorts of price distortions. They also note that the stated objectives of the liberalization programs included trying to overcome this situation by opening up the economies of the countries involved to foreign trade and to the international financial markets, and by eliminating other sources of price distortions.

On this score, what have been the results? Admittedly, in many cases we are in the presence of new price distortions. Moreover, these are not merely transitory phenomena, for they have lasted for extended periods. I think it is our duty to recognize this and to admit that we know very little, as Jacob Frenkel has said [see chapter 2] about the transition phase in stabilization-liberalization programs and how this transition could eventually lead to a first-best solution.

Before these programs there were very low, sometimes even negative, real interest rates. That was bad because it represented a wrong signal for the allocation of resources. Now we have heard from various symposium participants, who know the countries (and the monetary approach to the balance of payments) better than I do, that rates of interest did not converge and that they remain "too high." Of course, high rates also lead to distortions in the allocation of resources.

We have seen a persistent overvaluation of the rate of exchange in these countries. It has been going on for an extended period of time, and it has adverse consequences on the productive sector. The question was raised by Joseph Grunwald [see his comments in chapter 4]: to what extent have the policies in question not only adversely affected the capacity of these countries to export, but also contributed to deindustrialize an important region of Latin America? To some extent these programs are not only acting against inefficient industries but are also undoing learning accumulated during the period when present industrial capacity was being created.

I also believe that we should not be unduly fascinated with the apparent increases in output per worker of the so-called new industries. If we look carefully, we see that very little value is added in them. Some of the goods exported represent, largely, economic rents. It cannot be argued that these countries have now reached the "right" allocation of resources and are thus exporting more labor-intensive goods. That is not the case for fruits, wood, or for most of Chile's new exports. At a certain point, even the products of Argentina's "pampa húmeda" had great difficulty in being exported in spite of their obvious comparative advantage.

Thus, these programs have resulted, over extended periods of time, in situations representing disequilibria in the economy—of a different sign than before, but with equally severe distorting effects.

Similar considerations apply to real assets. I remember my own experience in going to Buenos Aires, before the application of the recent program, and finding that a two-bedroom apartment there was renting for US$10 a month. That rent was obviously out of line with any kind of international price comparisons one could imagine. But it is equally absurd that the same flat was recently renting for US$350 a month. I was not happy either with the recent price or with the former price, and a priori I do not see any good reason to have to choose between the two. The "true" price is probably somewhere in between. I think the question of the price of assets and the real estate "bubble" are critical ones, but to me the issue is not simply that today a capital loss will have to be taken, as Rolf Lüders has mentioned in relation to the Chilean case [see his comments in chapter 4]. We have to look at what happened (and why) in both instances—before and during the programs—as indications of price distortions and to avoid such situations in the future.

There have also been large losses of output and employment in the economies under consideration during the application of the policies under review, and we could discuss at length their impact on income distribution. Some analysts are very concerned with the concentration of income, assets, and ownership that has been caused by these programs. Others are very concerned with achieving privatization. Depending on the objective function, analysts may pay attention to these results and their equity implications or not. I would like to mention another point related not to equity but to a further loss in efficiency.

Given the distortions mentioned above and that the residents of these countries live day after day, month after month, under conditions of uncertainty because of potentially significant changes in economic policies, in such an environment decisionmakers end up developing the ability to make peculiar portfolio choices. These choices, which require a great deal of the time and energy of entrepreneurs, include whether to work or to take a prolonged vacation, to produce or to lend money out, to import or to produce locally, to go into debt locally or abroad or to do so in the short or the long run, and so on. There is a tremendous loss of efficiency in such a system. And this is not just a question of a once-and-for-all adjustment effect. For extended periods, firms and individuals must engage in such considerations. Mr. Lüders has given us a hint of recent circumstances in Chile in this respect.

CONCLUDING REMARKS

Some participants in the discussion have been trying to say that adjustment and stabilization should be considered separately from liberalization, but the experience we are analyzing is one of doing things at the same time. As a result, of course, there are numerous interactions and feedback effects.

We must also recognize that, although events do not have to occur in some particular way, they did take place in the way described several times at this symposium. That is, during the application of the programs under review, there existed severe distortions of prices for long periods of time, whereas the presence of such distortions was precisely one of the basic critiques levied against the economic policies pursued in the period before these attempts. In fact, the argument that these programs would lead to the elimination of distortions, to improvement in the allocation of resources, and to markets' functioning in a better way was precisely what led many people to support them.

Now, irrespective of how to denominate them—I think we have discussed nomenclature enough, and there is a consensus that it does not make much sense to try to stick to one label or another—in all cases and at various points in time these programs were characterized by substantial overvaluation of the exchange rate, by very high real interest rates, and by distortions in wages and in the price of real assets. I find some sort of perverse symmetry in what has happened. Equally adverse effects result from very high rates of interest—compared with what the interest rate should be in the long run in general equilibrium—as from very low and, in some cases, negative rates of interest. Of course the consequences are different, and the people affected are different, but I think we can agree that both situations will have adverse economic effects.

Another interesting feature of the severe distortions and of the interaction between, on the one hand, trying to stabilize and to adjust and, on the other, trying to liberalize is that one process may end up working against the other. We are all aware that the liberalization process necessarily includes a reduction in tariffs. Such reduction is expected to contribute to the elimination of the anti-export bias generally found in highly protected economies. However, one of the perverse results of these programs has been, due to the overvaluation of exchange rates noted above, to liquidate not only large sectors of industry, but in some cases also to kill the export capacity that had been growing in recent years.

Incidentally, I do not think that there is much basis for the claim repeatedly made here that—because observed levels of nominal protection vary greatly according to industry and, conse-quently, very different levels of effective protection exist—there must be a uniform tariff. We all know by now from experience and case studies that, because learning, technological develop-ment, and other skill-acquisition effects may demand extended periods of time and vary greatly among the different manufacturing industries, different infant industries may require different levels of protection and for different periods of time (Westphal 1982). Thus, there are no a priori theoretical or empirical grounds for claiming that equal levels of protection are required, and, if equal levels are not needed, then it will not be of much help to impose a low and uniform tariff level.

Neither am I impressed by the apparent results of nontraditional exports in Chile. I think that the only thing that is nontraditional about these exports is the name. I do not see a great difference between exporting copper products with limited degree of processing and exporting wood products or fruits. The point made above about the high rent content of certain activities applies here. They may have been discriminated against in the past, but these are also the only activities in which, after prolonged and substantial overvaluation, industrial exports subsisted.

Nor am I very impressed with the measures mentioned by Professor Harberger [see his comments in chapter 8] as successes in Chile. I think that they are largely rationalization measures. Those affecting the tax structure may be fine, but they are not inherent to the package of policies under review. We could have a system predicated on incomes policy, for example, and also have rationalization of the tax structure, and so on. Consequently, such results could not be a basis for saying that the program is succeeding.

Given the stage of our knowledge, I tend to agree with Jacob Frenkel's suggestion that a dose of prudence is required. For example, if there is a situation of extensive unused capacity, as in Chile recently, a devaluation could work and is not something totally to be discarded. I mention this merely to underscore that the mix of policies applied should be less doctrinaire. The capacity to adapt to changes in the real side of the national economy must also be included in these approaches, and we must learn how expectations of economic decisionmakers are really formed and changed. While we learn these lessons, it would be to our advantage to be a bit more humble in dispensing our advice.

Finally, I tend to agree with José María Dagnino Pastore [see chapter 3 and his comments in chapters 4 and 9]. If, when looking at the results of these experiments, we see that severe price distortions and large-scale unemployment of resources have taken place, and if, after recognizing that these distortions have persisted for a long period of time, those advocating these programs are not willing to admit that perhaps there should be a change in the policies because they are not working—then I think that the programs analyzed and the experts involved do not together constitute a package to be recommended to our countries.

REFERENCES

Inter-American Development Bank (IDB). 1982. _Economic and Social Progress in Latin America: The External Sector, 1982 Report._ Washington, D.C.

Ffrench-Davis, R. 1982. "External Debt and Balance of Payments of Latin America: Recent Trends and Outlook." In IDB 1982, pp. 162-80.

Westphal, Larry E. 1982. "Fostering Technological Mastery by Means of Selective Infant-industry Protection." In M. Syrquin and S. Teitel, eds., _Trade, Stability, Technology, and Equity in Latin America._ New York: Academic Press, pp. 255-79.

7

Policy Implications of the Monetary Approach and of Experiences in the Southern Cone

James A. Hanson

Various symposium participants have stated that they view the monetary approach to the balance of payments as a simple framework for analyzing the factors that produce a change in international reserves, an approach with which I agree.

RELEVANCE OF THE MONETARY APPROACH TO THE BALANCE OF PAYMENTS

This framework is based on the accounting identity of the central bank's balance sheet. The identity implies that the change in international reserves is equal to the difference between the changes in the money base, which is directly related to the money multiplier and the demand for nominal money, and in the central bank's domestic credit. Therefore, effects of exogenous shifts and policy changes in international reserves can be analyzed through their effects on either money demand, the money multiplier, or domestic credit. Obviously a stable, predictable money demand function is a necessary condition for this framework to be useful.

Viewed in this light, the issue raised by many participants of whether the "law of one price" holds is a red herring. For example, suppose there is imperfect substitutability between imports and domestic value added, so that the law of one price does not hold. In these circumstances a rise in the flow rate of emission of central bank credit can affect relative prices, the absolute price level, and output. However, the price _level_ will reach a new equilibrium, at which point continued emission of domestic credit at the same rate will produce a loss of reserves equal to the change in domestic credit—the result implied by the monetary model. All that is required to achieve this result is the household budget constraint and a fixed exchange rate with constant effective protection, as George Borts and I have pointed out elsewhere (Borts and Hanson 1979).

In sum, the monetary approach tells us something about the limitations of monetary policy in an open economy with fixed rates of effective protection. It does not, however, say much about how the effects of changes in domestic credit emission, or of devaluation, are divided between output and prices, unless we also make the strong but incorrect assumption that output or price are fixed. These questions are obviously of great importance but can be answered only by examining the individual country experiences.

THE SOUTHERN CONE EXPERIENCES: THE PROBLEM OF CONSISTENCY

What can we learn from the experiences of the Southern Cone countries? First, the policy package must be consistent in broad terms. The Argentine experience in particular shows the importance of achieving consistency between the fiscal deficit and the exchange rate path. One rough way to check this consistency involves assuming that the whole fiscal deficit will be financed by central bank emission. Then the ratio of the deficit to GNP, divided by the ratio of the money base to GNP, yields the _potential_ rate of money growth and inflation.[1] If the projected deficit equals, say, 4 percent of GDP, as was the case in Argentina in 1980, and if the ratio of the money base to GDP is 3 percent, then potential money growth because of domestic credit expansion will be 133 percent. Unless the exchange rate is devalued at approximately this rate, then the currency will become overvalued, or reserves will be lost, or both—just as the monetary model predicts. Further, local interest rates will rise as the expected rate of devaluation increases.

What about borrowing to cover the fiscal deficit? Local borrowings are likely to be small because of the narrowness of capital markets, and in any case the interest on existing, publicly held debt will approximately equal new debt issue. Foreign borrowings present more complicated problems.

At first, foreign borrowing may lead to increases in international reserves and to internal inflation if imports and capital inflows are limited. Such a policy can provide a short-run boost to aggregate demand if the fiscal deficit is increased, while generating a simultaneous increase in international reserves, because higher prices will force households to accumulate more nominal money to maintain their real balances at desired levels. Indeed, one interpretation of the growth in international reserves and of the relatively sticky inflation rate in all three countries during the initial phases of stabilization was that the devaluation was fairly rapid, given the greater openness to capital inflows and the slowdown in the growth of domestic credit. As a result, households and businesses exported more than they imported and even borrowed abroad to get the necessary working balances. This kind of inflation may be avoided by allowing additional imports and capital outflows, but then the economy may suffer a drop in output, as occurred in 1981-82.

At a later point in time, the economy may encounter a second problem if it relies on foreign borrowing extensively: servicing the debt. A rapid increase in borrowing is usually a stock adjustment, which goes on until foreign lenders reach a new equilibrium position relative to the economy. Once that new position is attained, interest payments on the existing debt are likely to exceed new capital inflows, especially in a world of high real interest rates. Thus, any jump in capital inflows must be combined with a macroeconomic policy that generates the capacity to earn additional foreign exchange commensurate with the additional debt service. Foreign borrowing can postpone a problem, but only at the risk of creating future problems.

For example, in the Argentine case rapid increases in borrowing were used to maintain the exchange rate and temporarily to hold down the interest rate. In both 1979 and 1980 Argentina doubled its outstanding debt, simultaneously maintaining output growth and reducing inflation by devaluing more slowly than inflation and by increasing imports. A large portion of the growth in debt was due to borrowing by the public sector or public enterprises. However, the public realized that further debt increases of this size were probably not feasible,[2] and consequently that the government's deficit would have to be monetized, with a corresponding change in the devaluation policy. Viewed in this light, the unwillingness of Viola's incoming government to extend the period of decreasing rates of devaluation was simply a recognition of reality and a minor contributor to the loss of confidence in the peso, which forced up real interest rates and produced the series of devaluations that continued through 1982.

The fiscal deficit must also be consistent with the projected financial reforms. If a large government deficit is to be monetized, then obviously reserve requirements cannot be cut simultaneously. Therefore, a large government deficit is likely to imply a large spread between deposit and loan rates at financial institutions. Further, this is not simply a question of achieving a balanced budget; the existing stock of low-interest government debt must be held by the banking system. This means that the government is faced with the difficult choice of raising enough revenue to cover higher interest payments on its existing debt or of cutting reserve requirements (which, as the monetary approach predicts, will produce inflation, a loss of international reserves, or both).[3]

In sum, these experiences indicate that countries should be realistic in their policies (for example, allowing the fiscal deficit and inflation to get too far ahead of the exchange rate policy is likely to produce disaster) and that countries should "get it right" at the beginning (for example, given the difficulty in computing the correct initial exchange rate and the lack of international reserves, it may be useful to use a "free float" for a time).

VARIATIONS IN THE EXCHANGE RATE

The foregoing discussion raises the question of the effectiveness of varying the exchange rate. In the long run, almost all models based on the monetary approach have the property that the long-run level of output is independent of whether the exchange rate is allowed to move freely or whether the exchange rate is fixed and the money stock and prices are allowed to vary. Thus, the choice of floating or of devaluing at a given moment depends on the short-run dynamics of the particular economy. For example, setting a floating rate initially may make sense when it is hard to select a "correct" fixed rate. Similarly, devaluing at a given moment may "oil the mechanism" that leads to the "correct" set of relative prices for tradables and nontradables.

One particular question of devaluation that has come up often in the symposium is the Chilean case. Here my own regression estimates agree with the results that Arnold Harberger [see chapter 8] and Vittorio Corbo [see chapter 4] obtained using other models—that the overall "home and import price index" increases by between 70 and 85 percent of the devaluation within one year.[4] Further, my estimates (Hanson 1982) suggest a negative short-run relation between output and devaluation. I attribute these results to the short-run dominance of the effects of rises in the cost of imported inputs and inelastically demanded consumer goods, relative to the positive effects of export expansion and reductions in consumer goods imports facing price-elastic demand, as well as to the backward indexation of wages. Clearly these results are based on historic data. The changed structure of the Chilean economy and its depressed state economy in 1982 might allow a devaluation to produce a greater movement of relative prices—as it apparently would in Argentina, Brazil, Colombia, and Uruguay, according to my estimates of the same type of model. The historical evidence suggests caution, however, in recommending a devaluation in Chile to change relative prices.

One must also wonder whether it is solely relative prices that are at fault. Certainly they have changed; but has the change been enough to account for a recession of the magnitude observed in 1982? An additional culprit is the high real interest rates produced by expectations of devaluation. If this is the case, then devaluation might be considered for financial reasons, but support for that argument is tenuous. Giving in to the speculators against the peso might lower interest rates and increase aggregate demand in the short run, if the flood of U.S. dollars into the country exceeds the rise in the demand for pesos because of the higher price level and the openness of the economy. But the reverse is equally possible—giving in to speculation might produce a fall in aggregate demand and output, as the historical evidence suggests occurs with devaluation. Moreover, capitulating to the speculators would encourage future runs on the peso and lower the long-run demand for pesos, and devaluation would temporarily cut real credit and reduce real wealth of those indebted in dollars.

REAL INTEREST RATES

High real interest rates are another common problem that seems to have arisen in all of the Southern Cone countries. My own feeling is that these were due, in roughly this order, to: (1) expectations of devaluation; (2) reserve requirements and institutional characteristics of the banking system; (3) speculative "bubbles"; and (4) previous lack of capital, world conditions, or restrictions on capital inflow. Support for the primacy of expectations of devaluation comes from the Chilean experience, in which real rates dropped sharply after the sharp devaluation of

1979 and then rose again in 1981, and from the Argentine experience, in which the yield curve was downward sloped before the April 1981 devaluation (a downward-sloping yield curve makes term transformation impossible). For the Argentine case, works by Blejer (1982) and by Mathieson (1981) suggest a more or less constant premium over LIBOR plus the actual devaluation, albeit with a period of over a year, 1980, with abnormally high real rates followed by three months with sharply negative real rates (1980 also reflected the effects of major bank failures in Argentina). Another important point supporting this view is that dollar-dominated interest rates on both loans and deposits in all three countries were about equal to U.S. levels, suggesting that households were indifferent between U.S. rates and high peso deposit rates. In this case the spread between rates on peso deposits and peso loans may also be an important factor in the interest rates on loans. Evidence from Argentina (Mathieson 1981); Chile (where the spread dropped sharply—by 1 percent per month to half its former level—when reserve requirements were lowered); and Uruguay (where rates also fell when reserve requirements were eliminated)[5] supports this view.

Clearly inconsistency in policies is an important factor in producing high real rates, as the Argentine case illustrates. A government simply cannot count on the exchange rate as a principal stabilization instrument in a fairly open economy for long because, if the exchange rate becomes too far overvalued, then speculation will produce a run on the currency. If one follows the monetary approach, then the result will be a loss of reserves and a "liquidity crunch" in which the interest rate will rise to equal LIBOR plus an expected rate of devaluation that far exceeds any government schedule of devaluation or the current rate of inflation—an outcome totally confirmed by the Argentine experience.[6] To put it another way, with the exchange rate fixed, the interest rate must absorb all of the short-run fluctuations in these highly variable economies.

Viewed in this light, Chile may have fixed the exchange rate too soon given the inertia of its wage and price dynamics. However, consistency and reserve requirements are not the whole answer—real rates in Uruguay have been fairly high despite a balanced budget and elimination of commercial bank reserve requirements in late 1979.

Another factor that can produce high real interest rates is a speculative bubble. Under such conditions not only does everyone borrow to buy foreign exchange, but businesses continue to borrow in hopes that the situation will turn in their favor. With no one being driven out of the loanable funds market, real interest rates are forced up to extremely high levels, until some borrowers are eliminated by bankruptcy. Moreover, old ideas die very slowly—businesses may borrow, and banks may lend, under the assumption that eventually the government will revert to business-as-usual practice and bail out firms, rather than permit bankruptcies or losses by depositors. Such elements were clearly present in Argentina in 1980 and early in 1981. Under these circumstances a speculative bubble can develop that will be eliminated only by allowing some bankruptcies.

One of the remedies for high real interest rates suggested at this symposium [see comments by Sebastian Edwards and Pablo Spiller in chapter 4] is the sale of forward exchange. I am certainly in favor of allowing the development of additional markets, and the existence of a forward market might substitute for some of the volatility of interest rates. I doubt, however, that this policy will have an important effect on interest rates, and it also carries some danger. Uruguay offered forward coverage free for some months in 1981 and at a price beginning in December 1981, but with little effect on real interest rates [see Pablo Spiller's comments in chapter 4]. This is because credibility problems remain even if forward exchange is offered. Further, if forward coverage is offered free of charge, then demand will be very great, generating negative international reserves for the central bank and possibly producing a spot run on the currency. If a charge is made for forward coverage, then demand will be reduced, but only a large charge will hold down demand in periods when devaluation is expected, a charge that probably will be reflected in real interest rates.

An alternative solution to the interest rate problem is to allow greater flexibility in the exchange rate to substitute for interest rate fluctuations. One approach to greater flexibility in exchange rates that has been proposed in this symposium is to fix the exchange rate against a basket of currencies [see discussion by Jacob Frenkel, chapter 2, and Larry Sjaastad, chapter 5]. This policy may produce more stability in the real exchange rate if fluctuations in the outside world continue at their current level. It has the defect, however, that it is not a simple rule to understand, especially if the basket is constructed to reflect the composition of the individual country's trade. Moreover, this policy does not get to the heart of the matter—until there is some experience with fixed rates and monetary stability, there may be waves of speculation against the currency that will produce sharp changes in real interest rates. After all, a 10 percent probability of a 30 percent devaluation in the current month—a probability that may be only tenuously related to relative price movements—implies a 3 percent monthly interest rate and is likely to eliminate term transformation.

I would suggest an alternative policy: to widen the band in which the price of foreign exchange is allowed to fluctuate without central bank intervention. This would allow for private traders to absorb some of the shifts in expectations about the exchange rate, without pressuring the short-term interest rate. For example, a 3 percent band would allow for variations of the kind just mentioned, with less pressure on interest rates. Moreover, by setting the target band some months in advance, larger fluctuations in relative prices could be smoothed. The defect of this proposal is, of course, that it subjects producers of tradables to more risk. However, if the alternative to greater risk is the recent recessions experienced by the Southern Cone, then the choice seems clear.

THE SEQUENCE OF LIBERALIZATION: TRADE OR CAPITAL MARKETS FIRST?

The appropiate order for liberalization—trade or capital markets first—is another question of dynamics. As Jacob Frenkel has said [see chapter 2], economists really do not have a great deal to contribute to this issue because in many cases we are still sorting out the comparative statics. In particular, the monetary approach to the balance of payments does not provide many guidelines. But the Southern Cone experience does provide some messy laboratory experiments by which to assess the issue.

The empirical evidence in the Southern Cone is mixed on the effects of the sequence of liberalization. For Uruguay, the general impression, which I believe is correct, is that the capital market was liberalized first. The macroeconomic data indicate an improvement from a near zero average growth rate in the 1960s and early 1970s to nearly a 5 percent average rate for five years, along with a simultaneous reduction in the dependence on imported energy and capital imports. Regression estimates for Chile, where trade liberalization came first, suggest that the underlying growth rate increased by between 60 and 100 percent of the underlying growth rate of the 1950s and 1960s. The Chilean estimates, however, are quite sensitive to the empirical treatment of the terms of trade and the 1975 recession, whereas the Uruguayan results are fairly robust. Argentine data do not indicate much liberalization of either kind: the fiscal deficit and money growth remained at abnormally high levels relative to pre-1974 figures; there were price control periods (the "tregua"—the truce on price and wage increases between March 1 and June 30, 1977); trade liberalization only began to bite in mid-1979; and the capital market liberalization only began in June 1977, when deposits were decentralized, and was affected by the failure of several large Argentine financial institutions in March 1980.

In the theoretical arguments regarding the order of liberalization, although the definition of goods market liberalization is clear, what is meant by capital market liberalization needs clarification. Is it:

- Public sector borrowing in world capital markets?
- Relaxation of regulations on holding U.S. dollars and dollar assets?
- Relaxation of restrictions on private foreign borrowing?
- Relaxation of requirements on reserves and allocations of credit along with reduced inflation?
- Freedom of entry?

Each of these measures has different implications for the behavior of interest rates and the functioning of the economy. For example, the principal costs associated with opening the capital market seem to be related to its apparent empirical association with high real interest rates, particularly recently. But once the general public is allowed to hold dollars, it seems to be impossible to prevent the interactions between the expected rate of devaluation and the interest rate of the kind cited earlier, which can produce high real rates.

One of the theoretical reasons that Jacob Frenkel cited [in chapter 2] for liberalizing the trade account first is that fixed investment is less flexible than financial capital. I disagree with this argument for the following reason. Capital inflows produce first an appreciation in the real effective exchange rate that will produce a balance of payments equilibrium, and then a depreciation as the debt service comes due. Thus, if the capital market is eventually to be opened up to foreign lenders, then traded goods producers necessarily will have to go through some hard times, which will be followed by a squeeze on nontradables to force the reallocation of factors of production back on to tradables. Indeed, one could argue that the capital market should be opened first, with the path of the exchange rate set to provide future incentives to those who invest in exporting. It seems to me that the failure to recognize this intertemporal relationship has been a major factor in the current Southern Cone problems.

Jacob Frenkel also raised the point that it is easier to alter the pace of trade liberalization than that of capital market liberalization, since that market depends so heavily on trust. This does not seem to be an important argument in light of his other recommendation, with which I agree, to liberalize rapidly.

The argument for rapid action is threefold. First, stretching out a program may reduce its credibility. It is doubtful whether import-substituting industries, let alone exporters, have reacted to the Argentine or Uruguayan five-year program of tariff reduction. Second, rapid action may be necessary to shock the system and to break the old modes of thought. Third, as Frenkel has pointed out, with gradualism inflation may increase rather than decrease. Day-to-day pressures favor spending and bailing out existing import-substituting industries and discourage taxation and dependence on the always-difficult-to-predict new exports. As Alfred Kahn (1979), the architect of U.S. airline deregulation, and Albert Hirschman (1965) have pointed out, new interests favoring the status quo are created at every step. At the same time, support for the government and its new directions is dissipated during initial periods of inaction. Both the Chilean and Argentine experience provide evidence for these phenomena. In Chile, the military government decided to take a gradual approach to inflation fighting until 1975, when the decline in the price of copper and in government revenue forced an anti-inflationary program and a sharp cut in imports, leading to a deep recession. In Argentina, inflation was stuck at about 150 percent for three years while various measures were tried to avoid costs of further stabilization, resulting in slow growth of output for three years and a loss of support for liberalization, although liberalization actually had not occurred.

NOTES

1. (Deficit/GDP)/(base/GDP) = potential change in base/base = potential growth in money stock, assuming a constant money multiplier. An increase in the base may lower the money multiplier, increasing the growth in the money stock if households shift from currency and demand deposits to interest-bearing deposits with lower reserve requirements. In addition to assuming a constant money multiplier, the formula ignores the effect of income growth, which is of second order in inflations of 100 percent a year. The formula refers to potential growth, since loss of international reserves may offset the rise in domestic credit.

2. The foreign debt would have had to rise from US$20 billion to US$40 billion in 1981 to continue the doubling. Further, much of the rise would have been necessary simply to cover debt service, which was rising sharply because of increases in the London interbank offered rate (LIBOR).

3. The only escape from this dilemma is if expectations of inflation are decreasing sharply. Then, prevailing interest rates will not be so far above those on existing government debt, and cuts in reserve requirements can be used to satisfy the growing demand for real money without a loss of international reserves—again, as the monetary approach would predict.

4. An elasticity of 0.85 would imply that the prices of tradables relative to those of home goods rise by 20 percent of the devaluation, assuming that the respective weights are 0.2 and 0.8 in the price index and that import and export prices move proportionately to the devaluation. Thus, a 100 percent devaluation would be necessary to raise the relative price of tradables 20 percent. Weights of 0.5 and 0.5 would imply that a 50 percent devaluation would raise tradables prices by about 21 percent relative to those of nontradables.

5. The reserve requirements could be lowered only after the Uruguayan fiscal deficit had been reduced. Further, in the Uruguayan case the cut in reserves was effective in "sterilizing" a capital inflow.

6. This result also assumes the "law of one interest rate," which is not a necessary part of the monetary approach but which seems to be borne out by the country experiences, although only Blejer (1982) has made a formal test. The relevant expected rate of devaluation may exceed the prefixed schedule, especially if macroeconomic policies are inconsistent. It also will exceed the actual or lagged inflation rate, at least until either the devaluation takes place or the output and price changes restore the current accounts to sustainable levels.

REFERENCES

Blejer, Mario I. 1982. "Interest Rate Differentials and Exchange Risk: Recent Argentine Experience." IMF Staff Papers, vol. 29, no. 2 (June), pp. 270-79.

Borts, George, and James A. Hanson. 1979. "The Monetary Approach to the Balance of Payments with Empirical Application to the Case of Panama." In Jere R. Behrman and James A. Hanson, eds., Short-Term Macroeconomic Policy in Latin America. Cambridge, Mass.: Ballinger/National Bureau of Economic Research.

Hanson, James A. 1982. "Inflation and Imported Input Prices in Some Inflationary Latin American Economies." Washington, D.C.: Industry Department, World Bank. Restricted circulation.

Hirschman, A. O. 1965. The Strategy of Economic Development. New Haven, Conn.: Yale University Press.

Kahn, Alfred. 1979. "Applications of Economics to an Imperfect World." American Economic Review, vol. 69, no. 2 (May), pp. 1-13.

Mathieson, Donald J. 1981. "Inflation, Interest Rates, and the Balance of Payments during a Financial Reform: The Case of Argentina." IMF Departmental Memorandum DM-81/47. Washington, D.C.: IMF Research Department. Revised in World Development, vol. 10, no. 9 (1982), pp. 813-27.

8

Commentary on Evaluation and Experience

Contributors to this chapter address recurrent issues that have emerged in the discussion of the monetary approach, issues that are identified for the reader by a set of subject headings made standard throughout the chapter. The analysis is from a regional perspective; it takes up the direction set in the last section of chapter 4 and followed in chapters 5-7.

RUDIGER DORNBUSCH

First I will offer an evaluation of the theoretical framework of the monetary approach, as characterized in Mario Blejer's paper [see chapter 1], take up two key problems with the approach, and propose an alternative to it. In my remaining remarks I will isolate four specific issues for comment—the exchange rate and the current account, the possibilities of devaluation, asset prices, and the sequence for economic liberalization—and make a concluding statement.

On the Monetary Approach and Its Applications

Mario Blejer has given us what sounds like a very eclectic perspective on economic stabilization policy in Latin America. What I want to do in this section of my remarks is to take his paper, isolate statements out of context, and piece them together to see what his paper tells us as a view of the world. Then I will ask if that is a reasonable presentation of a policy approach, argue why I think it may not be, evaluate the substantive questions surrounding what I see as the two key problems of the Southern Cone stabilization policies, and propose alternative policies.

Let me go through Mario's paper to isolate one question that must be addressed at the very beginning of any consideration of the monetary approach. In the first section of the paper we are told that a central tenet of the approach is that the overall balance of payments largely reflects monetary forces in the economy. I think that Mario, I, and everyone else here will agree that he really does not mean that. What he means is that the monetary approach is a way of looking at all the disturbances in the economy as they affect the balance of payments interpreted through their effects on the demand and supply for money.

Suppose that a firm has just discovered an oil well. That is hardly a monetary disturbance, except in how it affects money demand or money supply. So there can be no disagreement that the monetary approach is at best a way of filtering all the real and financial disturbances in their impact on the balance of payments. This is an important realization because the next question is whether the monetary approach also has a model of how all the real and financial disturbances interact in a general equilibrium framework. I find myself repeatedly saying that the monetary approach does in fact have a general equilibrium model, and that its general equilibrium model is dead wrong.

My first point, then, is that the monetary approach is a filter. It needs a supplementary general equilibrium model, and without such a model the approach will not be able to say what the discovery of an oil well—or anything else—will do to the balance of payments.

In this same opening section of the paper we are told that the monetary approach is a very eclectic framework. Mario, I think, leans over further than he would want when he says of the monetary approach that "in no way is it restricted to a specific set of assumptions." If we took that as literally as it is said, it would mean that the monetary approach as a scientific methodology must be totally empty. If it has no particular conjectures, then is cannot exclude any phenomena or the relevance of any variables—it is consistent with anything under God's sun. I think this characterization is exactly the opposite of the monetary approach. The monetary approach is a very specific, sometimes very useful, view of policy, with a quite narrow conjecture about how the world works. That conjecture may be true and it may not be. But I do think that what Mario asserts is exactly what the monetary approach is not. It is not a general, broadly eclectic framework in which anything possible can happen. I believe it is a much narrower macroeconomic model.

It is in the discussion of what Mario characterizes as the second central tenet of the monetary approach that we come to the crux of the approach. How do monetary disturbances—and these are the disturbances that are primarily analyzed here—how do they translate into an impact on the economy and on the balance of payments? I read the sentence out of context: "Equilibrium in the money market is attained by changes in the nominal money supply or the price level, or by a combination of both."

Now Mario is quite right if he says after my analysis that in the paper he repeatedly notes changes in output. But I would say that this emphasis on output changes was added almost as an afterthought in proofreading the paper. The basic view of the monetary approach really is that money, when it contracts, either goes through the balance of payments to come back or goes into prices; it does not predominantly go into a contraction of employment and output. That is perhaps the most serious issue—whether money works directly (and reasonably fast) primarily on prices, or whether it works primarily on output (and with endless slowness on prices). Surely that must be where the framework in its predictions is, first, very important for stabilization policy and, second, where the deciding issue really must lie.

There are subsequent statements to the same effect. In the section of the paper about the short-run effects of the approach, Mario says that "the effects of monetary disequilibrium will fall more heavily on the domestic price level and less on the balance of payments the lower is the degree of commodity and capital mobility." Again I would differ with him and say that the effects will fall more heavily on output rather than on prices.

My second problem, therefore, is with the implicit assumption of the monetary approach that output is a relatively minor channel—or perhaps relatively less systematic channel—through which monetary disturbances work. That view would set the approach very much at variance with another model, which says that, in the short run, prices are determined by cost and that disturbances in financial markets primarily go into output. If this second view is correct, there is an entirely different set of policies that should be looked at, not monetary policies but incomes policies. I will return to this issue.

I have a bit more discussion of the paper. In the section on the implementation of economic policy, there is an interesting point made about the extraordinary experience in Latin America, where the capital account has so dominant a role in the economy. Mario notes a puzzle. In the presence of domestic profit opportunities, there are capital inflows that lead to growth in high-powered money clashing with an unchanged real money demand such that inflation is created.

I will come back, in my discussion of interpretations of the high real interest rates, to the point that this phenomenon certainly is compatible with the monetary approach. Quite the contrary of what Mario says, it does not present a paradox.

The conclusions that Mario reaches in the last section of his paper are two. First, he notes that recessions are not part of the narrow viewpoint of the monetary approach (and I am not sure whether the monetary approach has much to say about them); second, that the Latin American stabilization policies do not offer a testing ground for the monetary approach (and Mario does not sharply delineate in what way the Latin American experience does not). But I interpret the gist of the paper to say, first, that the policies one would pursue under the approach were in fact not pursued rigidly, particularly in respect to domestic credit policy; second, that subsidiary policies were being pursued that might cloud the picture; and third, that attention must be paid to the oligopolistic nature of the markets, both the capital and trade markets. Oligopoly may have prevented substantial price discipline.

On Mario's second conclusion, if the Latin American experience is not a testing ground of the monetary approach, then we really should be worried what experience might be. All I can say is that the Southern Cone surely was a testing ground for a particular conception of monetary policy—namely, that financial discipline together with exchange rate discipline and the reliance on substantial international price connections should work well as a stabilization program. This is what I gather was behind the Chilean and the Argentine policies. Whether we call that conception of policy the monetary approach or whether we can call it the gist of University of Chicago macroeconomics—as we all learned it, and as every one of my classmates and myself certainly saw the way the world worked in 1971—I think it surely was being pursued there.

I am happy not to call all that the monetary approach, but I certainly think that it is a view of how the economy hangs together, and that it was being tested. And now we perhaps find that this view was really entirely erroneous.

Let me attempt a different way of looking at Mario's paper, extracting two central problems for discussion. What are the two key things that puzzle us as we look at these stabilization policies? Of course, there are an infinite number of things that are puzzling. But if we had to focus, I think there are two that stand out—first, the extraordinarily high real interest rates and, second, the substantial real appreciation of the exchange rate. Of the high real interest rates, we must ask where they come from, because they are so outlandish. If a real interest rate is 45 percent and remains so for more than a year, one must wonder how the economy can possibly be left intact. Of the substantial real appreciation of the exchange rate occurring in the process of stabilization, we must ask if that is an equilibrium path of the exchange rate or if it is an overvaluation and, if the latter, where the overvaluation might be coming from.

After discussing these puzzles, and before my final comments on several other issues, I want to address how things could have been done differently. There I return to an alternative model. One model says money works and that price discipline is there to help one; the other says that price discipline cannot be much relied on and that, if the latter is so, one must use direct controls.

High real interest rates. Let me make some fairly technical points about the high real interest rates. In 1981 in Chile the real interest rate was 45 percent on thirty-day commercial loans. That is the annual average, and it is by far higher—by a factor of two or three—than what we have seen in most industrialized countries. So we can agree that it was unusually high, and that it had been high in previous years. It has been high in Argentina; in Brazil it has been as high and higher.

There are a number of possible explanations. The first says that the real interest rate is high because there is anticipated currency devaluation. People think in the next month there will be a 10 percent probability of a 30 percent depreciation; therefore, people with domestic currency loans to offer require a 3 percent risk premium for the coming month, which annualized gives a 45 percent real interest rate. Since these numbers were made up to give a reasonable Chilean expectation, there is directly an easy answer. It is all expected depreciation.

But if one accepts this story, one would not think that every day has the same probability of a depreciation. One day things look really fierce; some days things look better. One would want to ask whether fluctuations in the real interest rate, or in what is now thought of as expected depreciation, really correspond with the events. There has been work done by Graciela Kaminsky (1982) for the Argentine case, and that work has cast some doubt on the hypothesis of expected depreciation.

The second explanation is that it is not expected depreciation that sets the interest rate high but, perhaps in addition, a risk premium. If there is variability in the anticipated real exchange rate, then in any portfolio model there would be a risk premium, and the risk premium depends on the relative supply of domestic assets—domestic-currency outside assets relative to other assets.

In a country where there is substantial budget financing by domestic debt and where, in fact, debt finance or a shift toward debt finance is a focal part of the policies, one expects substantial increases in the debt-to-net-worth ratio and from that an increase in the risk premium. If the variability of the real exchange rate is high and if risk aversion is large, there is practically no bound on the risk premium one can calculate from that. One really will not be able to separate, when all is said and done, what part of the increase is attributable to expected depreciation and what part to the level and the changes in the risk premium. But I do want to draw attention to the risk premium as an explanation separate from anticipated depreciation.

A third possibility is that interest rates are high because of capital controls. Suppose there are several assets: money, real capital, domestic debt, and foreign debt (access to the last being restricted by controls on borrowing). It is readily shown that, if constraints on capital inflows are effective, the value of the stock market will be less and home bond rates will be higher than under a regime of free capital flows. Liberalizing capital flows will produce a fall in lending rates and an increase in the stock market. Because this happens, real money demand increases. We therefore expect that liberalizing the capital account leads to noninflationary money expansion.

I come back to my earlier remark regarding Mario's thought that capital inflows attracted by profitability would not be explainable in the framework of the monetary approach. If the yield on capital inflows falls and the stock market booms, money demand would increase. So liberalization of the capital account does raise money demand.

Capital account controls, then, would certainly be an important potential explanation for the behavior of domestic interest rates. What one must be careful to do is not try to have only one of these explanations. What is likely, if one takes the Chilean case, is that one starts with capital controls as the important restriction, and it is quite possible in the initial phases that domestic interest rates are high because it has been very profitable in the denationalization process to buy up assets that were underpriced. So real interest rates are high basically from the financial profitability of capital or from the lower levels of saving. But then in the transition process (as the current account is deteriorating and capital controls are being liberalized), other things being equal, one would expect to see declining yields. What in fact happens is that over time expectations of devaluation and growing risk premiums come into play. So it is entirely possible that for a protracted period one has high real interest rates—at first because of capital controls, and then because of increasingly high risk premiums and anticipated depreciation.

The real interest rates have been so high that one wonders what happens to an economy in which this process is at work. One view of the effects relies on expected depreciation. Nominal interest rates are high at home if the exchange rate is anticipated to depreciate. The real interest rate is really not high—ex post it is, ex ante it is not. Therefore, one should not expect that there will be ruinous effects on domestic investment.

One must be very careful with that view because of the immediate first objection to it. If people anticipate depreciation and if, in fact, they anticipate real depreciation, then there will be different real interest rates for the traded goods sector and for the home goods sector. For the home goods sector the real interest rate is high because there is anticipation of real depreciation. Therefore, for the construction sector or the like, policies that allow real interest rates to be high would certainly be harmful.

But there is another way in which it is important to think of the link between real interest rates—realized real interest rates—and investment, and it is the following. Different businesses have different gestation periods. Firms produce output; they will sell it tomorrow, but they will have current outlays for labor, materials, and the like. So the firms, in their pricing, have to look at the present value of the prices at which they sell, compared with the current outlays. When one works that through, one gets a relationship between the real interest rate, the real wage, and the profitability of firms, the real interest rate now being the real interest rate at which firms finance themselves with the banks: $x = 1/(1+r)wa$, where x is the profit rate, r is the financial real interest rate, w is the real wage, and a is the union labor requirement, or the converse of productivity. What this says is that, one for one, a rise in the real interest rate reduces the profitability of firms unless there is an offsetting cut in real wages or a gain in productivity. So there is a direct link between the real interest rates that banks charge, for whatever reason, and the profitability of firms. The profitability of firms, of course, will affect investment—either because firms look ahead to the projects they can finance, or directly because of liquidity constraints.

This strikes me as the important fact of high real interest rates—the setting apart of bondholders on one side and operating firms on the other. Dagnino Pastore can comment on the Argentine case [see chapter 3, comments in chapter 4, and below], where this has been extraordinary, but I would think that in Chile this also must have been important.

I have talked about the real interest rate. It has been extraordinarily high. There are several reasons, but none of them leaves one very comfortable that the real rate has been just a market price that is so high because people are so madly wanting to invest. Quite the contrary, what may well be at issue is that the economy is slowly being decapitalized by an important disequilibrium or by an important risk premium that possibly is avoidable. The question is whether there is something one could do to avoid these consequences.

High real exchange rates. The next puzzle is the real exchange rate and how it is possible for it to have been appreciating so much, whether in Chile or in Argentina.

The first explanation is to say that productivity growth was so high that the Balassa effect was at work. In countries where productivity growth has been as high, the real exchange rate has appreciated, and this is simply a reflection of gaining external competitiveness. That is one of the hypotheses that Harberger has advanced [see his comments below]. It really is an ingenious one—who can argue with it?

If one takes that view, then one says that the real exchange rate has been appreciating and that that has been the equilibrium path. But if one considers real wages, one finds that the real wage, too, has been rising. One can even make a plausible case that the gain in real wages in a rough way corresponds to the gain in the real exchange rate and, therefore, that one is observing equilibrium real appreciation. I think it is very hard to reject that view.

Of course, one also can proceed on a sector-by-sector basis and possibly find different evidence. So here it is important to bear in mind that whenever the real exchange rate goes up significantly it does not necessarily mean that there is overvaluation.

The second possible explanation is that trade liberalization has changed the equilibrium real exchange rate. Taking the ratio of price indexes, one knows from trade theory that when tariffs are changed, equilibrium relative prices will change. One then must ask whether there is any presumption that a particular calculated real exchange rate one looks at should appreciate under liberalization.

On examining that question, one finds two effects. On the one hand, trade liberalization directly reduces the prices of importables relative to home goods, and to that extent it directly leads to real appreciation. On the other hand, there is an effect on export prices, which tend to fall relative to home goods prices. One then must ask whether the share of importables in traded goods is larger or smaller than some well-defined ratio of elasticities. Calculating these expressions, one finds that the case for appreciation becomes an extremely implausible explanation. The only way that case can work is if importables and home goods are extremely poor substitutes. So this second interpretation—that real exchange rate appreciation is not a disequilibrium but rather a response to trade liberalization—is theoretically plausible, but when one works out the numbers it is doubtful.

The third possible explanation is that real appreciation is a consequence of macroeconomic inertia and expectations—that, because of contracts affected by expectations about inflation and exchange rate policy, the growth rate of wages cannot be made to decline fast enough relative to the managed prices of traded goods. Therefore, the real exchange rate appreciates. That view, of course, is entirely obvious the moment one thinks of wage indexation. Vittorio Corbo has certainly made that point with force [see his comments in chapter 4 and below]— that any country that has backward indexation will have real appreciation mechanically in the process of exchange rate pegging. I take that to be an overwhelmingly persuasive explanation for the behavior of the real exchange rate.

The last possibility, of course, is the one that Mario favors. In his concluding remarks, he says that policies in the Southern Cone have not really been consistent with the model. The policies have on occasion been substantially expansionary, and then what one should expect is indeed real appreciation because the prices of home goods would tend to be rising relative to those of traded goods. But that, I take it, is inconsistent with the rapidly growing unemployment in these countries.

I have talked about the real interest rate and the real exchange rate. Both have shown large changes in the Southern Cone. We are accustomed to living in an environment where real economic variables do not move very much. When they move by 40 percent, we are puzzled. One explanation that is effective is to say that such movement reflects equilibrium because there have been disturbances in markets: it is a plain anticipated inflationary fact, productivity growth, or the like. However, when all is said and done, one cannot be assured that the real interest rate is _not_ excessively high, and one must certainly also assume that the real exchange rate is grossly overvalued. If these results are almost systematic outcomes of the stabilization programs, then one should look for alternative policies. But why should these be almost systematic outcomes? I figure the explanation must be that wages are substantially stickier than has been thought; that they can be sticky for years and years; and that the longer they are sticky the more they are correct—because the exchange rate will become so overvalued that in the end it has to be devalued, and then all the wage earners in retrospect will have done the right thing. So there may well be an expectational vengeance in these programs based on the monetary approach that makes the real exchange rate and the real interest rate high.

On Alternative Policies

How does one go about finding an alternative? If one believes that the behavior of wages is substantially the problem that stands in the way of economic stabilization—and that means that prices are not substantially flexible, governed not by international discipline but rather by the behavior of wages—then one looks for a three-part program (see Dornbusch 1982).

First, one would accept that what was done with the exchange rate in these countries was exactly right, because if stabilization is wanted, people must be given the expectation of stabilization—therefore, there should be targeted exchange rates. But, of course, what should be done is to sell forward, not to talk forward. The big difference between the success in Portugal in 1977—to which few here have given credit but which was a stabilization program that worked extremely well with very little social cost—and the experience in Argentina and Chile is that the Portuguese opened a forward market and told people that anyone who wanted to could buy as much foreign currency as he wanted. And to the protestations of the International Monetary Fund, the Portuguese managed happily for a year and managed in the process to stabilize the real wage with a cut of 15 percent. Why? Because nobody thought that a major outburst of inflation was ahead.

So fixing the forward rate, I think, is an essential part of stabilization policy because then one avoids the risk premiums; the high real interest rate; the adverse effects on investment and productivity; and all the problems that in the fourth year of stabilization programs become a vengeance because the economy cannot sustain the real wages that people want to have.

The second part of an alternative program, once the forward rate has been fixed, is to guarantee that one can live with the fixed forward rate. Surely this guarantee must come from appropriate incomes policy.

The third part is to use the public sector, after sanitation of public sector prices, to fix public sector prices—that is, to prefix public sector prices to give substantial support to the belief that inflation stabilization is being implemented.

If this program stands with any consistency—and there is no reason why it should not—then the result would be direct inflation stabilization, much more cheaply than could be had talking forward, without the large recession that comes whenever the economy is randomly attacked by substantially reducing money growth to see what happens.

In sum, I think there are two views of how the economy works. One is to say that if domestic credit contracts, sooner or later—and presumably very shortly—stabilization will be achieved. There is absolutely no doubt that fiscal and credit stabilization must be undertaken to reduce long-run inflation, but for the dynamics that approach is substantially wrong. I think all the evidence we have for the dynamics is that an economy gets by relatively cheaply with a consistent program, fixing the forward rate, incomes policy, and public sector prices. What is wrong with this policy mix? Nothing, except that it may worry policymakers while it is implemented because they have thrown all the keys away. But that is precisely the reason why the public might believe that the economy is in fact stabilizing.

With the foregoing in mind, I will direct my remaining remarks to four issues that have been raised in the discussion. I can afford to be brief because, as Jacob Frenkel [chapter 2] and Simón Teitel [chapter 6] have instructed, a certain humility suits us. I will make four rather narrow, technical points—with general reference to the Chilean experience.

On the Real Exchange Rate and the Current Account

My first remark concerns the real exchange rate and the current account. The suggestion is that, in the Chilean case, liberalization of the capital account should have required—or should explain—real appreciation. But the fiscal stabilization should also have required a real depreciation. One must weigh the two: the fiscal stabilization by itself to achieve full employment would have required a real depreciation; the capital account liberalization, a real appreciation. The two together would have required a constant real exchange rate.

Starting with 1976, one must give the Chilean fiscal stabilization some credit. I actually am concerned about the real exchange rate from 1965 to 1980. Surely, if real government spending is cut, as has happened, and taxes are increased, there has to be some effect on the equilibrium real exchange rate. The government cannot be so unimportant, or we would not worry so much about it.

On Devaluation

The second remark concerns the possibilities for a devaluation. It is agreed, I think, that when a tariff is imposed relative prices will change, that when a tax is imposed relative prices will change. So it must be possible that relative prices can change. What, then, is that story that a devaluation in a circumstance where relative prices are wrong should not be an important part of getting back to equilibrium? Of course, if there is wage indexation, devaluation is the very last thing one would want to do because it would do absolutely nothing.

There are two totally separate issues here. The first is indexation, which makes nominal exchange rate policies ineffective. The second is whether, barring indexation, equilibrium relative prices can be moved. Surely they can move—for one example, the Japanese real exchange rate in manufacturing has changed 60 percent in 1972-82.

On Asset Prices

The third set of remarks concerns the matter of asset prices and the suggestion that there was an asset price "bubble" in the case of Chile. [See also discussion by Rolf Lüders and Roberto Zahler (chapter 4), Simón Teitel (chapter 6), and John Williamson, Vittorio Corbo, and Arnold Harberger (below).] I think that is an important direction for analysis, particularly when the issue is liberalizing the capital account. What may well have happened in Chile is the following. Expectations about capital gains on assets made real interest rates (deflated by asset prices) look small, financed the actual capital gains, drove up wealth (and therefore consumption), and therefore exacted relatively little cost for the fiscal and trade stabilization.

If it is a bubble in the asset market that made the other policies have so little cost, one really has to worry when the bubble will burst. Now that the bubble idea has entered the debate, it may well explain why real growth was so extraordinarily high for so long. Surely, that is the surprising thing about Chile, and nothing is better than an asset market bubble to help explain events.

I am a bit concerned when it is suggested that when a bubble occurs it should be allowed to burst. Maybe it is a good idea for some banks to crack and for some companies to go bankrupt. Surely if there is a bubble, if assets are substantially overvalued, there must be a persuasive case for government intervention to engineer a soft landing. The case of Brazil should warn anyone of what happens when a crash is allowed to happen. Investments will not come back for a very long time. And Chile is certainly the last country one can think of for which lower investment is wanted.

One final remark on the bubble. We worry about whether capital inflows finance capital gains or whether they finance investment in prospective operating profits. It may well be the case that in Chile it was capital gains that were financed. I would add, too, that if there is an expectation of collapse, then of course the capital gains rate has to be much higher. The overvaluation has to go much further to compensate people for the possibility of a crash. Again, that may well be the case.

On the Sequence of Economic Liberalization

The fourth set of remarks concerns the proper sequence of liberalization. I want to offer some thoughts on a sequence of liberalization that is the reverse of the one some have recommended here. [See recommendations by Jacob Frenkel, chapter 2, and Guillermo Calvo, below; for further discussion of the issue, see Roberto Zahler, chapter 4, James Hanson, chapter 7, and Arturo Meyer, Jaime DeMelo, and Krishna Challa, below.]

Mr. Lüders' remarks [chapter 4], viewed in the right light, suggest that liberalizing the capital account last may well lead to circumstances that promote domestic oligopoly in capital markets. Such oligopoly may create distortions far outweighing the benefits of trade liberalization. If a small group can get access to the international capital market and to the real assets, liberalizing the capital account after the trade account is probably the last thing one would want to do, not only because it redistributes wealth frivolously but also because it leads to inefficient resource allocation by creating domestic oligopolies that may persist after the capital account does become liberalized. So, following that argument, one would want to start the process with liberalization of the domestic capital market and the capital account.

But it is argued that the moment one does that, of course, one gets the problem of high domestic real interest rates, and with capital inflows there may be exchange overvaluation.

What, then, to do about trade balance liberalization? I think the right answer is to have a fixed exchange rate on current account and to have a flexible exchange rate on capital account. Start with a flexible capital account rate. Then over time implement the properly sequenced trade liberalization. Last, unify the exchange rate. That eliminates much of the extreme overdeterminacy that may well happen on the way.

The criticism may arise that such a two-tier system will cause overinvoicing. But surely nothing can be less relevant as an observation, considering the economies in question.

Concluding Statement

In conclusion, and as a possible postscript to the symposium, I would add a final remark. The monetary approach has been represented as a broad perspective, and it has been vigorously asserted by several participants that the approach is not limited to any specific assumptions about the working of the economy and yet is not entirely empty as a scientific methodology. Surely the proponents of the monetary approach owe us an explanation of that puzzle. Specifically, which are the propositions of the monetary approach that are testable but are not identities that, of course, are common to any approach?

Unless proponents of the monetary approach can identify events or consequences inconsistent with their theory, they have unearthed either basic, incontestable truth or a vacuum. My impression is that, in the retreat from the model of the early 1970s, surviving monetarists confuse accounting identities with economic theories.

GUILLERMO A. CALVO

I will repeat some of the points I made earlier [see chapter 4], concentrating on policy recommendations. I agree completely with Jacob Frenkel [chapter 2] and James Hanson [chapter 7] that one has to be very modest, given the little knowledge—empirical knowledge—that we have. My remarks will concern various aspects of the functioning of a fixed exchange rate system.

On Devaluation

It seems that the limited empirical results indicate, and casual empiricisim also affirms, that there is little effect in real terms associated with devaluation. Yet there is still some effect, and I believe that there may be cases in which this effect can be important. One must take great care and caution with those empirical results because it can be proven in a formal way that, if there is an economic system where prices are not perfectly flexible but are set by individuals, rational individuals, who try to forecast the future, and if everybody in the economy expects a devaluation in the future, then the prices that can increase, in the sense that they are not subject to brisk international competition, will start to increase. One does not have to elaborate much to see the plausibility of that conclusion. Therefore, one may observe an economy in which there is appreciation of the real exchange rate and then a devaluation that works simply because people have already anticipated the devaluation. In this case devaluation works, albeit for the wrong reasons, because it already has been taken into account.

On the Real Interest Rate

The same kind of reasoning applies, or can be used, to explain the reason that the real interest rate is high. Because everybody expects a devaluation, the nominal interest rate is high; if the devaluation does not happen, then in the interim the real interest rate is high. When the devaluation occurs, the real interest rate goes down. But that does not mean that a devaluation by itself lowers the real interest rate. It is precisely the expectation that a devaluation will occur that raises the real interest rate in the first place.

One should be aware of those anticipatory effects because they may be important and may mislead the observer to think that devaluation in itself is effective.

On the Flexibility of Policy

It is much easier to attack another's position than one's own, so let me start in that way. Several points have been made that I would like to discuss. One is the issue of flexibility. It has been mentioned at several junctures that one should have flexible policies, but also that flexibility is perhaps the basis of some of the apparent implementation errors in the Southern Cone. And José María Dagnino Pastore [see his second set of comments in chapter 4] said that he was not clear why flexibility is being called for, or what the role of flexibility might be within the approach we are examining. I tend to agree with him in the sense that one must be careful with the issue of flexibility because there one confronts the issue of rules versus discretion. I presume that by "flexibility" is meant rules, very clear rules, that are contingent on the state of nature in the sense that, if there is a change, all understand that the change happens because something that is objective and understood by all has also changed. But if flexibility is interpreted as doing whatever is necessary when the time comes, that is very dangerous. We know that, if there is any rationality in the market, one simply confuses everyone by such action because no one will know what one is going to do. This kind of flexibility may create much confusion, and I do not think there is reason to expect that it will help in policymaking.

I believe that there is some value in flexibility, but one has to be very explicit about the meaning of the term. An advantage of the fixed exchange rate system is that it is a very simple rule. The issue is not that it is the only rule, but that it is a very simple one.

On the Sequence of Economic Liberalization

Rudiger Dornbusch [see preceding comments] has proposed a two-tier, double exchange rate system of one exchange rate for capital flows and another exchange rate for the trade balance operation. [See also José María Dagnino Pastore's second set of comments in chapter 4.] One also has to be very careful with such a proposal. I do not think much is known about this system theoretically, and the little that is known leads one to suspect that there may be problems with it.

It can be shown in a very simple model that—if there is a financial exchange rate, capital mobility, and a commercial rate used to clear the commodity market or the trade balance—the financial rate may be undetermined; but when it is determined, it may become quite volatile, quite sensitive to shocks in money supply. The small elasticity of the demand for money with respect to the interest rate—a feature, I believe, in some of the Southern Cone economies, given the relatively controlled banking system—may make the financial rate even more volatile.

My own suggestion about the optimal sequence of economic liberalization, with which most participants seem to agree, is that, if one has the choice, it is better to liberalize the trade account—to undertake trade liberalization—first and then to go on with the financial measures. Why would I endorse such a sequence? Because, as the experience of the Southern Cone attests, problems with appreciation of the real exchange rate have occurred that were not intended and that made the basic liberalization program more difficult. So long as control over the financial part of the system allows control of the price level in a tighter way, I would endorse not opening up the economy to capital mobility. That is the basic, and very simple reason that I recommend liberalization of trade first and then liberalization of the financial part of the system.

There is a twist here that I would emphasize, however, a sequence within liberalization of the financial sector that I mentioned in my earlier remarks [see chapter 4]. I believe that, leaving aside the distributional factors mentioned by Rudiger Dornbusch, I would tend first to open up capital mobility and then to decontrol the banking system. The reason again is very simple. Capital mobility in principle is a good thing. Not having it creates a distortion—the domestic economy is not allowed to take advantage of the credit provided by the rest of the world.

But if the banking system has already been decontrolled, capital mobility invites very short-term capital into the economy, given the decontrol of the interest rate in these countries and the relative control in other countries such as the United States. Capital comes in and out of the economy depending on the feeling of investors about potential capital controls—or controls to capital mobility, nationalization, and all kinds of things that have nothing to do with fundamental economic considerations. The economy, in effect, is subjected to rather erratic demand, because capital moves very quickly and, also, according to expectations that policymakers cannot control. From a formal point of view, something stochastic is added to the usual demand for money function. In any model that may be considered (for instance, a model that Carlos Rodríguez and I worked on for currency substitution), if there is a change in the composition of money demand and people move away from domestic money to foreign money, there is a transition in which the real exchange rate is affected. That is the effect that is undesirable—changes in the real exchange rate that are provoked by these kinds of uncertainty. Maybe from a purely economic point of view, such variability is a good idea, but the experience in the Southern Cone quite clearly shows that these kinds of fluctuation are not politically acceptable. So a good idea may have to be abandoned because of fluctuations that actually have very little to do with the basic program.

For these reasons, I would be very cautious in decontrolling the banking system in the first stages of the program. Decontrol in itself is a good idea—we know from basic economics that, in principle, the fewer distortions, leaving aside the "second-best" problems, the better. But there are transitional problems that should not be too quickly discounted.

On the Fixed Exchange Rate and Exchange Insurance

Let me mention two final points. I am not addressing the basic issue of whether a flexible or a fixed exchange rate system is wanted. I do not have an answer to that. But I can see problems, lots of problems, with a fixed exchange rate system. In a way it is like setting up a commercial bank. The high-powered money becomes like deposits of the bank. In effect, what the monetary authorities are saying is that they will be ready, if there is capital mobility, to exchange foreign money reserves for the deposits on call. We know from experience all over the world that this system has been tricky when applied in the absence of deposit insurance. Without some kind of exchange rate insurance, the fixed exchange rate may become an unpredictable system. I am not saying that this is a serious problem, but it is something that merits close attention.

The other problem with a fixed exchange rate system is the length of time the exchange rate is fixed. When a government administration comes to power and says there will now be a fixed exchange rate, at most what is meant is that the rate will stay fixed for as long as a particular minister of economics is in power. And that, as we have seen, can be for not very long.

JOHN WILLIAMSON

I wish to range over a variety of the topics that have emerged in this symposium: asset prices, the application of a "monetary approach" to policy, capital inflows, the sequence of liberalization, and exchange rate policy.

On Asset Prices

Of the two most revealing insights that I have obtained from this symposium, the first relates to what seems to be general agreement that there has been a big bubble in asset prices in Chile. I am still having some difficulty understanding how this explains the high real interest rates that one observes there in May 1982. My previous view of the relationship between asset prices and interest rates goes in the opposite direction: when real interest rates are high, I expect asset prices to be low. Now I am told that exogenously high real asset prices are causing high real interest rates, and I am trying to work out whether that is consistent.

I also wonder why the asset price bubble did not create more of an incentive than it appears to have done to expand the supply of real assets by an increase in the level of real investment. I guess there was some of that in real estate, but not in the economy as a whole.

On the Monetary Approach and Its Applications

My second revelation is that Arnold Harberger thinks that the Southern Cone countries have not made many "gross mistakes" in the last few years [see his comments below], and this I do find rather extraordinary. I look at Argentina in mid-1982, trying to abstract from my own British nationality, and I wonder just what the economy would look like if there had been a lot of gross mistakes. There is a very high rate of inflation once again; there is an incipient financial crisis; there is a severe recession.

One looks at Chile, and there are problems there as well. There appears to be general agreement that the real exchange rate is considerably overvalued. There also appears to be a strong view that a nominal devaluation would not do much about the overvaluation—a sure condemnation of where policy has got to. There is a 19 percent unemployment rate. Unless I am mistaken, if one extrapolates the trend rate of growth of Chile in the 1960s, one still obtains a level of something like 10 or 20 percent above where the Chilean economy is now, despite the years of rapid growth in the late 1970s. There is again the problem of high real interest rates, which presumably is threatening the viability of productive enterprises. There is the problem of unwinding the asset price bubble.

Unfortunately, I have not learned enough about Uruguay at this symposium to know whether closer acquaintance would suggest that there are similar problems there. But my reading of this record is that the Southern Cone is not a great economic success story. Even admitting that there are not many very successful economies around the world at the moment, I find it difficult to feel that the Southern Cone has performed above par.

I am asked: what are the "gross mistakes" that produced this situation? Let me just remark parenthetically that I am not sure if it is really worth going into whether it is monetarism or the monetary approach or just what semantic label we should stick on it, but there is a recognizable package of measures that has been applied here. The package is characterized by economic liberalization, something at least approaching laissez faire in comparison with what there has been in the past—an attempt to keep government out of markets; to avoid supply-side policies, incomes policies, and other interferences in the market mechanism; and to limit macroeconomic policy largely to the control of some supposedly critical nominal variable. In the Southern Cone, the control variable has been the exchange rate. In other countries where there have also been what I would label (perhaps too cavalierly) monetarist packages, it has generally been the money supply. The basic philosophy is that control of some particular nominal variable that is regarded as critical achieves what a government is capable of doing in the medium term, which is to get inflation under control and to keep it under control. There may be some unfortunate short-run consequences in terms of output effects and so on, but there is probably not much that can be done to reduce those effects anyway.

This type of strategy, concentrating on a part of the spectrum of potential policy variables, leads systematically to real appreciation. It does so by letting internal prices run ahead when one has the Southern Cone pattern, and it does so by a nominal appreciation when one has the U.S.-U.K. type of monetarist package, which controls the money supply.

I have great difficulty accepting that real appreciation is not a consequence of what Arnold Harberger [below] calls "monetary and wage dynamics." The only theory of inflation that I can make sense of in this context tells me that inflation is going to continue with its old inertia in the nontraded goods sector, longer than in the traded goods sector, and that this will systematically lead to a real appreciation. That is what we have seen in every case. And I do suggest that this consequence is not an accident that can be explained away by the Balassa effect, the "Sjaastad effect" [Arnold Harberger's term; see his comments below], or any other coincidence.

On Capital Inflows

It is true that capital inflow was something that sustained the real appreciation in the Southern Cone. Without the capital inflow, the overvaluation could not have gone on that long; something would have had to give. So the capital inflow permitted the perpetuation of the overvaluation. But that does not imply that the capital inflow is necessarily desirable. One has to ask what happened to these capital inflows. What I have gathered from this symposium is that in Chile the capital inflow financed an asset price bubble, which then made the people who normally save feel sufficiently rich that they did not have to save, and consequently domestic saving fell to very low levels. The capital inflow therefore replaced saving rather than increased investment. In Argentina, capital inflows financed a government deficit, and I perhaps rather naturally take a somewhat jaundiced view of some of the purposes for which the government deficit was used. But certainly the capital inflow to Argentina built up a situation that was unsustainable.

On the Sequence of Economic Liberalization

The relation between capital inflows and real appreciation leads me on to doubts about capital market liberalization and the way in which it has been applied in the Southern Cone. I do not have similar misgivings about trade liberalization—although I might want to criticize the speed with which trade was liberalized in the Southern Cone. But I have had increasing doubt, as I have listened to what has been said, as to whether the capital market liberalization was well conceived. It is one thing to borrow from the rest of the world to finance an increase in capital formation, but a country can do that without any general capital market liberalization. Brazil does not have a liberal capital account by any stretch of the imagination, but it borrowed vast sums until international bankers decided they were not willing to lend any more. (And more of the capital inflow to Brazil found its way into capital formation than did the inflows to the Southern Cone.)

An economy does not, therefore, need capital market liberalization to benefit from the world capital market by absorbing real resources to increase investment. When capital market liberalization does become essential is when a government wants its citizens to be able to gain the benefits of portfolio diversification. But that is something that becomes important to a country that is a capital exporter, or at least is approaching a position of a balanced capital account, and not to countries that are overwhelmingly capital importers. Of course, it is true that Argentine private nationals have a lot of foreign assets. That is quite clear from the sums in José María Dagnino Pastore's paper [see chapter 3], which I think showed that about US$17 billion was borrowed, whereas there was only a current account deficit of about US$7 billion over the period. So obviously, Argentines did build up large balances overseas. In the difference of US$10 billion is presumably included, for example, a lot of the real estate that was bought up in Brazil.

I am not saying that there is no yield from such outflows, but I am questioning whether that is a particularly wise use of resources on the part of a country that is still a heavy capital-importing country. The pattern of borrowing does not appear to be explicable on the basis of the rational expectations theory—rational expectations cannot lead to bubbles, practically by definition. James Hanson points out to me that there is some debate about whether one can conceive of a "rational bubble"—a price bubble that sustains itself for a while. Although I can conceive of it being rational for certain individuals to speculate on a path that they believe to be unsustainable, I must admit that the idea of it being collectively rational to choose any trajectory other than the stable root strikes me as paradoxical. So I am not completely reassured that I am wrong in my doubts about whether capital market liberalization is a particularly sensible part of the policy package at this stage. I am not sure, however, that I would want to include this miscalculation among the gross policy errors, so let me briefly turn to what I conceive those to be.

On Alternative Policies

The alternative macroeconomic strategy that I espouse has been outlined by Rudiger Dornbusch [above]. It is a balanced policy package—not restricted to monetary policies and supportive fiscal actions nor simply to liberalizing markets, but also consciously attempting to avoid what appear to be major distortions. Among these major distortions I include prices out of line with what is sustainable in the longer run—and I certainly include overvalued real exchange rates and real interest rates that threaten the financial viability of large parts of productive industry. Thus, I would say that having allowed such inappropriate prices to arise must be considered a gross policy error.

A realistic real exchange rate is a cause to which I have had a great attachment for many years. It seems to me to be essential for the credibility of any program, and I do not believe that credibility can be bought on the cheap by forward pegging. If economic policymakers peg forward rates as something that is not seen as part of a viable package, then that commitment itself eventually becomes incredible—and even before it becomes incredible it becomes very costly indeed. Experience of those costs is not limited to the Southern Cone; we had an example of it in the United Kingdom when the pound sterling was devalued in 1967.

If the attempt to achieve a realistic real exchange rate generates accelerating inflation, which is essentially what we are told would happen if Chile were to undertake a devaluation in an attempt to change the real exchange rate, then that tells us something very important about the inconsistency of real income claims. It is necessary to face the inconsistency directly, perhaps by modifying the wage indexation formula, as happened recently in Belgium after many years of the Belgians' saying that there was no point in their devaluing because devaluation would simply be reflected in higher prices. There are circumstances in which that is true, and if so there is no point in devaluing. But at the same time, that tells one that something else must be done about the economy; one cannot simply shrug off the need for action. I would say that it is a gross error to fail to face up to the necessity of changing inconsistent real income claims in an appropriate way. To simply stick to a policy of tight money in that situation and not attempt to change real income claims is using money to suppress symptoms rather than to cure the root causes of the problem.

Let me finish with a whimper rather than a bang. I just want to comment on Jacob Frenkel's remark [see chapter 2] about the cases for and against basket pegging. The case for basket pegging is essentially, as I see it, a macroeconomic case—that it avoids the sort of problem that Chile had when it got an unintended appreciation in the real exchange rate through pegging to an inappropriate currency. The case against basket pegging is a microeconomic case, and it is there that bilateral exchange rates, which Jacob talked about, become important. Pegging to a single major "international" currency gives domestic traders access to the facilities of an international market; it gives them something to invoice in with relatively little risk; it gives the possibility of access to the forward markets between the pegged currency and the other major currencies; and so on. These are all important causes.

So I agree with Jacob that there is an ambiguous choice at the moment. Of course, I would like to see a solution in which the Special Drawing Right (SDR) of the International Monetary Fund (IMF) would be made into something that could be used as an intervention currency and a major international currency. But whether the IMF will move along those lines in its current review of the SDR, I cannot say.

VITTORIO CORBO

I would like to make three points regarding the Chilean experience: on the asset price "bubble," on the exchange rate, and on devaluation.

On Asset Prices

My first point is in response to what John Williamson has asked [above] about the asset price bubble in Chile. The bubble developed mostly in the real estate market at the moment when the real interest rate in Chile was substantially reduced (in the second half of 1979 and early 1980, when there was a decrease of around 10 or 15 points in the real interest rate). So, the bubble started with a substantial decrease in the real interest rate.

Mr. Williamson has asked why the bubble did not affect real investment—indeed, it did strongly affect real investment, in the construction sector. The expansion of the construction sector in 1981 was 16.2 percent in real terms, and that was mostly in housing, in apartment buildings, and so on. There was a general price bubble in assets, but it was much stronger in the real estate sector.

On the Real Exchange Rate

As we have discussed, the fixing of the exchange rate in Chile, when inflation was at the annual rate of 35 percent, created a sharp peso appreciation and an important initial decrease in the real interest rate. The ensuing expansion of expenditure was validated—was financed—with borrowing from the rest of the world. The initial economic expansion, which was very strong in 1979 and 1980, was fueled by this tremendous decrease in the real interest rate. This expansion even carried over to early 1981; in 1981 the Chilean growth rate was still around 5 percent.

In this way, it looked as if one could reduce inflation and raise the growth rate simultaneously: fixing the official exchange rate allowed a decrease in the domestic inflation rate; at the same time the decrease in the domestic inflation rate and the increase in capital inflows allowed a tremendous rise in the domestic growth rate. Apparently, the problem of the tradeoff between reducing inflation and the costs of such reduction in loss of output was solved here in the right way. But clearly it was solved only on borrowed time. The costs came due the moment that the cumulative loss of competitiveness became so high that the recession in the tradables-producing sector and the large current account deficit triggered a large reduction in capital inflows. Chile must face this cumulative loss of competitiveness at a time when there is a large reduction in capital inflows from the rest of the world.

So, Chile comes to a juncture where it has to adjust to a large reduction in capital inflows by raising the relative price of tradables (to gain competitiveness). If the price of nontradables were flexible downward, Chile would make this economic adjustment without paying a large cost. But the problem becomes how to recoup the competitiveness, if some of the prices of nontradables are inflexible downward, as is shown by the wage rate and the recent figures reflecting a large increase in unemployment. There is no question that there is a problem here, and we have to face it. I think that in a symposium such as this, it is important to identify some of the problems. Chile has been successful in the liberalization of the commodity market, in improving tremendously the efficiency of the public sector, and in other fields, but I think that it failed in its macroeconomic policies. In the situation of mid-1982, with 100-percent-plus backward wage indexation, it is perhaps asking too much of the market to redress a loss of competitiveness of almost 25 to 30 percent, a change needed to adjust to the substantially reduced level of capital inflows.

On Devaluation

I strongly believe that, with the same level of capital inflow, a devaluation in the Chilean economy in 1979 or 1980 would have had little relative success. Whatever effect it may have had would have been largely transitory because the economy was booming and because, to absorb the capital inflow, it was necessary to have a deterioration of the real exchange rate. Thus, devaluation would not have had much effect in 1979 or 1980, or even at the beginning of 1981, as long as capital inflows stayed at the same level (see Corbo 1981).

Devaluation in mid-1982 would have some real effect—but again, as long as wage indexation is retained, a major part of the real effect would be lost very soon. There would be some gain because in Chile in May 1982 unemployment is 20 percent and rising. Devaluation would have a real effect—a much more important one—if wage indexation were eliminated, but I could not advise devaluing before eliminating indexation.

I think that the Argentine and Chilean situations are very different, and I also would not advise making simple interpolations from one case to the other. As I mentioned earlier [see chapter 4], it is important to take measures that will be publicly perceived to be feasible and thus influence the formation of public expectations. If I were advising devaluation in Chile in mid-1982, I would think very carefully about what might happen. A large devaluation would cause large bankruptcies—especially in the construction sector, the sector that had the price bubble. The entrepreneurs in this sector had previously been told that they would be kept alive by access to loans denominated in foreign currencies and would be offered cheap, ex ante interest rates. A large devaluation now would kill the construction sector. So, one must consider this redistribution of wealth. Devaluation in Chile today would have to entail a way to control expectations—say, an initial devaluation of perhaps 30 percent, with a subsequent "tablita" of two years that would follow the evolution of domestic and international inflation.

JOSÉ MARÍA DAGNINO PASTORE

I must confess that at times I have felt that we have not been talking about the Southern Cone—I have just heard about the successes. What are the criteria for measuring success and benefits against costs? Is it a success, a five-year-long, 20 percent unemployment? Is it a success, decreasing the net international position of Argentina by US$17 billion? Is it a success, the generalized bankruptcy of a nation's business sector? To me, those are relevant measures of costs and benefits beyond intellectual cabinet exercises, and I think those are the matters to address. And in addressing them, it is very important for one to be definite and not elliptical about the results of the policies implemented in the Southern Cone.

On the Monetary Approach and Its Applications

The results I have mentioned are the consequences of a policy package. I do not think it helps very much to give a specific name to this package. But what is clear is that we have heard participants make disclaimers about the relations between policies applied and some general frameworks of economic thought—some called "global monetarism" and some called "the monetary approach." These disclaimers are not well sustained by the historical evidence. Jacob Frenkel, for instance, has said [see chapter 2] that the monetary approach is a general framework in which one can fit several macroeconomic policies, and that somebody was going to fall flat on his face if he introduced additional assumptions, such as the "law of one price," and ignored real income effects.

In my paper [chapter 3, under "Limitations and Shortcomings of the Model"], I referred to what for some time was a kind of Bible of the monetary approach (Frenkel and Johnson 1976) to show the ease with which these disclaimers have been made and criticisms of the monetary approach dismissed. It is worth giving the full passages from Frenkel and Johnson here. The criticism of the assumption that real income is always at the full employment level was classified as "a red herring across the trail of scientific study and understanding" (Frenkel and Johnson 1976, p. 24). Then on the next page, there is a statement saying

> That the monetary approach largely assumes a fully employed economy is partly the result of the fact that in the context of a growing world economy in the long run the assumption of wage rigidity and variable employment becomes uninteresting; either employment expands into the full employment range and quantity adjustments yield to money price and wage adjustments, or it contracts and people either starve to death and go back to full employment numbers, or there is a revolution on Marxist lines, or more likely the public simply votes for the other political party than the one in power, since all of them promise to maintain full employment and the public expects them to do it. More fundamentally, the assumption of normally full employment reflects the passage of time and the accumulation of experience of reasonably full employment as the historical norm rather than the historical rarity that Keynes's theory and left-wing Keynesian mythology made it out to be. (Frenkel and Johnson 1976, p. 25.)

As these excerpts show, and contrary to Frenkel and Johnson's assertion (p. 24), the difference between the monetary approach and global monetarism is not so clear. Moreover, in chapter 6 of Frenkel and Johnson, the law of one price is fully included.

I do not particularly want to enter into these medieval discussions, but if the disclaimers we have heard about the relation of some kind of monetary approach and the policies applied in the Southern Cone are accepted, then the policy advice that may be taken from this symposium will be suspect. For the future, we have to establish policies that differentiate more from what has been done in the region in the recent past.

I do not think that discussion of the process is terribly important, except for trying not to repeat the mistakes. But I do think policy can be improved for these matters, and later I will make a few comments in this regard. Now I will argue the other side. To stabilize an economy is a very difficult task. There is no well-known recipe for how to do this. I think policymakers went into the kind of programs applied in the Southern Cone because other attempts had failed. But policymakers would be grossly mistaken not to take into account the costs of such programs—for a start, GNP levels. One must subtract the loss of net worth of a country that is due to its declining net international position to have a net result of the performance of a policy.

On the Real Exchange Rate and Exchange Insurance

In this sense, it is very clear that when the policies examined are applied, the result is an appreciation of the real exchange rate. Therefore, if additional policies are not put in place, one should be very careful about the exchange rate level at the start and begin with a good buffer to support the balance of payments during the time of this seemingly unavoidable appreciation. One must also be very careful about interest rates, and I think it would be worthwhile to try the exchange insurance scheme, to sell future U.S. dollars. [See also discussion by Jacob Frenkel (chapter 2), Vittorio Corbo, Sebastian Edwards, Pablo Spiller (chapter 4), and Rudiger Dornbusch (above).]

One of the advantages of exchange insurance is that it helps to solve the dichotomy between credibility and rigidity that is implied in the "tablita." A moving exchange insurance scheme confers more credibility because there is a legal commitment and, at the same time, probably more flexibility because the rate at which that insurance is sold changes daily. This seems a worthwhile avenue for progress.

To this extent, exchange insurance avoids what I think is the most costly phase of these experiments: when everyone sees that the preannounced exchange rate is unsustainable yet cannot be revised, then the rise in the interest rate hits the economy very, very hard.

My general experience is that, beyond theories, when policymakers hurt the economy badly is when one of the key macroeconomic variables is really thrown off equilibrium—be it the level of the deficit, of the interest rate, of the exchange rate, or of any other. Maybe this reflects a personal inclination toward the middle course. But when something is way off the expected long-term level, then one quickly gets into increasing costs and must leave open the possibility of going out without hurting credibility. The exchange insurance scheme is a way of doing that, but let us also remember that by procuring security it reduces the interest rates and that—by splitting the exchange rate at which U.S. dollars sold today will be paid at a future date t from the spot exchange rate that will prevail at that future date t—it permits daily exchanges in exchange insurance rates that cannot be matched by daily extensions of the tablita.

On the Real Interest Rate

The question of high real interest rates is a matter that goes beyond the subject of stabilization. It cuts to the quick of the capitalist system itself. The essence of the capitalist system is that there is someone who puts together the factors of production, takes risks, and gets a high return. Because he gets a high return on assets, he is able to get loans, to put together more capital, and to build the kind of large enterprises that exist in the capitalist world.

But when interest rates exceed the yield of assets, things turn completely around. Leverage works in reverse; it does not induce risk taking but causes an involution of the capitalist system. An economy can withstand this violence only for a short time. One cannot blame people for having expectations that such a situation cannot last very long. It is only rational to expect that the government will bail out private industry when the majority of the entire business sector is going bankrupt.

In this sense, it is not valid to assimilate such a process with the Schumpeterian "creative destruction." It is not progress to make it impossible for some firms to compete in the short run because the real exchange rate is half what it has to be. This cannot be sustained, and it is rational to expect that it will not be. Thus, it is also rational to try not to incur the capital losses of sending these enterprises into bankruptcy. When, after a very costly process of probably a 1,000 percent devaluation or so, the real exchange rate gets back to long-term parity, all those enterprises would again become competitive. But if they have been destroyed, then the economy suffers a net loss—in stocks, not in flows.

In sum, I think that the experience of the Southern Cone can be used, mixed with some other policy elements, not to stretch costs too long: to find ways (such as the exchange insurance scheme) to improve, or to make a compromise between, credibility and flexibility; to get out of untenable positions; and to avoid all these highly expensive transitional costs that we have seen incurred.

On the Sequence of Economic Liberalization and Stabilization

I want to supplement the foregoing and conclude by joining Larry Sjaastad [see chapter 5] in stressing the need to separate the three things that we have been discussing—adjustment of the balance of payments, economic stabilization, and economic liberalization. I think that trade liberalization has had a good record, and in this regard I want to mention again the Krueger study (1978). Of course, liberalization was easier when the world economy was expanding; it is a more difficult task now. But it is quite clear that—whatever one's economic prejudices—the performance, the track record, of liberalization is fairly good.

The sequencing, however, is very important. If the exchange rate is used for stabilization, it seems inescapable that there will be a period of appreciation; this runs counter to trade liberalization, which needs an initial period of undervaluation. So there is a choice to be made. Probably, as it happened in Argentina, if the two goals are pursued together, in the end the political, long-term fate of liberalization will be hurt because the liberalization will be considered a failure along with the stabilization measures—an unjust conclusion, but in the political arena the way things happen.

Balance of payments arrangements seem to be the next measures that will be needed after the failure of these policies in Argentina (and very likely in Chile and Uruguay). Of course, if a distortion in the real exchange of the magnitude we have seen is provoked, one cannot expect to solve it with a small devaluation. Once set free, the forces of disequilibrium are very difficult to control. In Argentina, the process was extremely disorderly, also because of political reasons. In any case, given such distortions one should expect a heavy impact on prices. Then it is important to talk not only about stabilization but also about how to handle the next stage, which is the balance of payments adjustment.

Despite Guillermo Calvo's remark [above] on some of its dynamics, it is here, I think, that the two-tier exchange market is a possibility worth exploring—not as an ideal solution, but as a transitional measure. Of course, there are the obvious problems of underinvoicing, overinvoicing, and other imperfections. [See also comments by Rudiger Dornbusch and John Williamson, above.] But given the other realistic alternatives, the costs and benefits tied with these other alternatives, and the two-tier market as a short-run thing, the proposal is attractive. I think Mario Blejer (personal communication 1982) has been doing some work on the proposal, and he has shown that a two-tier market is not that unstable if considered as a short-run measure.

ARNOLD C. HARBERGER

It will be fairly easy for me to be brief, since nearly everything has been said at least once so far. I will go through some notes that I have made, without making any attempt to put them in the kind of elegant, rational ordering that one does when one tries to write a paper.

On the Monetary Approach and Its Applications

The first thing that I have been asking myself as I have heard some of the discussion here (and I notice that others have also asked themselves the same question) is, what is the monetary approach all about? How has the monetary approach revealed itself in the setting of the Southern Cone countries? I was not present in Argentina at the time when these issues were being discussed, but I was present both in Chile and in Uruguay in the period from 1974 onward. The most obvious fact in each of those countries was that an anti-inflationary process was introduced. It was a process in which the initial rate of inflation was exceedingly high and in which any approach other than mini-devaluations would have been absurd. That is, mini-devaluation was the natural exchange rate policy to deal with the circumstances while the budget was got under control and the structure of the economy was put back together.

The mini-devaluation policy, however, has in itself an incredible inertia, a tendency for the rate of inflation to perpetuate itself. The move to the "tablita" was justified as a way of breaking expectations and getting out of that inertia. This tactic worked, I think, with reasonable success except in Argentina. In Argentina the problem was not the tablita but the way in which the tablita turned out to be inconsistent with fiscal and other aspects of the economy. It has been my view, looking at the Argentine situation, that if Argentina had started with six months of the tablita at 6 percent a month, had then gone to a second six months at 5 percent a month, and then had gone to yet another six months at 4 percent a month, it is conceivable that Argentina could have managed its problem without any great difficulty. There would not have been generated under those circumstances the possibility of bringing foreign currency to Argentina and, with total legality, having it earn 6 percent and more in pesos at a time when the tablita was being devalued at 1.5 percent or less per month.

Lots of fly-by-night capital did come to Argentina in the wake of those incentives. Huge quantities of reserves—US$10-12 billion worth—were built up. But why should any nation pay 4.5 percent per month in dollars for reserves? That was not something that was planned. It was something that came as an unwanted consequence of policies adopted for other purposes. The way it has been told to me is that, when the tablita was originally set up, it was set up with a fiscal program in mind that was completely compatible. The tablita got approved, but the fiscal program did not. There the policymakers were, left hanging, swinging slowly in the wind as some people have said.

We must recognize that, even under the mini-devaluation system, money is most of the time an endogenous variable. And certainly under the tablita and the fixed exchange rate system it is all the time an endogenous variable. Now, we should all also realize that the dramatic growth that took place in Chile and the somewhat less dramatic—but still in recent times unprecedented—growth that took place in Uruguay were associated with dramatic increases in the nominal and real quantity of money in these countries.

I think that having an endogenous money supply was almost a precondition to get that kind of expansion. If policymakers had been working in a monetary-growth-rule, quantity-theory framework, they would not have expanded the real money supply by 40 percent one year and by 50 percent the next. Thus, the endogeneity of money was a blessing and helped to grease the wheels for the substantial real advances that were made.

To me, in looking at this region, one of the things that impresses me—looking at something close to a decade, seven or eight years anyway, of economic policy—is how few gross, stupid mistakes were made. People make price controls whereby they keep prices at half of what they are supposed to be. Or they have agricultural price supports where they are paying four times the world price for something. People concoct all kinds of crazy rationing schemes. Black markets emerge with prices seven or eight times the official price. This is what we economists are good at, correcting those kinds of errors. We can diagnose them with relative ease, and at the same time we can speak with great confidence in telling people that what they are doing is wrong from an economic point of view. We do not have to become Hamlets and get all confused about it in the process.

I think in these three countries—Argentina, Chile, and Uruguay—one might find mistakes. Certainly the inconsistency between the fiscal deficit and the tablita in Argentina was a mistake. I think that allowing 15 percent of GDP to flow into Chile in one year was a mistake. And I am sure that one can find similar kinds of mistakes in Uruguay. But even these are not of the gross order of the other kinds of mistakes that I mentioned above. And the number of this kind of mistake made in the Southern Cone (during the years we are talking about) is, at the very least, quite limited.

Most of the mistakes that we identify for this period are mistakes that we only see in hindsight. It is therefore a fascinating time for an economist to observe. I hope that we as a profession are able to learn something by the obvious difficulties these economies are going through in 1982, so that next time we will be able to diagnose the problems a lot earlier.

Let me try to give a little more backing, a little more detail—to give a sense of the way I, at least, think about the subject. I believe that we in the economics profession, by and large, can tell good economic policy from bad. If those of us sitting around this table were to go to twenty countries at given times and try to give them a grade on their tax policies, on their exchange rate policies, on their price policies, on their public enterprise policies, I feel there would be a substantial clustering of the results—that we could tell the A's from the F's, the B's from the D's, and so on. We might argue between B and C, between B-plus and A-minus, but on the whole we would know. And these judgments that we would make about good and bad economic policy would not be conditional on the particular political color of a government. That is, over a wide range of governments, certainly from Frei to Pinochet, we could do our grading perfectly well.

It is in that sense that I feel that the Southern Cone countries in this recent period have not been making gross mistakes. They have been doing pretty good things. Now, I will give you some examples from Chile, which I know best, and then make a few remarks about Uruguay and Argentina. Perhaps others can then later fill in the gaps that I have left.

In Chile, a great mass of about 500 different excise and other indirect taxes was replaced by a well-designed value-added tax. An income tax reform was implemented that comes closest of any country in the world to putting into effect the Canadian Carter Commission's recommendations—which I believe income tax experts consider to be "the" standard against which to measure income tax achievements.

In Chilean agriculture there had for many decades been a prohibition on the planting of new vineyards. That was immediately repealed, and the vineyard industry has expanded. I believe most people think the repeal was a good move. In the public sector, both public sector production and pricing have been rationalized. Public sector prices today basically reflect economic costs. There is a pervasive system of cost-benefit analysis by substantially uniform criteria going on in all parts of the Chilean government. It is rather rigidly enforced, in the sense that if somebody comes to ODEPLAN [Oficina de Planificación] with a project that is not written in the right way, ODEPLAN will tell them whom they can work with to put the thing in the right form, so that it is in a language of cost-benefit analysis that is compatible with that of all the other projects.

On Chile's move (in 1979) to a uniform tariff, I have often said that the practical lesson of all that we have learned from effective protection theory is that a country must have a uniform tariff to know how much a given activity is protected, since the inputs and outputs differ even from factory to factory for the same product, and from product to product within the same factory. So, as a sort of pragmatic goal, the uniform tariff is something most of us, as technicians, would tend to recommend. Now, the level of a uniform tariff is a political decision that is much less of a technical decision than the decision to undertake uniformity.

A social security system that is designed to channel real saving into real investment, instead of spinning it off to finance government deficits and the like, and to have actual real assets behind the social security saving of people—that is what Martin S. Feldstein [chairman of the President's Council of Economic Advisers in the Reagan administration] is crying for in the United States; that is also the vision of the young, modern, public finance fraternity in this country. This is precisely the type of system that was recently implanted in Chile, in place of a costly and antiquated social security scheme that had been a thorn in the side of governments, and had resisted every attempt at reform, for decades.

So I am saying there are a lot of good things in the recent experience of the region. Also, one can tell when a system is being made worse. We have mentioned in conversation a situation in which negative interest rates in Brazil were being made more negative, in which high price supports were being made higher. Those are mistakes, and they are mistakes that we as technicians can put our fingers on and talk about, and, by and large, 80 or 90 percent of us will agree on any given one that it is in fact a mistake. It is that kind of mistake that I tend not to find in Chile. When Chile fixed the fixed exchange rate at 39, I was not particularly enthusiastic. I would rather have gone on with the tablita. But I could not say that fixing the exchange rate at 39 was a terrible or stupid move. It was a judgment that was made with a somewhat political motive in mind, I believe. Anyway, it was a decision about which one could not just say, "I call that a bad move."

Now, take Uruguay. I know Uruguay less well, but I remember talking at an early point in time to people and learning that there were Uruguayans, 50 years old, who were absolutely astounded by the proposal that they could go into any bank and buy all the foreign currency they wanted without limit and without even showing their identity cards. They had never had the experience of being able to buy foreign currency that way.

Obviously, it was a good thing for Uruguay to liberalize the currency market. Uruguay also had a major tax reform and introduced a very imaginative agricultural income tax, or substitute, called "Improme," which was based on the potential of a farmer's soil. It went up and down with the prices of outputs and inputs, but if a farmer made improvements, he did not pay any extra tax. It was a very interesting and technically sound tax, with good incentive effects. Uruguay also eliminated a huge discrimination against its principal exports that was built into the tax and exchange rate system, and the country has engaged in a gradual rationalization of both its export subsidy and import tariff schemes. These are positive things. I am still looking for the big mistakes on the other side.

Now, in Argentina, which I know still less, José María Dagnino Pastore has said [see chapters 3 and 4] that the Argentines started with 25 percent of the budget being financed by taxes, then moved that figure up to 75 percent. I believe that, and I also believe that in that process the quality of the taxes improved. That is, the new tax system would get a higher grade from the public finance experts than the old one.

I remember reading at some point that the huge railroad deficit in Argentina, which had been the bane of every government for years and years, was not eliminated, but that it was dramatically reduced, and a major rationalization of the Argentine railroads was accomplished during this period. I think that is the kind of policy success that we as economists, as technicians, ought to applaud.

What I mean when I say that these people have not made gross mistakes is that I do not find the negative counterparts to these positive things. If these correct decisions were balanced by an equal number of stupid ones, then I would give the region only a mediocre grade. But I do not find that counterbalance. The mistakes, if one is going to find them, are of the nature of a judgment call. The manager of one mutual fund buys one group of stocks, while the manager of another fund buys a different group of stocks. Both of them are following what seem to be reasonable criteria. Nobody can say that either of them at any moment is making a mistake, yet one of them might end up a big success and one of them a substantial failure. That is the sense in which I feel that, in all three of these countries, the policymakers have done a substantially sound, professional job of what they have undertaken.

In what follows I will be speaking in considerably greater detail about Chile than about the other countries because I know more about it. Some of these observations on various issues may carry over to other countries; some may not.

On the Real Exchange Rate

Question number one is, why is the real exchange rate so low?

The Balassa effect. The first reason is the Balassa effect. I agree with Sebastian Edwards [see his remarks in chapter 4]. I also made the same calculation, and I got something like 4 or 5 percent as what one might be able to explain by that effect.

Capital inflows. Second, the capital inflow effect is something that has been talked about. I would like to elaborate a bit on it. First of all, we must realize that, for the domestic economy to absorb a capital inflow, there must be a corresponding deficit in the other part of the balance, the balance on merchandise trade plus nonfinancial services. That is absolutely essential. There must be, in short, an excess of the demand for tradables over the supply of tradables in order to import real capital. But there is a trick here. If a country borrows abroad to buy Mirage jets, it does not have to make any adjustment in the domestic economy. Nor, if it buys other tradables such as John Deere tractors, does it have any adjustment to make. So, the amount of the adjustment, first of all, is limited to the amount of the borrowings that a country chooses to spend on nontradables.

Furthermore, in figuring out this kind of adjustment, a country should also net out the interest payments that are going back on its old debt.

So, I do not expect to find a close time-series correlation between borrowings abroad and the real exchange rate. I think that one has to refine the data to the point where one, first, nets out the interest payments and, second, tries to figure out how much of borrowings in each period is being assigned to nontradables versus tradables, an amount that will vary substantially from period to period. Therefore, I do not expect to be able to do much by way of econometric analysis on this. Nonetheless, I believe that our theory tells us flat out that there has to be an effect of this kind.

In addition, the issue concerns the country's total supply of tradables and its total demand for tradables, with tradables accounting for a third to a half of all goods in the system—tradables must be thought of here as a grand mass of goods, not just one or two at a time.

One thing we know: when it refers to the demand for such a grand mass of goods, an elasticity of 0.5 is high. Thus, there is not much mileage in elasticities of demand.

For some countries the supply of tradables, like the supply of manufactured goods, is quite high. In those countries one does not expect much up and down movement of the real exchange rate. Some of us have talked among ourselves about the Panama case. I think Panama has a high elasticity of supply of tradables. In Chile the tradables are orange trees, vineyards, copper mines—practically all the main tradables are things of very inelastic total supply. Therefore, I expect to see, and I believe I observe, considerable volatility in the real exchange rate of Chile, whereas I do not observe the same thing in the real exchange rate of Panama. I believe that the explanation is to be found in differential supply elasticities.

The Sjaastad effect. In addition to these two reasons—the Balassa effect and the capital inflow effect—we have what I like to call the "Sjaastad effect" [see chapter 5]. The Sjaastad effect refers to the recent appreciation of the U.S. dollar, and to what it has meant for currencies tied to the dollar.

Monetary and wage dynamics. With these three effects taken together, I think it is possible to explain the whole thing without recourse to monetary and wage dynamics. But that does not mean that monetary and wage dynamics were not in play, too. So there are at least four reasons—Balassa effect, capital inflow, Sjaastad effect, and monetary and wage dynamics—to explain why the real exchange rate is low.

On the Real Interest Rate

Why is the real interest rate high? It certainly is not because of government borrowing. It certainly is not because of a lack of contemporaneous capital movements. What do we have, then? I think we have an accumulated shortage of capital, a shortage of capital that in the Chilean case had already begun in the last years of the Frei administration, when the agrarian reform started to provoke disinvestment in land, and continued into the Allende period, when everyone was trying to get money out of the country (and some succeeded). Then it went on into the current period, when two quite important things happened. First, private saving was being used to buy back enterprises from the government; that was private saving but not national saving. Second, a powerful real wealth effect, with wealth being bid up dramatically, caused households to spend more than their income [see "On Asset Prices," below].

I am completely convinced by the recent national income data that say that households in Chile have been spending each year more than they earn. What convinces me is the real wealth effect on spending: as asset values doubled and redoubled in the post-1973 period, Chileans reacted by spending a bit more than their normal earnings.

On Devaluation

With respect to expectations of devaluation, I see things differently from some observers who have spoken here. I have watched how Chilean interest rates moved, let us say, in the course of the past year or so. When the Argentine crisis occurred in January 1981, there was a blip in the short-term interest rate in Chile. Then the short-term rate calmed down. Next came the crisis of a sugar company (CRAV) going bankrupt, and there was another blip, after which the short-term rate again calmed down. Then later on in the year there was a crisis with respect to the "intervention" (that is, placement in receivership) of the eight financial institutions by the central bank; this caused yet another rise in interest rates, after which they again started to come down.

For whatever reason, in May 1982 there has been another big blip in the short-term interest rate. These things can be averaged out over longer periods, but still I sense in these movements varying intensities of expectations of devaluation rather than any other single, dominant cause.

In a situation such as the Chilean one, I think Vittorio Corbo, Sebastian Edwards, Rolf Lüders [see chapter 4], and I all agree that devaluation would not work. Certainly with the link to wages that exists in the Chilean case, there is no hope of its working. In a little model that I constructed with parameters over a substantial range—that is, not dealing with pinpointed numbers for parameters but letting them vary over a factor of two or more—it still works out that a 20 percent devaluation in Chile would cause a rise of 14 to 18 percent, something like that, in home goods prices. The general price level would move by an average between the 20 percent for tradables and the, say, 14 percent for home goods. Who would want to undergo a 20 percent devaluation to have 17 percent price inflation? It is just not a sensible idea. Unless a persuasive case can be made that this whole line of reasoning is wrong—Vittorio Corbo has a different model [see chapter 4] in which similar results come out—I think that we professionals have got to stand together against the businessmen and others who, in my view, are acting viscerally. They say they want a devaluation because they are in trouble; they do not understand that the consequences of devaluation would not be the ones that they expect.

On the Money Supply

As a professional footnote, I would like to note that we have to think in these countries about big money. We ought to forget about M_1. When people can earn 3.0 or 3.5 percent a month on thirty-day deposits, they are going to squeeze their cash and their demand deposits down to the absolute minimum. Someone has noted that (in 1981) Chile's M_1 went down. But M_2 went up sharply, by something like 50 percent. So, one just has to be careful. I think relevant economic analysis must consider money as the counterpart of credit; that is, one must include in money whatever is on the other side (in a double-entry accounting sense) of that credit.

On Asset Prices

I think that Rolf Lüders and Roberto Zahler [see chapter 4] and others who have talked about the asset effect are absolutely right. I think that Chile has gone through a bubble in which asset prices were overblown and got beyond the point that was sustainable. People were thinking that the Chilean economy would grow at 8 percent a year forever. They were building the whole structure of asset prices on that assumption. It is a lovely assumption to make if only it stays true, but it has not. Some way has to be found to reconstitute a rational and reasonable structure of asset values, now that the bubble has burst, or at least receded. I like the idea Lüders has proposed as a private businessman, to sell assets to pay debts.

I think that, if there were ways to allow some bankruptcies to go through, it would not lead to a systemic collapse, but would be salutary for the system as whole. Furthermore, I think it was a big mistake for the Chilean government to guarantee totally the bank deposits of failed banks. The depositors in what were obviously very shaky banks should have suffered at least a slap on the wrist.

Roberto Zahler has commented about the social profitablity of funds borrowed from abroad that go into the private sector. [See his section of chapter 4, under "The current account"; see also under "Asset prices."] I agree in a certain sense. But "the gospel" would say that, if the people who make the investment are those who are going to suffer the loss, the rest of society does not have to worry about it. Do you follow me? There is not that much of a social problem to the extent that the investor who does something dumb suffers the consequences, so long as it does not have systemic repercussions.

But back to what I have called the "bubble" in asset prices: it has to be recognized that this wealth could not stay there. It had no underpinning. It was false wealth. John Williamson [above] has raised some questions about the asset price bubble. Think of it this way. When the Allende government came to power in Chile, income may have been 100, and private wealth may have been, let us say, 300, as an index. Before Allende ever reached power—I was there in September of 1970—the prices of used cars dropped to a fifth of their former level because people were selling them to leave the country. The prices of houses and apartments went down. Javier Vial bought a whole 60-hectare farm, with buildings and everything, for US$5,000 somewhere along the line.

Wealth collapsed, sort of like a black hole, in that period. When the change of government came in 1973, this wealth began to recreate itself. Nobody saved to do it. Wealth was just revalued because people had more confidence about its future income-generating power and the likelihood or nonlikelihood of its being taken away from them. And as this wealth blew up, somebody with an income of 100—starting, say, with a wealth of 100—had his wealth grow to 200 within one year. So he did not worry if he spent 105 or 110; do you follow me? Then, the next year, his wealth grew from 200 to 320, so he kept on spending more than his income. As this wealth inflated itself, first it got back to normal levels. That, I think, was a healthy, natural thing. But by the time wealth was getting back to normal levels of valuation, the economy had been growing at 8 and 9 percent for two or three years, and everybody was very euphoric, projecting ahead huge future rises in wealth and income. This process caused property values to blow up beyond the point that was sustainable. People kept spending during that period. So the growth in wealth was associated with a wealth effect upon consumption that led to negative household saving, which is what we have observed in the national accounts. That is the mechanism by which the bubble worked, in this apparently perverse way.

For the sake of a clear interpretation of events, it is very important to realize that there was no such thing as tight money at any time during the building up of the bubble and its subsequent peaking and shrinkage. M_2 more than doubled in nominal terms in 1977, nearly doubled in 1978, increased by two-thirds in 1979, by more than half in 1980, and by around 40 percent in 1981. Real M_2 increased over the whole five-year span by more than 150 percent, expanding by more than 10 percent in each single year and by more than 20 percent in most. In simple terms, money was not tight; it was very, very easy.

On Economic Interdependence

I have a short comment on Roberto Zahler's note [see his section of chapter 4, under "Economic interdependence"] on the integrated countries that amplifies my remarks on devaluation, above. Whether an economy has a high tariff or a low one, it still remains linked to the world market so long as its tariff is not prohibitive. That is true, but it is also true that the higher a country drives its tariffs, the smaller it squeezes its tradables sector. Therefore, in a sense, the process by which (under a fixed exchange rate) a given pulse of excess money spills out may be attenuated. With higher tariffs, it might take longer for excess money to spill out, and there might be somewhat of an overshoot in the process. But, more important than that, I would like to distinguish very much in this forum between something that was never quite realized clearly enough in the 1950s and 1960s.

We used to observe a fixed exchange rate that stayed in place for two, three, four years. Then internal inflation would run away from the fixed exchange rate, and there would be a big devaluation. We all talked very glibly about that. What we did not realize was that we were not dealing with Roberto Zahler's open economy. We were dealing with a situation in which a country would fix the exchange rate, would then pump in money, and would start to lose reserves. Then the policymakers would say: "let's impose licenses." With the licenses, they would often still lose reserves. Then they would turn to prohibitions, to prior deposits, and they would go on, piling one restriction on top of another. The restrictions were an intrinsic equilibrating variable in the system. Then when a devaluation finally took place, it was often a cleansing act. The economy would be rid of all those crazy restrictions at the same time. With this "corrective" (that is, devaluation plus the dismantling of many ad hoc trade restrictions), the economy would be back home again, so to speak, starting afresh.

That system is something that lives in the memory of all people in the Southern Cone. That is to say, when the average businessman thinks about a devaluation, that is the way he conceives of it as working. But that conception is completely inaccurate as a description of the systems that exist today.

On Unemployment

I agree with what has been said about the Chilean unemployment problem, that it is substantially unconnected with liberalization. In my own investigations I have become convinced that the lower half—let us say, the unskilled half—of the Chilean labor force has not had significant rises in real wages over the decade of the 1970s. The real wage has been governed, by and large, by a succession of cost of living readjustments, quasi-legal or truly legal. With high real interest rates and a construction industry that was most of the time on the rocks, at those real wages there just was insufficient demand for labor, and so there was unemployment.

I have finally "solved" the puzzle that I once saw when I thought that real wages for these people had been going up 50 percent or 60 percent or more over the decade. Widespread unemployment in conjunction with such wage rises was quite a puzzle. But the minute I convinced myself that their real wages had been more or less constant, or at least had stayed on a floor that was governed by actual or quasi-policy, then the puzzle ceased to exist, and I stopped worrying (at least about the problem of finding an analytical explanation of the observed levels of unemployment).

On Currency Reform

As I understand the situation of currency reform in the postwar European case, it involved the annulment of the old money. Annulment of the old money was something that was perfectly acceptable because it was black marketeers, war profiteers, prostitutes, pimps, and like people who were in possession of most of the old bills. The case of a currency reform that entails a simple relabeling of the old money is well known in the Southern Cone. The issue, I think, that has always arisen when the question of currency reform has come up in the Southern Cone countries is that policymakers there lack the moral consensus to annul the old money. The people who hold the old money are perfectly ordinary people who deserve that money; there is no sense in which these holdings are ill-gotten gains that should be taken away.

On Gradual versus Drastic Measures

Jacob Frenkel [chapter 2] and James Hanson [chapter 7] have brought up the issue of gradualism in policy implementation. Hanson speaks in favor of a kind of rapid-fire effect in trade liberalization. I guess by those terms I am on that side, too. But I think if one wants to characterize what has actually happened in the Southern Cone, it has been gradualism everywhere and all the way. The Argentine liberalization was to take place over five years. The Chilean liberalization went over five years, from 1974 to 1979. The Uruguayan schedule of liberalization was also for five years. On the monetary side, I have been at pains many times to point out that, up to 1981, there had not been a single year in which the Chilean money supply did not increase by more than 50 percent. And in 1981, M_1 may have gone down, but M_2, M_3, and M_4 were also going up very fast—M_2 by around 40 percent in 1981. Needless to say, one need not argue the case of gradualism for Uruguay, let alone for Argentina, on the monetary side. So the term "monetary crunch" simply does not describe the policies pursued in the Southern Cone, in the countries and periods that we have been discussing.

On Uruguay in May 1982

Finally, I will comment here in the role of another. Some of you may have noticed that earlier I received a peremptory note, and got up and walked out of the room, stayed out for five or ten minutes, and then came back. That was a colleague of ours, Bob Mundell, calling from Uruguay, to give me instructions on what to say to this group.

First of all, I am supposed to tell the World Bank and the International Monetary Fund that they should give Uruguay a very large grant, approximately half a billion U.S. dollars, at once; that this will enable Uruguay to surmount the crisis caused by the military actions [the Falkland Islands/Islas Malvinas conflict] and other recent events happening in the area and also to surmount the internal difficulties that that economy faces. Professor Mundell does not believe that a devaluation would do Uruguay any good; the Uruguayan situation is a little bit like that of Chile. But he does think that the tablita probably could and should be speeded up.

In addition, he would urge that the Uruguayan government raise taxes and impose a wage freeze. There is a budget deficit, he agrees, but the budget deficit has been caused by a shortfall in revenues due to the recession rather than to any underlying insufficiency of fiscal instruments to produce good revenue at high employment. Unemployment has gone from 5 percent to 11 percent in the last five months. So the Uruguayan situation seems to be like the Chilean situation in that respect.

Well, that is the message from Bob, and I consider my duty to have been done.

ENRIQUE LERDAU

I think that at this stage of the proceedings we have more or less reached the point in the professional joke tellers' convention, when—since the delegates all know each other's jokes— they dispense with the telling and just recite the numbers of the jokes. Then everybody laughs.

As Arnold Harberger has remarked, practically everything that is worth saying—and more— has already been said, and it is only possible at this point to express one's agreement by restating in different ways some of the things that have already been mentioned, although there may be a few jokes with new punch lines.

On the Monetary Approach and Its Applications

One thing that has not been sufficiently emphasized in the discussion—perhaps because everyone is fully aware of it—is the tremendous imbalances that prevailed in the three economies when the package of policies that is under analysis was introduced, and the inherent conflicts and inconsistencies that these imbalances imposed on the governments that had to deal with them. The rates of inflation were astronomical. The proportions of government deficits to GNP were far beyond the tolerable limits, and the external imbalances were very great indeed. One of the main problems that was faced by all three governments was, in fact, that they simultaneously tried to restore internal and external balance, and there is an obvious short-term conflict between improving a country's current account and reducing its rate of inflation.

On the Consequences of Economic Liberalization and Stabilization

I think it is not quite right just to lament the fact that liberalization got mixed up with stabilization policies by chance, because actually it was not by chance at all. Everyone here agrees that liberalization is a good thing, but there is some disagreement about stabilization. It has, therefore, been implied that it is unfortunate that the two policies had to come together and that liberalization got tarred with the brush of stabilization.

That implication is not entirely fair because I think that in all three cases—and especially in Chile—the attempt was made to reconcile the inconsistency between internal and external stabilization by opening up the economy and sucking in imports. The desire to use the flow of imports to bring down the rate of inflation was a perfectly sensible and understandable one, but it was in that context also that the liberalization policies were framed. Far from coincidentally, therefore, stabilization and liberalization were connected to the extent that both involved "opening" the economy to imports.

This has been a very technical discussion, and to some extent the appearance has been given that the issues discussed are purely technical questions. But from the discussion itself, I think, it has become clear that institutional and political factors have had a good deal to do with determining the results of economic policy. For one thing, frequent reference has been made to the crucial role that wage indexing has played in Chile in determining how the stabilization process works. Obviously, if the system of wage determination is that important, then it is no longer an entirely technical question but a question of whether policies have been viable or unviable according to the institutional framework and the political processes of the country concerned. I think that the Argentine experience in this respect is quite different from the Chilean one because the Argentine mechanism of wage determination was different.

I am sorry that Professor Mundell hung up when he made his collect call to Professor Harberger [see preceding commentary] from Uruguay during these proceedings (I assume it was a collect call, if only to collect some help) because there are a few peculiar features of the Uruguayan experience that I think have not been pointed out here. One is that suddenly nontradables became tradable. Housing is usually considered to be one of the most nontradable goods, but everyone knows what happened in Punta del Este, Uruguay—the extensive purchases of property by Argentines. I do not think that it has broader theoretical implications for the analysis, but the phenomenon of these purchases is a rather curious gloss on the Mundellian model.

I think the Uruguayan experience is unique in one respect, and that is that Uruguay seemed to function better than the other two economies of the region until the Argentine devaluation. What really happened there, I think, was that the same mistaken—if you will pardon me— policies of exchange rate overvaluation were followed in Uruguay as elsewhere, but they worked in Uruguay because its large neighbor followed these policies to an even greater degree. So, compared with Argentina, Uruguay was not overvalued, and the Punta del Este real estate purchases by Argentines were really one part of the consequences of Argentina's overvaluation. When that overvaluation came to an end, of course, it also became apparent that the Uruguayan problems were going to be similar, in the final analysis, to those of the other two countries.

On Devaluation

I am somewhat perplexed by the debate whether devaluation works. I am particularly bewildered because I thought that the whole discussion was being framed by people who believe in the important role of prices in making the economy work. If devaluation does not work, one would have to infer that overvaluation does. But the overall situation in the region—the bankruptcy of a large part of Argentine industry and of a part of Chile's as well, the bankruptcy of a substantial part of the Argentine livestock sector—is consistent with what we have heard during the discussion: that, at least in the producers' perception, the high exchange rate is part of their troubles. We have also heard that the producers are wrong, and that it is really the high interest rates that they ought to worry about. Yet I wonder whether they are not quite well placed themselves to know where the shoe pinches them.

It is rather strange that we are left in the three cases with very sophisticated rationalizations for a policy that ends up making export industries noncompetitive. If Arnold Harberger is looking for gross policy mistakes and has not found any, it may be because it is quite true that one cannot say that exchange rate overvaluation as such was an intended result. It was a result, instead, that was reached by a much more subtle and complex process, and one that presumably would have been avoided if the assumptions about factor mobility and wage flexibility had been more realistic. But the outcome was nevertheless one that would seem to be unacceptable from an economist's point of view.

GUY PIERRE PFEFFERMANN

Enrique Lerdau has said much of what I wanted to say. I will, however, comment on a few of the important issues that emerged during these informative proceedings.

On the Sequence of Economic Liberalization and Stabilization

One such issue is the need to distinguish between the phases of the adjustment process. I think that there is a difference in kind, not merely in degree, between going from hyperinflation to 30 percent inflation and going from 30 percent to zero inflation. And it is another thing again what to do then. As the revolution devours its children, I think in a kind of dialectical way, a certain set of policies gets invalidated by its own success. Once this point is reached, once inflation has been beaten, it is quite possible that rigid adherence to the previous set of policies is not tenable.

On Devaluation

I am therefore particularly worried about what I call the "devaluation pessimism" that I sense around the table. The greatest success that Chile had was after a tremendous real devaluation and while the exchange rate was still moving. Only when the exchange rate was pegged did things go sour.

Others may counter this estimation by asking what a small country can do if the terms of trade turn against it. But that would be the last moment, I would think, at which to discard one of the principal measures a country can use to adjust.

I do not think that, if one forgets about theoretical models and looks at economic history, there have been many successful devaluations. Even in Latin America, success depends on what policies accompany devaluation and what the particular circumstances are.

On the Flexibility of Policy

My own feeling is that perhaps this rigid adherence to the exchange rate betrays a certain political insecurity, that policymakers in the region have thought that if they start moving the exchange rate all the rest is going to unravel—the monetary side, the fiscal side, and so forth. This reminds me a bit of de Gaulle's stance: "It is either me or chaos." Many politicians, I believe, have kept themselves in place by posing this basically false dichotomy.

I do think, therefore, that, as soon as a country reaches a reasonable degree of economic stability, the way the problem is posed should be reconsidered. And I very much agree with Enrique Lerdau that, when an economy experiences 20 percent unemployment, it is the price of labor that must be reconsidered. Perhaps more attention should have been paid in the discussion to the price of labor and the wage indexation mechanisms. It is precisely when the emergency stabilization policies have begun to work that the time has come to decontrol various markets. What this implies is that with a fixed exchange rate an economy must have total liberalization. There cannot be a fixed exchange rate and only partial liberalization, especially if the one market that is not liberalized is an extremely important one.

Thus, it would be very interesting to look back, for instance, at the experience of Brazil in 1964, 1967, and so on, when the Brazilian labor market was fairly free—or perhaps to examine certain experiences of Korea. Simón Teitel has said [see chapter 6] that a country should protect certain of its industries for various reasons—indeed, Korea has done just that. But the point is that Korea has done it on an extremely selective basis. I think that, just as with the exchange rate, the reason that there is such dogmatism in the Southern Cone about these other policies is that, perhaps in the political context of the Southern Cone, things do fall into all-or-nothing, yes-or-no kinds of categories. There is a reluctance among policymakers to decide that, say, seven factories and products will be protected and that the rest will not.

What I am pleading for, essentially, is more empirical and less theoretical analyses of both the exchange rate policy and the consistency of partial liberalization within the monetary approach.

ARTURO MEYER

I would like to comment briefly on the monetary approach and how it was applied in Argentina, and then to compare the experiences of Argentina and Chile with respect to the appropriate sequencing of liberalization and stabilization measures.

On the Monetary Approach and Its Applications

José María Dagnino Pastore has shown very clearly [see chapter 3] that in Argentina approximately US$17 billion has somehow been misused. I say "misused" in the sense that this increase in the external debt of the country did not correspond with an increase in productive capacity and repayment capacity.

There is no doubt in my mind that the inconsistent fiscal policies that were pursued in Argentina had something to do with this misuse of external resources; in this respect a sensible conclusion would be that the liberalization of the capital account should have waited until the stabilization effort was more advanced. But I also cannot avoid the nagging suspicion that, if US$17 billion was misused, somehow incentives must have been wrong.

On the Sequence of Economic Liberalization

Of course this leads to the issue of trade reform, and in this connection I would like to pursue the comparison of the trade liberalization processes in Chile and Argentina. I think that what has been said about the sequence of the trade liberalization process relative to the liberalization of the capital account is quite important. It appears very clear that Chile started with trade liberalization and then followed with capital account reform. For the case of Argentina, we have heard two different accounts. According to Roberto Zahler [chapter 4], capital reform was undertaken first and trade liberalization after; Larry Sjaastad [chapter 5] and José María Dagnino Pastore [chapter 3 and comments in chapter 4] seem to think that the two things were done more or less at the same time. According to my recollection of those days, when I was an official of the Central Bank of Argentina, Mr. Zahler's perception is the more accurate.

But this particular difference is immaterial. What is important is that in Argentina trade liberalization did not precede the capital account liberalization, and this had an undesirable effect. To put it in very simplistic terms, when external resources became available in substantial amounts as a result of the capital account liberalization, investment just did not take place—I am thinking particularly of the Argentine manufacturing sector—simply because investment was not sufficiently attractive. This was so partly because the exchange rate was not right, but especially because the trade liberalization process was not complete at the time. The latter factor created great uncertainty for the Argentine manufacturing sector. The government announced that there would be a program of tariff reform in April 1976, but no meaningful action was taken until late 1978. Would any sensible businessman invest when a change in the rules of the game has been announced, but the new rules are not yet known?

Other differences in the trade liberalization processes in Argentina and Chile are worth noting. First, trade liberalization was meant to go deeper in Chile. If I remember correctly, Chile ended with a 10 percent uniform tariff, and Dagnino Pastore has said that the goal in Argentina—which was not reached, of course—was a 30 percent tariff. (It was not clear to me whether that tariff was supposed to be uniform or simply a 30 percent average.)

Second—and little has been said about this difference—the trade liberalization process in Argentina was incomplete not only in the sense that it was eventually abandoned or postponed, but also in the more important sense that broad classes or groups were excluded from the liberalization process. I am thinking, obviously, of goods that are produced by the Argentine industrial-military complex, the most important of which are steel and petrochemicals. How meaningful is a process of tariff reform when major industrial inputs are excluded from it? Or, to put it in slightly different terms, if the trade liberalization process is going to be incomplete because the political realities in a country determine that it must be so, is tariff reform still the optimal policy for trade liberalization, or should policymakers be thinking of supplementing tariff reform with export rebates and subsidies?

CARLOS ELBIRT

I would like to refer to external capital inflows in the framework of stabilization programs. Two cases are evident. In one case external funds are channeled mostly to the public sector; in the other to the private sector.

On Capital Inflows: To the Public Sector

The first case is illustrated by the Jamaican experience one observes in mid-1982. The final outcome of a stabilization program in such case largely depends on the quality of the public sector investment program, on the wise or unwise manner in which the money from abroad is spent by the public sector.

On Capital Inflows: To the Private Sector

In the Southern Cone's experience, external funds were channeled mostly to the private sector. This experience proves, in my view, that the private sector does not necessarily spend money more wisely than the public sector, apparently for reasons related to imperfections and distortions, especially in the financial market. Therefore, I would like to leave a question on the floor: what policy recommendation can we make to a country in which large capital inflows are taking place through the private sector, since in that case control of the quality of the public investment program is not so relevant?

JAMES A. HANSON

I would like to raise three points in my remarks.

On Capital Inflows

First, I want to to take up a point that Carlos Elbirt has raised [preceding comments]. That is, the question of how a country adjusts to capital inflows—in particular, as Vittorio Corbo has discussed [above and in chapter 4], what happens to the real exchange rate. If a country receives an increased capital inflow and has a nontraded goods sector, then it will experience a rise both in the relative price of nontradables to tradables and in its price level relative to world prices. However, after the ratio of capital inflow to output stabilizes, the country generally will be unable to cover the interest on its debt out of new capital inflows. As a result, the country will in most cases have to experience a fall in the relative price of nontradables, to a value below the initial level. To the extent that the country also attemps to protect its domestic market, the magnitudes of these upward and downward movements of relative prices can become even worse in some sectors. It also is very tempting for a country to use this process in the short run. When the capital market is opened up, a country can finance a temporary boom with a sharp rise in borrowing.

In the initial phases of liberalization-stabilization—for example, in Argentina and in Colombia—the first phase of the price movement occurred. However, the policy also has created a problem of readjusting relative prices and curtailing the nontradables sector in response to the inevitable slowdown in foreign lending.

My question is: what are policymakers going to do to smooth the adjustment? After all, such capital inflows are initially going to wipe out some exporting and import-competing activities so that resources can be shifted into nontraded goods activities. But then a shift of resources back into traded goods activities will be necessary to service the debt.

We must think more about this question. If a permanently higher level of net capital inflows (including interest) is expected, then some sort of relative appreciation is desirable. It is desirable to wipe out some exporting and import-competing industries to get more nontradables. This, I think, is the point Vittorio Corbo has made [see chapter 4] about absorbing the capital flow. But, when the net capital flows are fluctuating, the real question is what policy can do to smooth the shocks and the back-and-forth shifts of resources.

On the Sequence of Economic Liberalization

Second, I want to reemphasize a point I made earlier [see the preceding chapter]. At this symposium many people have said that a country should liberalize its capital market after trade liberalization has taken place. The arguments I just made suggest that this would resolve some of the problems of economic liberalization. The country initially could bring in some imported inputs, for example, which would allow output to expand.

But the question I am asking now is a prior one: what is meant by capital market liberalization? Does it mean government borrowing from abroad? Does it mean allowing public holding of U.S. dollars and dollar assets? Does it mean trimming banking regulation, including reserve requirements and credit allocations, or does it mean free entry to the banking system? Just what is the combination of measures that is meant?

The measures I have mentioned are quite different, and each has quite different implications for what is going to happen to domestic interest rates. The term "capital market liberalization," it seems to me, has been used far too loosely in our discussions of the optimal sequence of capital liberalization measures compared with those for goods market liberalization. Before we can say whether goods or capital market liberalization should be "first," we must define what is meant by capital market liberalization.

For example, Arnold Harberger has said that one of the benefits of capital market reform in Uruguay was that Uruguayans could hold U.S. dollars [see his comments above]. Allowing residents of a country to hold dollars is a benefit in some ways, but when the public can hold dollars, the domestic interest rates are tied to the rate of devaluation the public expects. Governments must recognize this limitation on interest rate policy, difficult though it may be.

On Devaluation

My third point is merely a clarification regarding the effects of devaluation. It may work in some countries, it may not work in others. The empirical results for Chile that I cited earlier [chapter 7] suggest that relative prices do not change much after a devaluation. For Argentina, Colombia, and Uruguay, the same kind of regression equations suggest that devaluation produces a much larger change in relative prices. This in turn suggests that one must look at the institutions and what is going on in a country to estimate the effects of a devaluation. Why is the effect of devaluation on relative prices so different? Part of the reason may be that money gets sucked into the country by the devaluation. Reserves are accumulated, and that accumulation bids up local prices. The speed with which this occurs may vary among countries. There also are many other possible reasons; for example, de facto or de jure indexing of wages and prices. The point is that in Chile, taking the period 1952-70, one finds empirically that about 70 percent of a devaluation gets translated into a rise in domestic prices. If one takes the 1952-80 period, one finds the figure to be 85 to 90 percent. This is the empirical result that one must confront before recommending devaluation.

JAIME DE MELO

When we have discussed the order in which economic reforms should be undertaken, we have spoken primarily about whether a country should first liberalize its trade account or its capital account. Other discussants have emphasized that stabilization and liberalization should be distinguished, but I do not think sufficient attention has been paid to whether a country should not first stabilize its economy, and if so, how much it should stabilize.

On the Extent of Economic Stabilization

As Enrique Lerdau has said [above], one should keep in mind that the Southern Cone countries started from situations of extreme disequilibrium, in that inflation rates were much higher than what they had been historically. The question then is whether it is sufficient to bring down inflation to 50 or 60 percent, which would be equivalent (in comparison with the average world inflation rate) to what Korea did when it liberalized in 1963-65. Korea maintained a rate of inflation of about 30 to 40 percent while world inflation was about 5 to 10 percent. So, Korean inflation was about 25 percentage points above the world level at the time.

On the basis of the Korean example, the issue then is to what level the rate of inflation should be brought down, given that it appears very costly in terms of unemployment to bring it down below the 50 percent range in countries with a history of high inflation. Among the reasons for bringing down inflation is that, when inflation is high, people commit otherwise productive resources to seeking stores of value that are alternatives to money. Inflation is also reflected in higher relative price variability, which makes it difficult for entrepreneurs to forecast correctly changes in relative prices and, hence, to choose the appropriate factor proportions. In other words, how much should a country stabilize? Is it sufficient in the world of the 1980s to stabilize down to 40 or 50 percent inflation and from there to go on to liberalize? I would answer that question affirmatively in the light of the Southern Cone experience. Then, one may be able to avoid the unemployment costs that countries have incurred in bringing down domestic inflation to levels that were close to the world level at the time.

On the Extent of Factor Market Rigidities during Liberalization

Another example drawn from the liberalizations that took place in the East relates to getting prices right. Certainly arriving at "correct" relative prices was a primary ingredient in these Asian reforms, but one must not forget that in those countries labor markets worked fairly well. That may have been one of the reasons why the liberalizations could in effect translate themselves into changes in output, which may occur if labor markets do not function properly. If a country's factor markets do not function well, then even if the country gets prices right, nothing much is going to happen.

A related issue is protection, about which there is disagreement between Simón Teitel and Larry Sjaastad, as Guy Pfeffermann has noted [above]. It is true that in Japan and Korea there has been selective protection of infant industries on a highly selective basis, but at relatively high tariff rates. What is different, perhaps, in what happened with the Southern Cone reforms is that in the Asian case there also were incentives or orders for the infant industries to go out and to export. When there was a removal of biases against exporting in the Southern Cone, the decontrol was not sufficient, and a bias remained against the promotion of exporting activites. In contrast with the Asian case, the Southern Cone countries did not provide subsidies to exports while they continued to maintain some protection from import competition.

SEBASTIAN EDWARDS

I want to make just two brief comments—one related to the effects of a devaluation, which I think to some extent have been misinterpreted here, and the other related to the effects of high capital inflow on the real exchange rate.

On Devaluation

I think that there are two questions one has to ask when one wants to know if a devaluation is going to have any effect at all. The first is whether relative prices are out of line. In the cases where devaluation seems not to have worked, devaluation has taken place when relative prices were not out of line. In the case of Chile in May 1982, of course, it is fairly clear that prices are out of line, and in that sense a devaluation might work.

The second question is whether institutional arrangements are adequate. In this respect, the wage indexation law in Chile would, I think, have a negative effect in that devaluation would be partially offset by an increase in prices of nontradables through the wage indexation clause.

A policy recommendation that emerges quite clearly here, and one that has been mentioned earlier, is that the wage indexation law in Chile should be abolished. Once this law is abolished, it is quite certain that, at the present time, a devaluation would work in Chile.

On Capital Inflows

The second point I want to make is about the effect of higher capital inflow on the real exchange rate. As I said earlier [see chapter 4], I think there is no question that a higher capital inflow will cause a real appreciation. That is the only way to effect, as James Hanson has said [above and preceding chapter], the higher capital flow.

Now, the problem in the case of Chile is that in 1981 the higher capital inflow was not an equilibrium one. Fifteen percent of GDP is not an equilibrium capital flow. So, the question that we must ask is how did it happen that in 1981 Chile had such a massive capital inflow, now that in mid-1982—clear from the data available—the level of capital inflow going down.

What makes the adjustment painful in Chile is not that there was going to be a higher equilibrium capital inflow, but rather that in 1981 capital inflow overshot, as it were, its new postliberalization level. What we must do, then, is to look for an explanation for this overshooting. The bubble and increase in prices of real assets might give us the clue to an answer.

What we should emphasize in the case of Chile is that in one particular year there was a huge mass of capital flow. I do not think there is any theoretical presumption that this will happen in other countries that undertake capital liberalization. It might happen and it might not.

JOSÉ B. SOKOL

My comment relates to a neglected aspect of economic liberalization—the nonregistered (illegal) importation of goods and capital. A situation may have existed in some countries in the 1970s—Colombia, in particular—where sizable illegal activities took place that affected both the current and capital accounts of the balance of payments.

On Illicit Inflows and the Current Account

In the particular case of a country accumulating a sizable amount of foreign exchange reserves that continued to increase over a number of years, if these activities were to have benefited only the current account (through illegal imports), this problem would actually have been a kind of blessing. The economy would have been opening up, and the inflationary pressures produced by the monetization of these reserves would have ameliorated.

On Illicit Inflows and Both Current and Capital Accounts

If, however, the illegal activities were to exist both in the capital account (through illegal capital inflows) and in the current account (through illegal imports), the country would find itself in a situation in which, on the one hand, it would in fact be undergoing a process of economic opening up while, on the other hand, it would have to stabilize. Thus, the two effects would pull in opposite directions and produce more distortions in the economy. This situation existed in Colombia during the late 1970s and points to a particular case in which de facto liberalization of the external sector in both the current and capital accounts is not beneficial to the economy.

KRISHNA CHALLA

We have discussed what should have come first, liberalization of the capital market or liberalization of the product markets, but I am wondering what comes next. I seriously ask myself whether the countries of the Southern Cone can afford to liberalize any longer. I think, to borrow Arnold Harberger's phrase [above], that if these countries continue liberalizing they may end up in a black hole. And I am not certain whether there will be another asset price bubble to come out of. In Argentina in mid-1982, a large segment of the industrial sector is threatened by bankruptcy, and the portfolios of the banks are very weak. If one adds up all the debt-equity ratios, there is considerably more debt than equity.

On the Extent of Economic Liberalization

If liberalization is to continue, on what basis? I think that in the past the private sector has not responded to the incentive framework provided by the government as the government had expected. I was happy to see at least one representative of the private sector, Rolf Lüders, in attendance here. I think much more of his kind of analysis [see chapter 4] will be required—and not only what he has done for the past, telling how the private sector saw the situation in Chile four or five years ago and what it did, but also for economists to listen now to our own advice and to the response the private sector has to it.

In Argentina, certainly, it was financial wizardry that was practiced, and financial survival techniques that were honed, not those fiscal attributes that economists would like to see strengthened to improve productivity and to restructure the economy. I cannot fully agree with José María Dagnino Pastore [see chapters 3 and 4 and his comments above]; I have seen in Argentina little restructuring, increases in productivity, and effect of liberalization. We have already discussed the uses of the increased Argentine debt and where the investment, if at all, has gone—to the public sector, and to the protected private industrial sector, but not to the industries in which one would think Argentina has a comparative advantage. In Argentina, a massive number of companies are going bankrupt, but at the same time they are still investing in real estate outside the country.

On Alternative Policies

As regards future policies, it is not a question of technicalities, of devaluation or nondevaluation. It is a question of how much a government is willing to condone the behavior, and how much it is willing to risk the displeasure, of those who have taken advantage in the past. It is a question of to what extent it might be possible now to get back, in significant amounts, assets that must be abroad. It is a question, finally, of how much the government wants, and is capable, to address again this tremendous redistribution of wealth that has taken place.

SIMÓN TEITEL

I would like to comment on the question of capital inflows and the role of indebtedness in the recent adjustment process in Latin American countries.

On Capital Inflows

In a recent Inter-American Development Bank report (IDB 1982), we noted that in the 1970s a large apparent increase took place in the openness of Latin America as measured for the region by the ratio of the sum of exports and imports of goods and services to GDP, with the regional average for this indicator going from 26 percent in 1970 to approximately 50 percent in 1980. If the content of trade is examined, however, we note that, whereas exports plus imports of goods as a proportion of GDP increased between 1971-73 and 1980 by 79 percent, services as a proportion of GDP increased by 100 percent. This is, to a large extent, a reflection of the increased importance of foreign indebtedness.

Examining the change in the importance of the external sector in the Southern Cone countries, we see that during the last decade Argentina, Chile, and Uruguay all improved their ranking within the Latin American region on the openness indicator. Chile went from thirteenth place in 1970 to ninth in 1980, Argentina from twenty-first to seventeenth, and Uruguay from nineteenth to fifteenth. The ratio of trade of goods and services to GDP increased from 39 percent to 80 percent for Chile, 21 percent to 51 percent for Argentina, and 27 percent to 59 percent for Uruguay.

If one looks at the use to which external financing was put in Latin America, one finds indications of problems in the region. Looking at the data for the incremental capital required to increase output (over the period 1960-80), one sees a clear break at the point after the first oil shock. The efficiency of investment apparently comes down, since the incremental capital-output ratio increases significantly. The implication is that the debt contracted may not always have been applied efficiently in productive investment and may in part have been used to finance domestic or foreign consumption (Ffrench-Davis 1982; IDB 1982, ch. 2).

On the Future Role of External Debt

For several reasons, it is quite unlikely that external debt will play such an important role in the adjustment process in Latin America in the near future as it has in the recent past. One important reason is that the financial surplus of the OPEC countries, which made possible this high and growing degree of indebtedness, will not be available in the near future.

A substantial reduction in the level of external debt available to Latin America, however, will create serious problems for these countries. The estimates of economic analysts in all scenarios require high doses of debt to sustain even moderate economic growth for the region. To the extent that Latin American countries will not have access to the required external financing, they should be able to increase their exports proportionally. Given that investment to increase the capacity to export has not been growing, that in some cases these countries have reduced their export capacity because of overvalued exchange rates, and that protectionism in the industrialized countries is on the rise, the economic prospects for the region are quite bleak for the short run.

Even so, given its enormous resource potential, both natural and human, Latin America should be able to overcome this difficult spell and return to a more satisfactory economic performance in the medium to longer run.

PABLO T. SPILLER

I would like to continue the discussion Enrique Lerdau began [above] about some of the institutional arrangements that can complicate stabilization policy. In Uruguay in mid-1982 there are two, I think, quite bad arrangements of this kind. One is in the labor market, and the other is in the public enterprise sector. In both sectors there is an implicit kind of backward indexation.

On Uruguayan Labor Market Policy and Stabilization

In the labor market, sometimes policy goes to extremes. For example, there was a wage raise of 10 percent by the end of 1981, which translated into an immediate and substantial loss of reserves, which was completely rational given the institutional circumstances. Certainly, this type of institutional constraint should be avoided in the future.

On Uruguayan Public Enterprise Policy and Stabilization

The other inappropriate arrangement concerns public enterprise pricing, which has been adjusted to inflation with a lag of approximately three months. The pricing is for nontradable goods and creates pressure on the internal price level. These two issues—labor market and public enterprise policies—clearly should be analyzed in more depth for each country in the region.

REFERENCES

Corbo, Vittorio. 1981. "Inflation in an Open Economy: The Case of Chile." Paper presented at the Latin American Meeting of the Econometric Society, Rio de Janeiro. Cuadernos de Economía (Santiago), vol. 19, no. 56 (April 1982).

Dornbusch, Rudiger. 1982. "Stabilization Policies in Developing Countries: What Have We Learned?" World Development, vol. 10 (September), pp. 701-08.

Ffrench-Davis, Ricardo. 1982. "External Debt and Balance of Payments of Latin America: Recent Trends and Outlook." In IDB 1982, pp. 162-80.

Frenkel, Jacob A., and Harry G. Johnson, eds. 1976. The Monetary Approach to the Balance of Payments. Toronto: University of Toronto Press; London: Allen and Unwin.

Inter-American Development Bank (IDB). 1982. Economic and Social Progress in Latin America: The External Sector, 1982 Report. Washington, D.C.

Kaminsky, Graciela Laura. 1982. "Essays on Expectations and Real Exchange Rate Variability." Ph.D. dissertation. Massachusetts Institute of Technology, Cambridge, Mass. (August).

Krueger, Anne O. 1978. Foreign Trade and Economic Development: Liberalization Attempts and Consequences. Cambridge, Mass.: Ballinger/National Bureau of Economic Research.

Further Reading

The works listed here augment those supporting the chapters of the volume and are presented to facilitate and stimulate further analysis of the issues. The word "processed" describes works that are reproduced by mimeography, xerography, or any means other than conventional typesetting and printing; such works may not be cataloged or commonly available through libraries.

Aliber, Robert Z. 1980. A Conceptual Approach to the Analysis of External Debt of the Developing Countries. World Bank Staff Working Paper no. 421. Washington, D.C., October.

_____. 1982. National Monetary Policies and the International Financial System. Chicago: University of Chicago Press.

Allen, P. R., and Peter B. Kenen. 1978. The Balance of Payments, Exchange Rates, and Economic Policy. New York: International Publications Service.

Anjaria, S. J., and others. 1982. Developments in International Trade Policy. IMF Occasional Paper no. 16. Washington, D.C., November.

Argy, Victor. 1982. Exchange Rate Management in Theory and Practice. Princeton Studies in International Finance no. 50. Princeton, N.J.: Princeton University, October.

Arriazu, Ricardo H. 1983. "Policy Interdependence from a Latin American Perspective." In IMF (1983).

Artus, Jacques. 1983. "Toward a More Orderly Exchange Rate System." Finance & Development, vol. 20, no. 1 (March), pp. 10-13.

Auernheimer, Leonardo, and Robert B. Ekelund. 1982. The Essentials of Money and Banking. New York: Wiley.

Bacha, Edmar. 1983. "Vicissitudes of Recent Stabilization Attempts in Brazil and the IMF Alternative." In Williamson (1983a), pp. 323-40.

Balassa, Bela. 1980. The Newly Industrializing Developing Countries after the Oil Crisis. World Bank Staff Working Paper no. 437. Washington, D.C., October.

_____. 1981a. Adjustment to External Shocks in Developing Countries. World Bank Staff Working Paper no. 472. Washington, D.C., August.

_____. 1981b. Structural Adjustment Policies in Developing Economies. World Bank Staff Working Paper no. 464. Washington, D.C., July.

_____. 1981c. "Policy Responses to External Shocks in Selected Latin American Countries." Quarterly Review of Economics and Business, vol. 21, no. 2 (Summer), pp. 131-64. Also published as World Bank Reprint Series no. 221 (Washington, D.C.).

_____. 1982. "Disequilibrium Analysis in Developing Economies: An Overview." World Development, vol. 10, no. 12, pp. 1027-38. Also published as World Bank Reprint Series no. 241 (Washington, D.C.).

_____. 1983. "The Adjustment Experience of Developing Economies after 1973." In Williamson (1983a), pp. 145-74.

Balassa, Bela, and others. 1981. The Balance of Payments: Effects of External Shocks and of Policy Responses to These Shocks in Non-OPEC Developing Countries. Paris: OECD.

Balassa, Bela, and associates. 1982. Development Strategies in Semi-Industrial Economies. Baltimore, Md.: Johns Hopkins University Press.

Bautista, Romeo M. 1980. Exchange Rate Adjustment under Generalized Currency Floating: Comparative Analysis among Developing Countries. World Bank Staff Working Paper no. 436. Washington, D.C., October.

Behrman, Jere R. 1976. Foreign Trade Regimes and Economic Development: Chile, Book 8. Jagdish N. Bhagwati and Anne O. Krueger, eds., Special Conference Series. New York: Columbia University Press/National Bureau of Economic Research.

_____. 1977. Macroeconomic Policy in a Developing Country: Chilean Experience. Contributions to Economic Analysis, vol. 109. Amsterdam: North-Holland; New York: Elsevier.

Behrman, Jere R., and James A. Hanson, eds. 1979. Short-Term Macroeconomic Policy in Latin

America: Conference on Planning and Short-Term Macroeconomic Policy in Latin America. Cambridge, Mass.: Ballinger/National Bureau of Economic Research.

Bergsten, C. Fred, and others. 1970. Approaches to Greater Flexibility of Exchange Rates: The Burgenstock Papers. Princeton, N.J.: Princeton University Press.

_____. 1981. The World Economy in the 1980s. Lexington, Mass.: Lexington/D.C. Heath.

Bhagwati, Jagdish N. 1974. Illegal Transactions in International Trade. Amsterdam: North-Holland; New York: Elsevier.

_____. 1978. Anatomy and Consequences of Exchange Control Regimes. Cambridge, Mass.: Ballinger/National Bureau of Economic Research.

_____, ed. 1982. Import Competition and Response. Chicago: University of Chicago Press.

Bhatt, Vinayak, and Alan R. Roe. 1979. Capital Market Imperfections and Economic Development. World Bank Staff Working Paper no. 338. Washington, D.C., July.

Bigman, David, and Teizo Taya. 1982. Exchange Rate and Trade Instability: Causes, Consequences, and Policies. Cambridge, Mass.: Ballinger.

Black, John, and Brian Hindlin, eds. 1980. Current Issues in Commercial Policy and Diplomacy. New York: St. Martins.

Blough, Roy, and Jack N. Behrman. 1968. Regional Integration and the Trade of Latin America. New York: Committee for Economic Development.

Bond, Marian E. 1980. "Exchange Rates, Inflation, and Vicious Circles." IMF Staff Papers, vol. 27, no. 4 (December).

Bos, P. C. 1969. Money in Development: The Functions of Money in Equilibrium and Disequilibrum, with Special Reference to Developing Countries. New York: International Publications Service.

Branson, William H. 1983. "Economic Structure and Policy for External Balance." In IMF (1983).

Brundenius, Claes, and Mats Lundal, eds. 1982. Development Strategies in Latin America. Boulder, Co.: Westview.

Brunner, Karl, and Allen H. Meltzer, eds. 1976a. Institutional Arrangements and the Inflation Problem. Carnegie-Rochester Conference Series on Public Policy, vol. 3. Amsterdam: North-Holland; New York: Elsevier.

_____. 1976b. Institutions, Policies, and Economic Performance. Carnegie-Rochester Conference Series on Public Policy, vol. 4. Amsterdam: North-Holland; New York: Elsevier.

_____. 1977. Stabilization of the Domestic and International Economy. Carnegie-Rochester Conference Series on Public Policy, vol. 5. Amsterdam: North-Holland; New York: Elsevier.

_____. 1978. The Problem of Inflation. Carnegie-Rochester Conference Series on Public Policy, vol. 8. Amsterdam: North-Holland; New York: Elsevier.

_____. 1979. Policies for Employment, Prices, and Exchange Rates. Carnegie-Rochester Conference Series on Public Policy, vol. 11. Amsterdam: North-Holland; New York: Elsevier.

_____. 1982. Economic Policy in a Changing World. Carnegie-Rochester Conference Series on Public Policy, vol. 17. Amsterdam: North-Holland; New York: Elsevier.

Bryant, Ralph C. 1980a. Financial Interdependence and Variability in Exchange Rates. Washington, D.C.: Brookings.

_____. 1980b. Money and Monetary Policy in Interdependent Nations. Washington, D.C.: Brookings.

_____. 1981. Notes on the Analysis of Capital Flows to Developing Nations and the "Recycling" Problem. World Bank Staff Working Paper no. 482. Washington, D.C., August.

Buiter, William H. 1980. "Monetary, Financial, and Fiscal Policies under Rational Expectations." IMF Staff Papers, vol. 27, no. 4 (December).

Cagan, Philip. 1972. The Channels of Monetary Effects on Interest Rates. New York: Columbia University Press/National Bureau of Economic Research.

Calvo, Guillermo A. 1981. "Trying to Stabilize: Some Reflections Based on the Case of Argentina." Paper presented at the Conference on Financial Problems and the World Capital Market, Mexico City, March 27. Processed.

Chipman, J. S., and C. P. Kindleberger, eds. 1981. Flexible Exchange Rates and the Balance of

Payments: Essays in Memory of Egon Sohmen. Studies in International Economics, vol. 7. Amsterdam: North-Holland; New York: Elsevier.

Chu, Ke Young, and Andrew Feltenstein. 1978. "Relative Price Distortions and Inflation: The Case of Argentina, 1963-76." IMF Staff Papers, vol. 25 (September).

_____. 1979. "Extraordinary Inflation: The Argentine Experience." Finance & Development, vol. 16, no. 2 (June), pp. 32-35.

Cizauskas, Albert C. 1980. The Changing Nature of Export Finance and Its Implications for Developing Countries. World Bank Staff Working Paper no. 409. Washington, D.C., July.

Clausen, A. W. 1982a. Global Interdependence in the 1980s. Remarks before the Yomiuri International Economic Society, Tokyo, January 13. Washington, D.C.: World Bank.

_____. 1982b. The World Bank and International Commercial Banks: Partners for Development. Remarks to the International Monetary Conference, Vancouver, May 25. Washington, D.C.: World Bank.

_____. 1983. Third World Debt and Global Recovery. The 1983 Jodidi Lecture at The Center for International Affairs, Harvard University, Boston, February 24. Washington, D.C.: World Bank.

Cline, William R. 1975. International Monetary Reform and the Developing Countries. Washington, D.C.: Brookings.

_____. 1983a. International Debt and the Stability of the World Economy. Washington, D.C.: Institute for International Economics.

_____. 1983b. "Economic Stabilization and Developing Countries: Theory and Stylized Facts." In Williamson (1983a), pp. 175-208.

Cline, William R., and associates. 1981. World Inflation and the Developing Countries. Washington, D.C.: Brookings.

Cline, William R., and Sidney Weintraub. 1981. Economic Stabilization in Developing Countries. Washington, D.C.: Brookings.

Crockett, Andrew D. 1981a. "Stabilization Policies in Developing Countries: Some Policy Considerations." IMF Staff Papers, vol. 28, no. 1 (March).

_____. 1981b. "Determinants of Exchange Rate Movements: A Review." Finance & Development, vol. 18 (March), pp. 33-37.

Cuthbertson, Keith. 1979. Macroeconomic Policy: The New Cambridge Keynesian and Monetarist Controversies. New York: Wiley.

Dagnino Pastore, José María. 1967. Income and Money, Argentina 1935-60. 3 vols. Buenos Aires: Fundación de Investigaciones Económicas Latinoamericanas (FIEL). Spanish and English.

_____. 1968. Towards a Sustained Expansion. Buenos Aires: Ministerio de Economía, Provincia de Buenos Aires.

_____. 1970. Argentine Economic Policy, 1969-70. Buenos Aires: Ministerio de Economía y Trabajo de la República Argentina.

_____. 1974a. The Argentine Financial System. Argentine National Group, publication no. 2. Washington, D.C.: Latin American Program for Capital Markets Development, Organization of American States. Spanish.

_____. 1974b. "Medium- and Long-Term Financing under High Inflation." In Central Bank of Uruguay, Capital Markets Seminar. Montevideo. Spanish. Processed.

_____. 1980. "Structural Change within Nations." In World Congress of the International Association of Financial Executives, proceedings. Sydney. Processed.

_____. 1983. "Optimal Public Investment Programs under Capital Rationing." Revista Española de Economía (Madrid), forthcoming.

Dagnino Pastore, José María, and Ana María Vartalitis de McCallum. 1982. "Definiciones y mediciones de efectos de una zona libre comercio." Integración Latinoamericana (Buenos Aires), no. 69 (June), pp. 49-60.

Dale, William B. 1983. "Financing and Adjustment of Payments Imbalances." In Williamson (1983a), pp. 3-16.

Dam, Kenneth W. 1976. The Role of Rules in the International Monetary System. Coral Gables, Fla.: Law and Economics Center, University of Miami.

Dell, Sidney. 1983. "Stabilization: The Political Economy of Overkill." In Williamson (1983a), pp. 17-46.

Dell, Sidney, and Roger Lawrence. 1980. The Balance of Payments Adjustment Process in Developing Countries. Elmsford, N.Y.: Pergamon.

DeMelo, Jaime, and Sherman Robinson. 1980. Trade Adjustment Policies and Income Distribution in Three Archetype Developing Economies. World Bank Staff Working Paper no. 442. Washington, D.C., December.

_____. 1981. "Trade Policy and Resource Allocation in the Presence of Product Differentiation." The Review of Economics and Statistics, vol. 63, no. 2 (May), pp. 169-77. Also published as World Bank Reprint Series no. 214 (Washington, D.C.).

Dervis, Kemal, Jamie DeMelo, and Sherman Robinson. 1981. A General Equilibrium Analysis of Foreign Exchange Shortages in a Developing Economy. World Bank Staff Working Paper no. 443. Washington, D.C., January.

Desai, Meghnad. 1982. Testing Monetarism. New York: St. Martins.

Dhonte, Pierre. 1979. Clockwork Debt: Trade and the External Debt of Developing Countries. Lexington, Mass.: Lexington/D.C. Heath.

Diaz-Alejandro, Carlos F. 1970. Essays on the Economic History of the Argentine Republic. New Haven, Conn.: Yale University Press.

_____. 1983. "Country Studies: Comments." In Williamson (1983a), pp. 341-46.

Dooley, Michael P. 1983. "An Analysis of Exchange Market Intervention of Industrial and Developing Countries." IMF Staff Papers, forthcoming.

Dornbusch, Rudiger. 1976. "Expectations and Exchange Rate Dynamics." Journal of Political Economy (December).

_____. 1980. Open Economy Macroeconomics. New York: Basic.

_____. 1981. "Portugal's Crawling Peg." In Williamson (1981).

_____. 1983a. "Issues Relating to Conditionality: Comments." In Williamson (1983a), pp. 223-30.

_____. 1983b. "Flexible Exchange Rates and Interdependence." In IMF (1983).

Dornbusch, Rudiger, and Jacob A. Frenkel, eds. 1979. International Economic Policy: Theory and Evidence. Baltimore, Md.: Johns Hopkins University Press.

Dornbusch, Rudiger, and Stanley Fischer. 1980. Macroeconomics. 2d ed. New York: McGraw-Hill.

Dow, Sheila C., and Peter E. Earl. 1982. Money Matters: A Keynesian Approach to Monetary Economics. Totowa, N.J.: Barnes & Noble.

Dreyer, Jacob S., Gottfried Haberler, and Thomas D. Willett. 1982. The International Monetary System: A Time of Turbulence. Washington, D.C.: American Enterprise Institute.

Feder, Gershon, Richard Just, and Knud Ross. 1981. "Projecting Debt-Servicing Capacity of Developing Countries." Journal of Financial and Quantitative Analysis, vol. 16, no. 5 (December), pp. 651-69. Also published as World Bank Reprint Series no. 237 (Washington, D.C.).

Feltenstein, Andrew. 1980. "A General Equilibrium Approach to the Analysis of Trade Restrictions, with an Application to Argentina." IMF Staff Papers, vol. 27, no. 4 (December).

Ferber, R., ed. 1980. Consumption and Income Distribution in Latin America. Washington, D.C.: ECIEL Program, OAS.

Fernandez, Roque B., and Carlos A. Rodríguez, eds. 1982. Inflación y estabilidad. Buenos Aires: Ediciones Macchi.

Ffrench-Davis, Ricardo, and Ernesto Tironi. 1982. Latin America and the New International Economic Order. New York: St. Martins.

Finch, C. David. 1983. "Adjustment Policies and Conditionality." In Williamson 1983a, pp. 75-86.

Finch, M. H. 1981. A Political Economy of Uruguay since 1870. New York: St. Martins.

Fischer, Douglas. 1980. Monetary Theory and the Demand for Money. New York: Halsted/Wiley.

Fischer, Stanley, ed. 1980. Rational Expectations and Economic Policy. Chicago: University of Chicago Press.

Fleming, Alexander. 1981. Private Capital Flows to Developing Countries and Their Destination: Historical Perspective, Recent Experiences, and Future Prospects. World Bank Staff Working Papers no. 484. Washington, D.C., August.

Foxley, Alejandro, and others. 1979. Redistributive Effects of Government Programmes: The Chilean Case. Elmsford, N.Y.: Pergamon.

Foxley, Alejandro, and Lawrence Whitehead, eds. 1980. Economic Stabilization in Latin America: Political Dimensions. Elmsford, N.Y.: Pergamon.

Frank, Isaiah. 1981. Trade Policy Issues for the Developing Countries in the 1980s. World Bank Staff Working Paper no. 478. Washington, D.C., August.

Franko, Lawrence G., and Marilyn J. Seiber. 1979. Developing Country Debt. Elmsford, N.Y.: Pergamon.

Frenkel, Jacob A., and Harry G. Johnson. 1978. Economics of Exchange Rates. Reading, Mass.: Addison-Wesley.

Friedman, Irving S. 1983. "Private Bank Conditionality: Comparison with the IMF and the World Bank." In Williamson (1983a), pp. 109-24.

Friedman, Milton, and others. 1974. Essays on Inflation and Indexing. Washington, D.C.: American Enterprise Institute.

Fry, Maxwell, ed. 1983. World Development special issue. Oxford: Pergamon, forthcoming.

Galbis, Vincente. 1982. "Inflation: The Latin American Experience, 1970-79." Finance & Development, vol. 19, no. 3 (September), pp. 22-26.

Garcia-Zamora, Jean-Claude, and Stewart E. Sutin. 1980. Financing Development in Latin America. New York: Praeger.

Ghatak, Subrata. 1981. Monetary Economics in Developing Countries. New York: St. Martins.

Glenday, Graham, Glenn P. Jenkins, and John C. Evans. 1980. Worker Adjustment to Liberalized Trade: Costs and Assistance Policies. World Bank Staff Working Paper no. 426. Washington, D.C., October.

Goldstein, Morris. 1980. Have Flexible Exchange Rates Handicapped Macroeconomic Policy? Special Papers in International Economics no. 14, International Finance Section. Princeton, N.J.: Princeton University.

Goldstein, Morris, and John H. Young. 1979. "Exchange Rate Policy: Some Current Issues." Finance & Development, vol. 16, no. 1 (March), pp. 7-9.

Gordon, Raoul. 1976. Foreign Capital in Latin America. New York: Gordon.

Gregory, Peter. 1967. Industrial Wages in Chile. International Report Series no. 8. Ithaca, N.Y.: ILR Publications.

Griffiths, Brian, and Geoffrey E. Woods, eds. 1981. Monetary Targets. New York: St. Martins.

Group of Thirty. 1980. Foreign Exchange Markets under Floating Rates. New York.

Grunwald, Joseph. 1978. Latin America and the World Economy: A Changing International Order. Beverly Hills, Calif.: Sage.

Guisinger, Stephen E., ed. 1973. Trade and Investment Policies in the Americas. Dallas, Tex.: Southern Methodist University Press.

Guitián, Manuel. 1981a. "Fund Conditionality and the International Adjustment Process: The Changing Environment of the 1970s." Finance & Development, vol. 18 (March), pp. 8-11.

_____. 1981b. "Fund Conditionality and the International Adjustment Process: A Look into the 1980s." Finance & Development, vol. 18 (June), pp. 14-17.

Gutierrez, Alfredo, and others. 1979. Uruguay: Economic Memorandum. Washington, D.C.: World Bank, January.

Haberler, Gottfried. 1969. Money in the International Economy: A Study in Balance of Payments Adjustment, International Liquidity, and Exchange Rates. Cambridge, Mass.: Harvard University Press.

_____. 1974. Economic Growth and Stability: An Analysis of Economic Change and Policies. Atlantic Highlands, N.J.: Humanities.

Hanson, James A. 1971. Growth in Open Economics. Lecture Notes in Economics and Mathematical Systems, vol. 59. New York: Springer-Verlag.

_____. 1983. "Contractionary Devaluation, Substitution in Production and Consumption, and the Role of the Labor Market." Journal of International Economics, vol. 14, no. 1 (February), pp. 1-11. Also published as World Bank Reprint Series no. 257 (Washington, D.C.).

Harberger, Arnold C. 1976. Project Evaluation: Collected Papers. Chicago: University of Chicago Press.

_____. 1978. Taxation and Welfare. Chicago: University of Chicago Press.

_____. 1983. "Conclusions and Policy Implications: Panel Discussion." In Williamson (1983a), pp. 578-80.

Harberger, Arnold C., and Martin J. Bailey, eds. 1969. The Taxation of Income from Capital. Washington, D.C.: Brookings.

Havrilesky, Thomas, and John T. Boorman. 1982. Money Supply, Money Demand, and Macroeconomic Models. Arlington Heights, Ill.: Harlan Davidson.

Heller, Peter S. 1980. "Impact of Inflation on Fiscal Policy." IMF Staff Papers, vol. 27, no. 4 (December).

Herring, R. J., and R. C. Marston. 1977. National Monetary Policies and International Financial Markets. Amsterdam: North-Holland; New York: Elsevier.

Hicks, John R. 1967. Critical Essays in Monetary Theory. New York: Oxford University Press.

Higonnet, Rene P., and Antonio Jorge, eds. 1982. External Debt and Latin American Economic Development. Elmsford, N.Y.: Pergamon.

Hirsch, Fred, and John H. Goldthorpe, eds. 1978. The Political Economy of Inflation. Cambridge, Mass.: Harvard University Press.

Hope, Nicholas C. 1981. Developments in and Prospects for the External Debt of the Developing Countries. World Bank Staff Working Paper no. 488. Washington, D.C., August.

Hughes, Helen, and Jean Waelbroeck. 1981. "Can Developing-Country Exports Keep Growing in the 1980s?" The World Economy (June), pp. 127-47. Also published as World Bank Reprint Series no. 194 (Washington, D.C.).

Humphrey, Thomas M., and Robert E. Keleher. 1982. The Monetary Approach to the Balance of Payments, Exchange Rates, and World Inflation. New York: Praeger.

International Monetary Fund (IMF). 1977. The Monetary Approach to the Balance of Payments: A Collection of Research Papers by Members of the Staff of the International Monetary Fund. Washington, D.C.

_____. 1979a. Annual Report on Exchange Arrangements and Exchange Restrictions. Washington, D.C.

_____. 1979b. International Financial Statistics. Yearbook. Washington, D.C., September.

_____. 1979c. Balance of Payments Statistics. Yearbook. Washington, D.C., December.

_____. 1979d. Direction of Trade Statistics. Yearbook. Washington, D.C., July.

_____. 1979e. Government Finance Statistics. Yearbook. Washington, D.C.

_____. 1981, 1982a. World Economic Outlook. IMF Occasional Papers nos. 4 and 9. Washington, D.C., June.

_____. 1982b. Adjustment and Financing in the Developing World: The Role of the International Monetary Fund. Washington, D.C.

_____. 1983. Exchange Rate Regimes and Policy Interdependence. Washington, D.C.

Jackendoff, Nathanial. 1968. Money, Flow of Funds, and Economic Policy. New York: Wiley.

Jasperson, Frederick. 1981. Adjustment Experience and the Growth Prospects of the Semi-Industrial Countries. World Bank Staff Working Paper no. 477. Washington, D.C., August.

Johnson, Harry G. 1972. Macroeconomics and Monetary Theory. Chicago: Aldine.

_____. 1973. Further Essays in Monetary Economics. Cambridge, Mass.: Harvard University Press.

Johnson, Omotunde, and Joanne Salop. 1980. "Distributional Aspects of Stabilization Policies in Developing Countries." IMF Staff Papers, vol. 28, no.1 (March).

Jones, R. W., and Peter B. Kenen, eds. 1983. Handbook of International Economics. Vol. 1. Amsterdam: North-Holland, forthcoming.

Joshi, Vijay. 1981. International Adjustment in the 1980s. World Bank Staff Working Paper no. 485. Washington, D.C., August.

Jud, Gustav Donald. 1978. Inflation and the Use of Indexing in Developing Countries. New York: Praeger.

Kaldor, Lord. 1982. The Scourge of Monetarism. New York: Oxford University Press.

Keesing, Donald B. 1979a. World Trade and Output of Manufactures: Structural Trends and Developing Countries' Exports. World Bank Staff Working Paper no. 316. Washington, D.C., January.

_____. 1979b. Trade Policy for Developing Countries. World Bank Staff Working Paper no. 353. Washington, D.C., August.

Kenen, Peter B., and others, eds. 1982. The International Monetary System under Flexible Exchange Rates: Global, Regional, and National. Cambridge, Mass.: Ballinger.

Khan, Mohsin, and Malcolm D. Knight. 1981. "Stabilization Programs in Developing Countries: A Formal Framework." IMF Staff Papers, vol. 28, no. 1 (March).

Killick, Tony, ed. 1981. Adjustment and Financing in the Developing World: The Role of the International Monetary Fund. Washington, D.C.: IMF, October.

Kincaid, G. Russell. 1981. "Inflation and the External Debt of Developing Countries," Finance & Development, vol. 18 (December), pp. 45-48.

Krueger, Anne O. 1977. Growth, Distortions, and Patterns of Trade among Many Countries. Princeton Studies in International Finance no. 40. Princeton, N.J.: Princeton University.

_____. 1978. "Alternative Trade Strategies and Employment in LDCs." American Economic Review, Papers and Proceedings (May).

_____. 1979a. "Devaluation and Its Consequences in Developing Countries." Intereconomics (January-February).

_____. 1979b. The Development Role of the Foreign Sector and Aid. Cambridge, Mass.: Harvard University Press.

_____. 1980a. "Role of Relative Prices in Economic Development." In Ferber (1980).

_____. 1980b. "Trade Policy as an Input to Development." American Economic Review, Papers and Proceedings (May).

_____. 1981a. "Opening Up: The Case for Cutting Tariffs and Eliminating Quotas." Economic Papers, vol. 68 (October), pp. 16-21.

_____. 1981b. "Effects of Trade Regimes and Factor Markets Distortions on Resource Allocation in LDCs." Paper presented at the Second Regional Meeting of the Econometric Society, Rio de Janeiro, July. Processed.

_____, ed. 1981c-83a. Trade and Employment in Developing Countries. 3 vols. Chicago: University of Chicago Press/National Bureau of Economic Research.

_____. 1982b. "Analysing Disequilibrium Exchange-Rate Systems in Developing Countries." World Development, vol. 10, no. 12 (December), pp. 1059-68.

_____. 1982c. "The Role of the World Bank as an International Institution." Paper presented at the Carnegie-Rochester Conference on Public Policy, University of Rochester, Rochester, N.Y., April. Processed.

_____. 1983b. Exchange-Rate Determination. New York: Cambridge University Press.

_____. 1983c. "Trade Policies in Developing Countries." In Jones and Kenen (1983).

_____. 1983d. "Analyzing Disequilibrium Exchange Rate Systems in Developing Countries." In Fry (1983).

_____. 1983e. "The World Bank and a World Financial System under Strain." Paper presented at the London Times Conference on World Banking, London, December 9. Processed.

Krueger, Anne O., and Jagdish N. Bhagwati. 1973. "Exchange Control, Liberalization, and Economic Development." American Economic Review (May).

Krueger, Anne O., Jagdish N. Bhagwati, and Chaiyawat Wibulswasdi. 1974. In Bhagwati (1974).

Kyle, John F. 1976. The Balance of Payments in a Monetary Economy. Princeton, N.J.: Princeton University Press.

Laidler, D. E. 1979. Essays on Money and Inflation. Chicago: University of Chicago Press.

Laker, John E. 1981. "Fiscal Proxies for Devaluation: A General Review." IMF Staff Papers, vol. 28, no. 1 (March).

Letiche, John M. 1982. International Economic Policies and Their Theoretical Foundations: A Source Book. New York: Academic.

Levin, Jay H. 1970. Forward Exchange and Internal-External Equilibrium. Michigan International Business Studies no. 12. Ann Arbor: Division of Research, Graduate School of Business Administration, University of Michigan.

Levy, Fred D., and others. 1980. Chile: An Economy in Transition. Washington, D.C.: World Bank, January.

Lucas, Robert E., Jr., and Thomas J. Sargent, eds. 1981. Rational Expectations and Econometric Practice. 2 vols. Minneapolis, Minn.: University of Minnesota Press.

McKinnon, Ronald I. 1973. Money and Capital in Economic Development. Washington, D.C.: Brookings.

_____. 1976. Money and Finance in Economic Growth and Development. New York: Dekker.

Mallon, Richard D., and Juan V. Sourrouille. 1975. Econometric Policymaking in a Conflict Society: The Argentine Case. Cambridge, Mass.: Harvard University Press.

Mamalakis, Markos J. 1976. The Growth and Structure of the Chilean Economy: From Independence to Allende. New Haven, Conn.: Yale University Press.

Marshall, Jorge, José Luis Mardones, and Isabel Marshall. 1983. "IMF Conditionality: The Experience of Argentina, Brazil, and Chile." In Williamson (1983a), pp. 275-321.

Matthiessen, Lars, and Steiner Strom, eds. 1981. Unemployment: Macro- and Micro-Economic Explanations. London: Macmillan.

Mayer, Thomas. 1978. The Structure of Monetarism. New York: Norton.

Medina, J. J. 1980. Evaluación del plan de apertura de la economía argentina 1979-84. Documentos de Trabajo 15. Buenos Aires: Centro de Estúdios Macroeconomicos de la Argentina (CEMA), June.

Medley, Richard, ed. 1982. The Politics of Inflation: A Comparative Analysis. Elmsford, N.Y.: Pergamon.

Meier, Gerald M. 1982. Problems of a World Monetary Order. 2d ed. New York: Oxford University Press.

_____. 1983. Pricing Policy for Development Management. Baltimore, Md.: Johns Hopkins University Press.

Miles, Marc C. 1978. Devaluation, the Trade Balance, and the Balance of Payments. New York: Dekker.

Minford, P. 1978. Substitution Effects, Speculation, and Exchange Rate Stability. Studies in International Economics, vol. 3. Amsterdam: North-Holland; New York: Elsevier.

Nashashibi, Karim. 1983. "Devaluation in Developing Countries: The Difficult Choices." Finance & Development, vol. 20, no. 1 (March), pp. 14-17.

Neuhaus, Paulo. 1982. "Floating Interest Rates and Developing Country Debt." Finance & Development, vol. 19, no. 4 (December), pp. 37-38.

Nowzad, Bahram. 1982. "Debt in Developing Countries: Some Issues for the 1980s." Finance & Development, vol. 19, no. 1 (March), pp. 13-16.

Odling-Smee, John. 1982. "Adjustment with Financial Assistance from the Fund." Finance & Development, vol. 19, no. 4 (December), pp. 26-30.

Okun, Arthur M. 1981. Prices and Quantities. Washington, D.C.: Brookings.

Organisation for Economic Co-operation and Development (OECD). 1979. Monetary Targets and Inflation Control. Paris.

Organization of American States (OAS). 1974. Flujos de financiamento oficial externo a America Latina. Washington, D.C.

_____. 1978. Methods for Evaluating Latin American Export Operations. Washington, D.C.

Pablo, Juan Carlos de. 1979. "Reflexiones sobre la cuestión arancelaria." Ensayos Económicos no. 9 (March).

_____. 1981. El proceso económico: Como lo vi y como lo veo. Buenos Aires: Ediciones El Cronista Comercial, March.

_____. 1983. "El enfoque monetario de la balanza de pagos en la Argentina: Análisis del programa del 20 de diciembre de 1978." El Trimestre Económico (Mexico), vol. 50(2), no. 198 (April-June), pp. 641-69.

Pfeffermann, Guy P. 1982. "Latin America and the Caribbean: Economic Performance and Policies." The Southwestern Review of Management and Economics, vol. 2, no. 1 (Winter), pp. 129-72. Also published as World Bank Reprint Series no. 228 (Washington, D.C.).

Pfeffermann, Guy P., and Richard C. Webb. 1979. The Distribution of Income in Brazil. World Bank Staff Working Paper no. 356. Washington, D.C.

Poole, William. 1978. Money and the Economy: A Monetarist View. Reading, Mass.: Addison-Wesley.

Putnam, Bluford H., and D. Sykes Wilford, eds. 1979. The Monetary Approach to International Adjustment. New York: Praeger.

Randall, Laura. 1977. An Economic History of Argentina. New York: Columbia University Press.

Ribas, Armando P. 1980. Inflación—La experiencia argentina 1976-80. Buenos Aires: Ediciones El Cronista Comercial, November.

Riechel, Klaus-Walter. 1978. Economic Effects of Exchange-Rate Changes. Lexington, Mass.: Lexington/D.C. Heath.

Rietti, Mario. 1979. Money and Banking in Latin America. New York: Praeger.

Robichek, E. Walter. 1980. "Official Borrowing Abroad: Some Reflections." Finance & Development, vol. 17 (March), pp. 14-17.

Salazar-Carillo, Jorge, and Juan J. Buttari. 1982. The Structure of Wages in Latin American Manufacturing Industries. Gainesville, Fla.: University Presses of Florida.

Sansón, Carlos E. 1981. "Latin America and the Caribbean: A Medium-Term Outlook." Finance & Development, vol. 18 (September), pp. 34-37.

Sapir, André, and Ernst Lutz. 1981. Trade in Services: Economic Determinants and Development-Related Issues. World Bank Staff Working Paper no. 480. Washington, D.C., August.

Sarnat, Marshall. 1978. Inflation and Capital Markets. Cambridge, Mass.: Ballinger.

Silva Lopes, José da. 1983. "IMF Conditionality and the Standby Arrangement with Portugal of 1978." In Williamson (1983a), pp. 475-504

Solomon, Robert. 1982. The International Monetary System 1945-81. New York: Harper and Row.

Stallings, Barbara. 1978. Class Conflict and Economic Development in Chile, 1958-73. Stanford, Calif.: Stanford University Press.

Steinherr, Alfred. 1981. "Effectiveness of Exchange Rate Policy for Trade Account Adjustment." IMF Staff Papers, vol. 28, no. 1 (March).

Stern, Ernest. 1983. "World Bank Financing of Structural Adjustment." In Williamson (1983a), pp. 87-107.

Stewart, Frances, and Arjun Sengupta. 1982. International Financial Cooperation: A Framework for Change. Boulder, Co.: Westview.

Stuart, Brian C. 1981. "Stabilization Policy in Portugal, 1974-78." Finance & Development, vol. 18 (September), pp. 25-28.

Subercaseaux, Benjamin. 1976. Monetary and Banking Policy of Chile. New York: Gordon.

Syrquin, Moises, and Simón Teitel. 1982. Trade, Stability, Technology, and Equity in Latin America. New York: Academic.

Tait, Alan A., and Peter S. Heller. 1982. International Comparisons of Government Expenditure. IMF Occasional Paper no. 10. Washington, D.C.

Tanzi, Vito. 1977. "Inflation, Lags in Collection, and the Real Value of Tax Revenue." IMF Staff Papers, vol. 24 (March).

——. 1980a. Inflation and Personal Income Tax. New York: Cambridge University Press.

——. 1980b. "Inflationary Expectations, Economic Activity, Taxes, and Interest Rates." American Economic Review (March).

——. 1982a. "Tax Increases and the Price Level." Finance & Development, vol. 19, no. 3 (September), pp. 27-30.

——. ed. 1982b. The Underground Economy in the United States and Abroad. Lexington, Mass.: Lexington/D.C. Heath.

Tanzi, Vito, and others. 1970. Taxation: A Radical Approach. Institute of Economic Affairs, Readings in Political Economy Series no. 4. Levittown, N.Y.: Transatlantic.

Teitel, Simón. 1978. "The Strong Factor-Intensity Assumption: Some Empirical Evidence." Economic Development and Cultural Change, vol. 26, no. 2 (January). Also published as Inter-American Development Bank Reprint Series no. 101 (Washington, D.C.).

——. 1981. "Productivity, Mechanization, and Skills: A Test of the Hirschman Hypothesis for Latin American Industry." World Development, vol. 9, no. 4 (April). Also published as Inter-

American Development Bank Reprint Series no. 107 (Washington, D.C.).

_____. 1982. "Acerca del Informe de la Comisión Brandt." El Trimestre Económico, vol. 49, no. 109 (January-March). Also published as Inter-American Development Bank Reprint Series no. 110 (Washington, D.C.).

Thorn, Richard S., ed. 1981. Monetary Theory and Policy. Lanham, Md.: University Press of America.

Tobin, James, ed. 1983. Macroeconomics: Prices and Quantities. Essays in Honor of Arthur Okun. Washington, D.C.: Brookings.

Tullio, Giuseppe. 1980. The Monetary Approach to External Adjustment. New York: St. Martins.

United Nations. Various years. Economic Survey of Latin America. New York: Unipub.

Vane, Howard R., and John L. Thompson. 1979. Monetarism: Theory, Evidence, and Policy. New York: Halsted/Wiley.

van Houten, Jan. 1981. "Book Notices." Review of Thorp and Whitehead 1979. Finance & Development, vol. 18 (March), p. 41.

van Wijnbergen, S. 1982. "Stagflationary Effects of Monetary Stabilization Policies: A Quantitative Analysis of South Korea." Journal of Development Economics, vol. 10, pp. 133-69. Also published as World Bank Reprint Series no. 236 (Washington, D.C.).

Virmani, Arvind. 1982. The Nature of Credit Markets in Developing Countries: A Framework for Policy Analysis. World Bank Staff Working Paper no. 524. Washington, D.C.

Wallich, Henry C. 1982. Monetary Policy and Practice: A View from the Federal Reserve Board. Lexington, Mass.: Lexington/D.C. Heath.

Weston, Rae. 1980. Domestic and Multinational Banking: The Effect of Monetary Policy. New York: Columbia University Press.

Williams, R. C., with G. G. Johnson. 1981, 1982. International Capital Markets: Recent Developments and Short-Term Prospects. IMF Occasional Papers nos. 7 (June) and 14 (July). Washington, D.C.

Williamson, John. 1977. The Failure of World Monetary Reform, 1971-74. New York: New York University Press.

_____. 1981. Exchange Rate Rules: The Theory, Performance, and Prospects of the Crawling Peg. New York: St. Martins.

_____, ed. 1983a. IMF Conditionality. Washington, D.C.: Institute for International Economics.

_____. 1983b. The Exchange Rate System. Washington, D.C.: Institute for International Economics, forthcoming.

World Bank. 1979-83a. World Development Report. New York: Oxford University Press.

_____. 1980b. World Tables. 2d. ed. Baltimore, Md.: Johns Hopkins University Press.

_____. 1983b. World Debt Tables: External Debt of Developing Countries. 1982-83 ed. Washington, D.C.

Wynia, Gary W. 1978. Argentina in the Postwar Era: Politics and Policymaking in a Divided Society. Albuquerque: University of New Mexico Press.

Yeager, Leland B., and associates. 1981. Experience with Stopping Inflation. Washington, D.C.: American Enterprise Institute.

Nicolás Ardito Barletta is vice president, Latin America and the Caribbean Regional Office, of The World Bank. Mario I. Blejer is an economist in the Fiscal Affairs Department of the International Monetary Fund and associate professor of economics in the Graduate School of Business, New York University. Luis Landau is senior departmental economist in the Country Programs Department I, Latin America and the Caribbean Regional Office, of The World Bank.